PRAIRIE STATE COLLEGE

3 2783 00125 8790

Trauma and the Therapeutic Relationship

D0082666

Trauma and the Therapeutic Relationship

Approaches to Process and Practice

Edited by

David Murphy

and

Stephen Joseph

PRAIRIE STATE COLLEGE
LIBRARY

© Selection, editorial matter: David Murphy and Stephen Joseph 2013
Foreword © John C. Norcross 2013
Individual chapters © Respective authors 2013

All rights reserved. No reproduction, copy or transmission of this
publication may be made without written permission.

No portion of this publication may be reproduced, copied or transmitted
save with written permission or in accordance with the provisions of the
Copyright, Designs and Patents Act 1988, or under the terms of any licence
permitting limited copying issued by the Copyright Licensing Agency,
Saffron House, 6–10 Kirby Street, London EC1N 8TS.

Any person who does any unauthorized act in relation to this publication
may be liable to criminal prosecution and civil claims for damages.

The authors have asserted their rights to be identified as the authors of this
work in accordance with the Copyright, Designs and Patents Act 1988.

First published 2013 by
PALGRAVE MACMILLAN

Palgrave Macmillan in the UK is an imprint of Macmillan Publishers Limited,
registered in England, company number 785998, of Houndmills, Basingstoke,
Hampshire RG21 6XS.

Palgrave Macmillan in the US is a division of St Martin's Press LLC,
175 Fifth Avenue, New York, NY 10010.

Palgrave Macmillan is the global academic imprint of the above companies
and has companies and representatives throughout the world.

Palgrave® and Macmillan® are registered trademarks in the United States,
the United Kingdom, Europe and other countries.

ISBN 978–0–230–30455–0

This book is printed on paper suitable for recycling and made from fully
managed and sustained forest sources. Logging, pulping and manufacturing
processes are expected to conform to the environmental regulations of the
country of origin.

A catalogue record for this book is available from the British Library.

A catalog record for this book is available from the Library of Congress.

Printed in the UK by Charlesworth Press, Wakefield

Contents

Foreword

John C. Norcross

The culture wars in psychotherapy dramatically pit the treatment method against the therapy relationship. Do treatments cure disorders or do relationships heal people? As every half-conscious practitioner should have learnt in graduate school, the obvious answers to all such complex questions are 'Both' and 'It depends'.

Yet, despite decades of clinical experience and research findings to the contrary, manualized treatment methods have come to dominate our discipline. In the United States and especially in the United Kingdom, manualized treatments on the 'approved list' have come to determine, in large part, what gets reimbursed for psychotherapy, what gets funded for research and what passes for evidence-based practice. If one reads these compilations literally, the inescapable conclusion is that disembodied therapists apply manualized interventions to discrete DSM or ICD disorders.

Tragically, one rarely hears in professional circles advocates for 'both' the therapeutic relationship and the treatment method. The relationship receives only token acknowledgement or lip service in randomized clinical trials which routinely conflate the 'treatment' with the individual therapist and the relationship. As my colleague Bruce Wampold has repeatedly demonstrated in empirical research, what is typically attributed to the treatment method is, in fact, the salubrious effects of the person of the therapist and his/her cultivation of a nurturing relationship.

Colleagues will frequently chide me: 'John, of course, we recognize the importance of the relationship as part of the treatment.' I smile and respond, 'That's great. So do I. Can you also see it the other way: The treatment method is an important part of the healing relationship?' That's usually met with an uncomfortable silence or a puzzled expression.

Even here I am guilty of perpetuating the artificial and polarizing distinction between relationships and methods. Words like 'relating' and 'interpersonal behaviour' are used to describe how therapists and clients behave towards each other. By contrast, terms like 'technique' or 'intervention' are used to describe what is done by the therapist. We often treat the how and the what – the relationship and the intervention, the interpersonal and the instrumental – as separate categories. In reality, of course, what one does and how one does it are complementary and inseparable. To remove the interpersonal from the instrumental may be acceptable in research, but it is a fatal flaw when the aim is to extrapolate research results to clinical practice.

In other words, the value of a treatment method is inextricably bound to the relational context in which it is applied. Hans Strupp, one of my first research mentors, offered an analogy to illustrate the inseparability of these constituent elements. Suppose you want your teenager to clean his or her room. Two methods for achieving this are to establish clear standards and to impose consequences. Fine, but the effectiveness of these two evidence-based methods will vary on whether the relationship between you and the teenager is characterized by warmth and mutual respect or by anger and mistrust. This is not to say that the methods are useless, merely how well they work depends upon the context in which they are used.

Perhaps in no other behavioural disorder is the inseparability of the relationship and the method in such compelling relief than in trauma. The world becomes unsafe; a human betrays fundamental trust; restful sleep morphs into nightmares; close relationships turn sour and anxious; daily life becomes a continual threat. Do treatments cure trauma or do relationships heal traumatized people? 'Both' should be the immediate crescendo and the evidence-based response!

In *Trauma and the Therapeutic Relationship*, David Murphy and Stephen Joseph have astutely put the relationship at the heart of trauma therapy, which has heretofore been narrowly focused on the brand-name treatment package. The scholarly result is a balanced 'both' of interpersonal and instrumental strategies that will enhance clinical care and ultimately heal traumatized patients. The therapy relationship is not prized as better than or instead of the acronym-plagued treatments, but as alongside and in optimal combination with them. Not as the polarizing either/or but as the both/and – just as the research evidence consistently attests.

This volume comprehensively covers a relationship-driven, research-guided therapy for trauma survivors. A bevy of international experts convincingly demonstrate how the common factor of the relationship can be effectively applied to trauma work and how it successfully operates with affective – cognitive processing and emotional regulation. The chapter on facilitating posttraumatic growth poignantly reminds us that some of our traumatized clients finish the process stronger than ever. The person of the therapist is, thankfully, accorded space and respect here in three separate chapters: the impact of vicarious trauma, our tendency to retreat inwards ourselves and the need for ongoing peer supervision and support. After all, the curative contribution of the person of the therapist is, arguably, as empirically supported as any psychotherapy method.

Beyond the valuable content and practice guidance on treating trauma, what appeals to me in this scrumptious book is the overarching effort to reduce the insidious false dichotomy of relationship versus method. In doing so, Murphy and Joseph deliver a cherished and overdue correction to our preoccupation with method at the expense of relationship in traumatology. We have so often confused the transcendent message – we care, we feel your pain, we are here with you, we will help you through this hellish experience – with the quotidian intervention.

Trauma and the Therapeutic Relationship shows us the way towards a mature discipline: science and practice, method and relationship, working together as expert companions. Just as we should have learnt in graduate school, and just as we should be doing to improve the lives of trauma survivors.

John C. Norcross, PhD, ABPP

Acknowledgements

We are grateful to Catherine Gray and India Annette-Woodgate at Palgrave Macmillan for their support in the production of the book and to the anonymous readers who provided helpful feedback. Thanks also to the counselling team at the University of Nottingham for their continued support and to students of the trauma masters course for the lively discussions which have enriched our thinking around the issues in this book. Finally, many thanks to John Norcross for his encouraging foreword and to all the contributors to this volume who kindly took time out to write for us.

Notes on Contributors

Maryann Abendroth, PhD, is an Assistant Professor at Northern Illinois University School of Nursing and Health Studies. Her area of research includes well-being among formal and informal caregivers, secondary traumatic stress and instrument development. She developed a conceptual model of caregiver strain among families caring for persons with Parkinson's disease. She is a compassion fatigue educator and a former hospice nurse.

Sandra L. Bloom, MD, is a Board-Certified Psychiatrist, Associate Professor of Health Management and Policy and Co-Director of the Center for Nonviolence and Social Justice at the School of Public Health of Drexel University in Philadelphia, USA. Dr. Bloom is the founder of the Sanctuary Institute, and Distinguished Fellow at the Andrus Children's Center. She is a former president of the International Society for Traumatic Stress Studies and author of several books including the trilogy about trauma-informed service, *Restoring Sanctuary: A New Operating System for Trauma-Informed Systems of Care.*

Lawrence G. Calhoun, PhD, is Professor of Psychology at UNC Charlotte, and a licensed clinical psychologist. For many years, his scholarly work has been focused on the responses of persons encountering major life crises, particularly the phenomenon of posttraumatic growth. He is co-author, with Richard Tedeschi, of *Posttraumatic Growth in Clinical Practice.*

Martin J. Dorahy, PhD, DClinPsych, is a clinical psychologist and Associate Professor in the Department of Psychology, University of Canterbury, Christchurch, New Zealand. He has a clinical, theoretical and research interest in complex trauma and dissociative disorders. He maintains a clinical practice focused primarily on the adult sequelae of childhood relational trauma.

Charles Figley, PhD, is a university professor in the fields of psychology, family studies, social work, traumatology and mental health. He is the Paul Henry Kurzweg, MD Distinguished Chair in Disaster Mental Health and Graduate School of Social Work Professor at Tulane University, USA (formerly a distinguished professor at Florida State University, USA, where he was the Traumatology Institute Director). He is a full professor at the Florida State University College of Social Work, USA.

Julian D. Ford, PhD, is a clinical psychologist and Professor of Psychiatry at the University of Connecticut School of Medicine, USA, where he directs the Child Trauma Clinic and the Center for Trauma Response Recovery and Preparedness (www.ctrp.org). Dr. Ford has co-edited three books recently: *Treating Traumatized Children, the Encyclopaedia of Psychological Trauma and Treatment of Complex Traumatic Stress Disorders*; authored a textbook on PTSD, *Posttraumatic Stress Disorder: Scientific and Professional Dimensions*; and is co-authoring a *Clinician's Guide to Treatment of Complex Traumatic Stress Disorders* (October 2012) and co-editing a child/adolescent companion volume (April 2013). He developed and conducts research and dissemination projects on the Trauma Affect Regulation: Guide for Education and Therapy (TARGET©) psychosocial intervention for adolescents, adults and families (www.advancedtrauma.com).

Landa C. Harrison, LPC, MEd, is Senior Project Manager, Sanctuary Institute, Andrus Children's Center, where she is responsible for the development, execution and practice of Sanctuary in an array of human service organizations in the United States and abroad. She is the creative force behind and primary contributor to the institute's new initiatives and offerings. As a trauma therapist and educator, Ms. Harrison frequently speaks across the globe on a variety of mental health and organizational culture topics.

Stephen Joseph, PhD, is a professor in psychology, health and social care at the University of Nottingham, UK. Stephen is a registered Counselling and Health Psychologist and on the British Psychological Societies Register of Psychologists Specializing in Psychotherapy. His research interests are psychological trauma, the person-centred approach and positive psychology. He is co-editor of *Positive Psychology in Practice* (2004), *Trauma, Recovery and Growth* (2008) and author of *What Doesn't Kill Us: The New Psychology of Posttraumatic Growth* (2011).

Janice L. Krupnick, PhD, is a professor in the Department of Psychiatry at Georgetown University School of Medicine, USA and the founder and director of the psychiatry department's Trauma and Loss Program. She has been involved in psychotherapy research as well as clinical practice for more than 30 years, specializing in the development or adaption of treatments for patients with posttraumatic stress disorder and/or major depressive disorder. She also maintains a private psychotherapy practice in Chevy Chase, MD.

Donald Meichenbaum, PhD, is Distinguished Professor Emeritus, University of Waterloo, Ontario, Canada, from which he took early retirement 15 years ago to become Research Director of the Melissa Institute for Violence Prevention in Miami, Florida (see www.melissainstitute.org). He is one of the founders of cognitive behaviour therapy, and in a survey of clinicians reported in the American Psychologist he was voted 'one of the 10 most influential psychotherapists of the 20th century'. He has received a Lifetime Achievement Award from the Clinical Division of the American Psychological Association.

David Murphy, PhD, is a registered counselling psychologist and on the Register of Psychologists Specializing in Psychotherapy. He works as a client-centred psychotherapist in the field of trauma and is Honorary Psychologist in Psychotherapy at the Centre for Trauma, Resilience and Growth Nottinghamshire Healthcare NHS Trust. He is the programme leader for the MA in Trauma Studies at the University of Nottingham, UK. David co-edited *Relational Depth: New Perspective and Developments* (2012) and is currently editor for *Person-Centered & Experiential Psychotherapies.*

Richard G. Tedeschi, PhD, is a professor of psychology at the University of North Carolina at Charlotte, USA. With his colleague, Lawrence Calhoun, he has published several books on posttraumatic growth, an area of research that they have developed. Their books include *Trauma and Transformation (1995)* and *The Handbook of Posttraumatic Growth (2006)*. Dr. Tedeschi is a consultant to the American Psychological Association on trauma and resilience.

Sarah Yanosy, LCSW, is Director of the Sanctuary Institute at ANDRUS in Yonkers, NY. Ms. Yanosy has overseen the implementation of Sanctuary, a system-wide holistic organizational intervention, for over 250 organizations across the United States and in five other countries. She has published several articles and book chapters and has been a keynote and featured speaker on trauma and organizational culture at both national and international conferences.

1

Putting the Relationship at the Heart of Trauma Therapy

David Murphy and Stephen Joseph

Psychological trauma is a thriving and growing field of study and practice attracting interest from professionals working across a range of disciplines from psychology and psychotherapy through to psychiatry, counselling and social work to nursing, medicine and the armed forces. But what is trauma? The term has different meanings in different contexts. For instance, ask a medic what they mean by trauma, and this usually refers to something involving significant damage to the physical integrity of the person, such as being severely burned or breaking or losing a limb. In this book, however, we are concerned with experiences that cause damage to the psychological integrity of the person. Different events, such as car accidents, violent assault, robbery or domestic violence, will affect people differently because of the nature of those events and how their meaning to the person is influenced by issues such as power, control and gender. However, regardless of the type of event, there are common psychological reactions that all survivors seem to experience because of the universal human needs for affective and cognitive processing. It is in light of this understanding that we are able to bring together authors from different perspectives, working in different contexts, to focus discussion around the role of the therapeutic relationship.

The therapeutic relationship and its role in recovery from psychological trauma are topics which we think are important to scholars and practitioners. As the world has been changing at a fast pace, so too has our understanding of mass trauma. There is now more media attention placed on the devastating effects of natural disaster, manmade, technological or organizational events, accidents, war and terror. All such events are widely reported. New media and the Internet have meant that people have insider access to the lives of others as they unfold. Stories of people's trauma of a more personal nature are also widely available. Physical assaults, sexual violence and child maltreatment are often front-page news. All this means that trauma has become a focal point for not only those directly affected but also those who are increasingly made witness through our interconnected and globalized world. As the awareness of trauma in people's lives has increased, so too has the need to provide help and support to those affected. The demand to provide services has increased at a time where resources have also been put under strain.

The therapeutic relationship has however been neglected as a topic for research and scholarly activity. The field of trauma therapy has been required to respond to the standards of evidence-based practice and empirically supported treatments. While we are in agreement that empirical evidence should guide how we practise and what treatments we choose to use, the absence of research must not be mistaken for evidence against the therapeutic relationship. Research that is based on a diagnostically based medical model approach to understand trauma has left little room for consideration of the most human element of responding to trauma – interpersonal relationship between the client and therapist. This book aims to address this gap. For those who have always felt that the relationship with the client is important, we hope that this book provides new inspiration, confidence and even courage to develop their relational focus. It is our aim to put the therapeutic relationship at the heart of trauma-related work.

First, we need to understand why relationship-based approaches have been overlooked because of the emphasis on the diagnostically based medical model approach. There is a long history to the field of trauma studies, but recently it's been dominated by the development and influence of the diagnostic category for Posttraumatic Stress Disorder (PTSD). PTSD was first introduced into the third edition of the *American Psychiatric Association's Diagnostic and Statistical Manual for Mental Disorders* (DSM-III: American Psychiatric Association, 1980). Over the subsequent decades, the diagnostic category of PTSD has been the focus for research and theory within the field of trauma studies. Consequently, the ideology of illness has by and large become the dominant narrative among practitioners, with the attendant implication that the therapist is the expert on the client, rather than clients being experts on themselves. As such the diagnostic category of PTSD determines a specific therapist–client style of interaction that precludes other forms of psychotherapeutic interaction taking place.

However, there has been a shift in the field in the last decade. We have seen positive psychology and the concept of posttraumatic growth (PTG) begin to challenge the illness ideology that has for so long permeated the psychological professions (Maddux, Snyder, & Lopez, 2004). The idea that traumatic stress involves a process of growthful adjustment is not totally new, but this way of conceptualizing traumatic stress has only comparatively recently gained the attention of psychologists and psychotherapists as well as many other professional practitioners. Adopting the stance of PTG provides a more congenial approach to therapeutic work.

Through this book, we want practitioners to connect with a sense of relatedness to their clients within trauma therapy and to see the full range of ways in which the relationship can possibly be important. Whether one conceptualizes traumatic stress from within an illness or growth paradigm is not a trivial issue. In trauma therapy, our conceptualization informs everything we do within therapy and also what we are trying to achieve (Joseph & Wood, 2010). This includes the stance we adopt within building the therapeutic relationship with our clients. For example, from within the growth paradigm, the therapeutic relationship is seen as beneficial in its own right. In contrast, from within an illness ideology, the therapeutic relationship will *always* be utilitarian in the sense that it is a precursor to the delivery of therapeutic intervention. As a consequence, psychotherapy in the trauma field has followed that of the wider field of psychotherapy. We have seen therapeutic techniques to treat PTSD at the forefront of research and clinical development.

In both the United Kingdom, through the development of clinical guidelines by the independent body the National Institute for Health and Clinical Excellence (NICE), and the United States, through the empirically supported treatments initiated by the American Psychological Association (APA), some approaches to therapy are considered as more preferable first-line treatments than others. Some examples of the technological developments that have emerged through the illness ideology include Trauma-Focused Cognitive-Behavioral Therapy (TF-CBT), Eye Movement Desensitization and Reprocessing (EMDR) and emotional freedom techniques (EFT), to name but a few. While acknowledging that survivors can find the use of therapeutic techniques helpful, has the illness ideology underpinning their use meant that therapeutic technologies come at the expense of the therapeutic relationship?

The answer to this last question seems to be yes. There is a huge body of evidence that has established therapies of all persuasions are broadly equally effective. Consequently, and as some researchers have stated for many years, the therapeutic factors that are most effective are those that must be common to all therapeutic approaches (Duncan, Miller, Sparks, & Hubble, 2004; Frank & Frank, 1976; Wampold, 2001; Wampold, Minami, Baskin, & Tierney, 2002). Regardless of the brand name of the therapy, there are a variety of ingredients common to all 'bona fide' therapies; for example, they provide the opportunity to talk, education about PTSD, encouragement, teaching coping skills and the opportunity for exposure (Wampold et al., 2010). As such, perhaps the most significant common factor, and the one that has been most consistently associated with therapy outcome, is the therapeutic relationship (Norcross, 2012).

Where once experiential and humanistic therapies were the major proponents of the significance of the therapeutic relationship, all psychological therapies now recognize the important role that relationship has in psychotherapy. Over the recent years, the therapeutic relationship has been shown to be a predictor of outcome in cognitive behavioural therapy (CBT) and interpersonal psychotherapy (IPT) (Zuroff & Blatt, 2006), process experiential psychotherapy (Watson & Geller, 2005) and the effectiveness of relationship-based non-directive client-centred psychotherapy has also been evidenced (Bedi et al., 2000; Greenberg & Watson, 1998; Murphy, 2010). The therapeutic relationship has been shown to be important not only for outcome across different therapeutic approaches but also with different client groups and presenting problems including, for example, depression (Watson et al., 2003), couples and family therapy (O'Leary, 1999) and psychotic states (Traynor, Elliott, & Cooper, 2011). It might be expected, therefore, that in trauma therapy the therapeutic relationship also plays a significant role in the process of recovery.

The relevance of the therapeutic relationship might not be apparent from the perspective of the illness ideology, but if we consider trauma as those experiences that shatter our fundamental beliefs about the world and our sense of self (Janoff-Bulman, 1992) then it becomes clear in what way the therapeutic relationship may be involved. It is the process of rebuilding shattered assumptions that therapeutic relationships seem most directly relevant – as it speaks to people's needs to make sense of their experiences, to talk and be listened to by others and to engage in the process of constructing new and more adaptive stories about themselves and the world. Indeed, understood this way, we can see how the therapeutic relationship may be central to the facilitation of PTG (Joseph, 2011).

In this book, we have brought together renowned authors from the field of psychological trauma, in its broadest sense, both to focus on posttraumatic stress and posttraumatic growth and to consider the role of the therapeutic relationship in working with traumatized clients. It is clear from the range of approaches represented across the chapters contained within this book that the therapeutic relationship is considered an important factor in all areas of trauma studies. However, we hope that by exploring the role of the therapeutic relationship across these different approaches we will be able to highlight the significant place it occupies. We also hope to clarify a range of different perspectives on the therapeutic relationship and show how they are tied to different meta-theoretical perspectives that underpin our understanding of the nature of psychological trauma.

This book aims to address the issue of the therapeutic relationship in trauma therapy. We have assembled some of the most eminent researchers, scholars and practitioners in the field of trauma studies to share their views on these two interrelated topics. The contributors have been selected as they represent the broad range of therapeutic approaches in which the therapeutic relationship is important and also as they are representative of new and emerging alternative visions for trauma studies that go beyond the illness ideology and incorporate more contemporary perspectives on both the theory and practice of trauma therapy, such as the focus on PTG. Consequently, this book will be of interest to practitioners and researchers from all schools of psychotherapy that have practitioners in the field of trauma studies.

There are of course many aspects to the therapeutic relationship that we can consider. In humanistic therapies, Rogers' (1957) six necessary and sufficient therapeutic relationship conditions have contributed significantly to the field of psychotherapy. In psychodynamically informed therapies, the concept of the therapeutic alliance (Bordin, 1979) has become a focus of psychotherapy research. The alliance concept was seen to extend across theoretical approaches. As such the alliance became the focus of therapeutic relationship research and has been cited within thousands of psychotherapy process-outcome research studies as a reliable predictor of outcome (Orlinksy, Ronnestad, & Willutzki, 2004). In addition, the psychoanalytic concepts of transference and countertransference have also been widely researched (see Norcross, 2012 for a review) and present a complex picture in their association to outcomes. The 'real relationship' discussed recently in work by Gelso (2002, 2009) is also important to developing understanding regarding therapeutic relationship factors.

As a result of the above theory and research, most therapists nowadays regardless of their theoretical orientation recognize the importance of the therapeutic relationship. However, as we have begun to show, this might be for different reasons. Broadly speaking, there are three main explanations for the association between the therapeutic relationship and psychotherapy outcome. First is the view that the therapeutic relationship creates rapport between the client and therapist in order to increase compliance on the part of the client with the treatment provided. This view considers the therapeutic relationship to be important but not directly causal in therapeutic outcome. Second is the view that the therapeutic relationship is important because it is the vehicle for the delivery of the treatment and as such does contribute to outcome because it enables unconscious processes in the client to be made conscious. Third is the view that the therapeutic relationship is directly causal in therapeutic change because the relationship is considered to *be* the therapy. Here the therapist's task in the relationship is to communicate understanding and acceptance and by so doing will lessen the blocks the client has in congruently experiencing their needs for traumatic stress processing.

Within this book, our authors represent these different theoretical orientations and consider some of the most important and relevant aspects of the therapeutic relationship and their specific role in therapy with traumatized clients. In the following chapter, Donald Meichenbaum provides a solid base for the argument that in the field of trauma there are, what he terms, a range of 'acronym therapies', and the evidence for their effectiveness in the treatment of PTSD suggests broad equivalence. He goes on to draw the conclusion that it is not the specific elements of each therapy which makes trauma therapy effective but the general and non-specific factors common to all of the approaches. Meichenbaum identifies the central role of the therapeutic alliance in making therapy work, whatever particular brand or orientation the practitioner adopts. Meichenbaum argues that healing takes place within the therapeutic relationship and shows that in trauma therapy a significant facilitative feature of the therapeutic relationship is its ability to support the process of re-narrativizing the self.

Having established the central role of relationship as a pan theoretical construct in trauma therapy, Chapter 3 puts the spotlight on the therapeutic alliance construct. Janice Krupnick provides a detailed and up-to-date review of the literature looking at the therapeutic alliance in the field of trauma therapy. The alliance is presented as a key element of the therapeutic relationship and one that is positively associated with successful therapeutic outcomes for traumatized clients. As in the case of psychotherapy generally, and in therapy for other specific mental health diagnoses, the alliance appears to be a reliable predictor of outcome across therapeutic approaches including cognitive, behavioural and person-centred and experiential psychotherapies.

Most psychological approaches have adopted the latter view by focusing on cognition and behaviour as the targets for intervention. The affective–cognitive states of the person have all too often been neglected within the literature which seems somewhat at odds with the significant role that emotion plays in human responses to trauma (Wastell, 2005). Both with regard to guiding the human organism through encounters with environmental stimuli and specifically in the case here of traumatic events, emotion plays a significant and central role in guiding the individual through the posttrauma period.

In Chapter 4, we (Stephen Joseph and David Murphy) present a model of affective–cognitive processing. The model supposes that successful affective–cognitive processing enables new meaning and purpose in life to be found, resulting in a sense of personal and psychological growth. We consider the role of therapeutic relationship in removing the threats to trauma processing and thus creating a non-directive therapeutic environment in which the client experiences being facilitated in their PTG.

In Chapter 5, the role that emotion plays in developmental trauma is considered further by Julian Ford. In this chapter, Ford argues that the role emotion plays in psychotherapy is to help create the relational environment most conducive to constructive development and socialization. All psychotherapy practitioners in the trauma field will recognize that clients have all too often experienced and been exposed to social environments where the conditions for constructive emotional regulation have been missing and are instead replaced by unpredictable, volatile or even toxic forms of interpersonal relations. As a result, trauma survivors often have difficulty in recognizing, interpreting and regulating their affective states in response to event cognitions and other environmental stimuli. However, it is within the therapeutic relationship. Ford suggests that the therapist acts as an essential part of a 'co-regulating' system of the affective states experienced by the client.

The therapist is able to facilitate emotional expression, support deeper processing of emotional schemes and help in gaining access and giving rise to primary emotion schemes. The client ultimately comes to process affective states for themselves and consequently is then able to function more optimally and live with lower levels of distress. Clients and therapists are able to co-construct a relational environment that enables this therapeutic work to take place. The client internalizes the relationship and learns that emotional processing is something they are able to manage and ultimately do for themselves, in a more constructive way, after therapy has ended.

As Ford's chapter shows, trauma therapy can be difficult emotionally. Working with traumatized clients is often challenging for the therapist. When people have been harmed through trauma, the emotional work has to be empathically tuned in to the client's needs, and with care, compassion and sensitivity to the client's processing. Questions about the therapists' readiness and resourcefulness are central as are the client's resilience and readiness to work on traumatic issues from their past. In Chapter 6, Martin Dorahy discusses the therapeutic process when working within the therapeutic relationship with a deeply traumatized male client, caught within a fragile process. Dorahy explores the client's defensive strategies to retreat from a close intimate relationship and the therapist's response being to complete the task and goal of building a therapeutic relationship that can help bring new understanding and insight for the client. There are many challenges for therapists and clients alike. Can the client trust the therapist in order to be open, vulnerable and face the traumatic events? Can the therapist find the right balance of support and encounter to help the client face their anxiety and hold on to a sense of self? In this chapter, Dorahy shows that trauma therapy needs to move at the client's pace, and this is especially the case when the client experiences a fragile process.

The field of trauma studies has been largely concerned with the therapeutic relationships' potential for healing from the wounds caused by the devastating effects of trauma. However, as we discuss in Chapter 4, it is not uncommon for people to also report experiences of personal and psychological growth. In Chapter 7, Richard Tedeschi and Lawrence Calhoun pick up the theme of PTG. Tedeschi and Calhoun provide an example of the type of relationship that facilitates the process of PTG. In their expert companion approach, the therapist provides close empathic tracking of the client as they explore the impact of their trauma. The explicit aim is to facilitate the rebuilding of the assumptive frameworks that are shattered through the trauma event and to find the new meanings that can emerge following trauma. The concept of PTG is consistent with the growth paradigm of psychological practice, and the relationship here is aligned with the principled position outlined earlier in this introductory chapter.

These seven chapters have considered the collaborative and mutual bond required for successful psychotherapy in the field of trauma and the tasks of affective–cognitive processing of traumatic events. Through these chapters, we also hope to have illustrated the broad ways in which the therapeutic relationship can be important. First, the relationship provides only the context – the therapeutic relationship enables appropriate therapeutic techniques to be applied. Second, the relationship is the means for delivering specific interventions such as interpretations. Third, the relationship is the vehicle for therapeutic change itself. The therapeutic relationship is healing in its own right. These three different perspectives on how the therapeutic relationship contributes to constructive change following trauma are evidence for the universal need for trauma therapists to be mindful in their practice of how the relationship is being formed and of its contribution to the client's change.

In the next two chapters, the focus turns to how working therapeutically and forming close and often deep emotional connections with survivors can be difficult. One of the effects of bearing witness to other people's trauma can be that helpers themselves become vicariously traumatized. Chapter 8 discusses the process of vicarious traumatization. Maryann Abendroth and Charles Figley show how trauma work often extends beyond that of the psychotherapy consulting room including other workers such as palliative care and hospice nurses, social workers and those in child protection services. They discuss how, much like psychotherapy practitioners, professionals from other fields are similarly affected. The lessons here are valuable as the field of trauma studies has become of interest to those far beyond psychotherapy. As a result of reading this chapter, practitioners from all fields will be better equipped to cope and manage their own well-being while working relationally if they are aware of the risks of such work. Because the process of vicarious trauma results in the eventual erosion of compassion, and the inability to empathize, the needs for caution and self-care are clear. Abendroth and Figley offer some helpful strategies for professional helpers to support themselves and increase their awareness of the signs of vicarious traumatization.

Finally, an effective way to self-manage in the field of trauma work is through regular engagement in supervision. This is especially the case where the supervisory process is informed and guided by relational factors. Chapter 9 by Sandra Bloom, Sarah Yanosy and Landa Harrison examines the role of supervision in maintaining a healthy therapeutic relationship. The therapeutic relationship within the context of trauma therapy is often put under intense pressure and is at a high risk of being affected in many ways. The role of supervision is, under a heightened and intensely pressurized circumstance, to ensure the continued safe and ethical practice of the therapist. A traumatized client can often present to the therapist difficult and complex issues to understand. As such, the self-awareness of the practitioner is important for keeping the worker emotionally stable and grounded. Supervision provides the opportunity for reflection on the work, for maintaining their own emotional regulatory processing and to support them being genuine within that relationship.

The same pressure can also be applied to the wider organizational context. It is not uncommon for those working in the trauma field to introject experiences, laden with values and feelings from trauma victims. Bloom, Yanosy and Harrison's sanctuary model of supervision is one way of working with this relational dynamic within a trauma therapy organization where the risks can be high for worker well-being. The model involves the whole therapeutic system where supervision takes place within an egalitarian relational environment.

This book has emerged from the career-long commitment to the therapeutic relationship of both editors. Our work is grounded in the *principle* of relationship as being the essence of all our therapeutic work – whether it is with clients in the clinic, with supervisees or with students on our courses. The relationship *is* the work. As such, we are encouraged that the importance of the therapeutic relationship in trauma therapy is now gaining recognition.

We thank all of our eminent contributors for their work in this endeavour. Each has bought their own take on the important role of the therapeutic relationship in trauma therapy. It is with thanks to such scholars that the field of trauma studies continues to grow. Despite technological developments, reliance on techniques and medications, increasingly we are recognizing the greater importance of authentic human-to-human contact to successful psychotherapy for survivors of even the most traumatic events.

Summary points

- The therapeutic relationship makes a significant contribution to the outcome of therapy for trauma survivors.
- The therapeutic relationship is relevant in all therapy but plays different roles in the different therapies for trauma survivors.
- Researchers and practitioners alike are called to focus their attention on the role of the therapeutic relationship in their trauma-focused work.

Suggested reading

Joseph, S. (2011). *What doesn't kill us: The new psychology of posttraumatic growth.* New York: Basic Books.

Norcross, J. C. (2012). *Psychotherapy relationships that work: Evidence-based responsiveness.* New York: Oxford University Press.

Norcross, J. C., & Wampold, D. E. (2010). Adapting the relationship to suit the individual patient. In: J. C. Norcross (Ed.), *Evidence-based psychotherapy therapy relationships* (pp. 27–33), http://www.nrepp.samhsa.gov/pdfs/Norcross_evidence-based_therapy_relationships.pdf, accessed on 11 March 2011.

References

American Psychiatric Association. (1980). *Diagnostic and statistical manual of mental disorders* (3rd Edition). Washington, DC: American Psychiatric Association.

Bedi, N., Chilvers, C., Churchill, R., et al. (2000). Assessing effectiveness of treatment of depression in primary care. *British Journal of Psychiatry, 177*, 312–318.

Bordin, E. S. (1979). The generalizability of the psychoanalytic concept of the working alliance. *Psychotherapy: Theory, Research and Practice, 16*, 252–260.

Bozarth, J. D. (2002). Empirically supported treatment: Epitome of the specificity myth. In J. C. Watson, R. N. Goldman & M. S. Warner (Eds.), *Client-centered and experiential Psychotherapy in the 21st Century: Advances in theory, research and practice* (pp. 168–181). Ross-On Wye: PCCS Books.

Duncan, B. L., Miller, S. D., & Sparks, J. A. (2004). *Heroic clients, heroic agencies: Partners for change – A manual for client-directed outcome-informed therapy and effective, accountable, and just services.* E-Book: ISTC Press.

Frank, J., & Frank, J. (1976). *Persuasion and healing: A comparative study of psychotherapy.* Baltimore, MD: Johns Hopkins Press.

Gelso, C. J. (2002). The real relationship: The 'something more' of psychotherapy. *Journal of Contemporary Psychotherapy, 32*, 35–40.

Gelso, C. J. (2009). The real relationship in a postmodern world: Theoretical and empirical explorations. *Psychotherapy Research, 19*, 253–264.

Greenberg, L. S., & Watson, J. C. (1998). Experiential therapy of depression: Differential effects of client-centered relationship conditions and process-experiential interventions. *Psychotherapy Research, 8*, 210–224.

Janoff-Bulman, R. (1992). *Shattered assumptions: Towards a new psychology of trauma.* New York: Free Press.

Joseph, S. (2011). *What doesn't kill us: The new psychology of posttraumatic growth.* New York: Basic Books.

Joseph, S., Murphy, D., & Regel, S. (2012). An affective–cognitive processing model of posttraumatic growth. *Clinical Psychology and Psychotherapy.* Doi. 10.1002/cpp.1798.

Joseph, S., & Wood, A. (2010). Assessment of positive functioning in clinical psychology: Theoretical and practical issues. *Clinical Psychology Review, 30*, 830–838.

Luborsky, L., Rosenthal, R., Diguer, L., Andrusyna, T. P., Berman, J. S., Levitt, J. T., Seligman, D. A., & Krause, E. D. (2002). The dodo bird verdict is alive and well – mostly. *Clinical Psychology: Science and Practice, 9*, 2–12.

Maddux, J. E., Snyder, C. R., & Lopez, S. J. (2004). Toward a positive clinical psychology: Deconstructing the illness ideology and constructing an ideology of human strengths and potential. In P. A. Linley & S. Joseph (Eds.), *Positive psychology in practice* (pp. 320–334). Hoboken, NJ: Wiley.

Murphy, D. (2010). Psychotherapy as mutual encounter: A study of therapeutic conditions. *Unpublished PhD Dissertation Thesis.* Available at http://hdl.handle.net/2134/6627.

Norcross, J. C. (Ed.) (2002). *Psychotherapy relationships that work: Therapist contributions and responsiveness to patients.* New York: Oxford University Press.

Norcross, J. C. (Ed.) (2012). *Psychotherapy relationships that work: Evidenced-based responsiveness* (2nd ed.). New York: Oxford University Press.

O'Leary, C. (1999). *Counselling couples and families: A person-centred approach.* London: Sage.

Orlinsky, D. E., Ronnestad, M. H., & Willutzki, U. (2004). Fifty years of psychotherapy process-outcome research: Continuity and change. In M. J. Lambert (Ed.), *Bergin and Garfield's handbook of psychotherapy and behaviour change* (5th ed., pp. 307–389). New York: Wiley.

Rogers, C. R. (1957). The necessary and sufficient conditions of therapeutic personality change. *Journal of Consulting Psychology, 21,* 95–103.

Traynor, W., Elliott, R., & Cooper, M. (2011). Helpful factors and outcomes in person-centered therapy with clients who experience psychotic processes: Therapists' perspectives. *Person-Centered & Experiential Psychotherapies, 10,* 89–104.

Wampold, B. E. (2001). *The great psychotherapy debate: Models, methods and findings.* Mahwah, NJ: Lawrence Erlbaum.

Wampold, B. E., Minami, T., Baskin, T. W., & Tierney, S. C. (2002) A meta-(re)analysis of the effects of cognitive therapy versus 'other therapies' for depression. *Journal of Affective Disorders, 68,* 159–165.

Wampold, B. E., Imel, Z. E., Laska, K. M., Benish, S., Miller, S. D., Fluckiger, C., Del Re, A. C., Baardseth, T. P., & Budge, S. (2010). Determining what works in the treatment of PTSD. *Clinical Psychology Review, 30,* 923–933.

Wastell, G. (2005). *Understanding trauma and emotion.* Maidenhead, Berks: Open University Press.

Watson, J. C., & Geller, S. M. (2005). The relation among the relationship conditions, working alliance, and outcome in both process-experiential and cognitive-behavioral psychotherapy. *Psychotherapy Research, 15,* 25–33.

Watson, J. C., Gordon, L. B., Stermac, L., Kalogerakos, F., & Steckley, P. (2003). Comparing the effectiveness of process experiential with cognitive-behavioral psychotherapy in the treatment of depression. *Journal of Consulting and Clinical Psychology, 71,* 773–781.

Zuroff, D. C., & Blatt, S. J. (2006). The therapeutic relationship in the brief treatment of depression: Contributions to clinical improvement and enhanced adaptive capacities. *Journal of Consulting and Clinical Psychology, 74,* 130–140.

2

The Therapeutic Relationship as a Common Factor: Implications for Trauma Therapy

Donald Meichenbaum

Here is the challenge. I recently retired from my university to assume the position as Research Director of the Melissa Institute for Violence Prevention (see www.melissainstitute.org). In this capacity, I am invited to consult and train clinicians on ways to work with clients who have experienced traumatic events and victimizing experiences. The clients usually have received a diagnosis of Post Traumatic Stress Disorder (PTSD) and an array of comorbid disorders such as substance abuse and depressive disorders. For instance, I have been training clinicians who are working with returning service members, torture victims, Native populations who have been sexually abused, as well as clinicians who work in Residential Treatment Centres. If you were in my shoes, what advice would you offer these clinicians? What specific interventions would you recommend?

Consider the treatment options that can most succinctly be summarized in a list of acronyms. I have come to the conclusion that you cannot formulate a treatment for patients with PTSD and related disorders unless you have an acronym. In fact, I think that therapists must come up with the acronym first, and then develop the therapy. You can choose from the following list:[1]

---

[1] DTE: Direct Therapy Exposure; VRE: Virtual Reality Exposure; CPT: Cognitive Processing Therapy; EMDR: Eye Movement Desensitization and Reprocessing; SIT: Stress Inoculation Training; AMT: Anxiety Management Training; MBSR: Mindfulness-Based Stress Reduction; MAGT: Mindfulness and Acceptance Group Therapy; ACT: Acceptance and Commitment Therapy; CR: Cognitive Restructuring; TF-CBT: Trauma-Focused Cognitive Behaviour Therapy;

DTE, VRE, CPT, EMDR, SIT, AMT, MBSR, MAGT, ACT, CR, TF-CBT, IBT, CP, CMT, IPT, IRT and others.

In addition, you can select from an additional array of treatment approaches that have been developed to address the presence of comorbid disorders such as SS, TARGET and STAIR-MPE.[2] This list of treatment options could be extended if we consider specific interventions that address patient-dominant emotional concerns such as complicated grief, guilt, shame, anger, moral injuries and spiritual-based interventions.

Remember, as a consultant I am getting paid to help psychotherapists choose the 'best' most-effective interventions. The catch-words are 'evidence-based' and 'evidence-informed' interventions.

Now, here is the rub. In my desire to be an 'honest broker' and not a specific advocate of any one acronym therapy, I find myself on the 'horns of dilemma'. On the one hand, there is the report of the Institute of Medicine (2008) of the efficacy of exposure-based therapies with patients who suffer from PTSD and the Veteran's Administration endorsing and training their clinical personnel on Direct Therapy Exposure and Cognitive Processing Therapy.

On the other side of the debate, there are a number of meta-analytic reviews that question the relative differential efficacy of so-called evidence-based therapies *versus* bona fide comparison groups that are 'intended to succeed'. Reviews by Benish et al. (2008), Imel et al. (2008), Keijsers et al. (2000), Norcross (2002) and Wampold et al. (1997, 2010) have seriously challenged the proposition that any one acronym form of treatment is the 'winner of the race' and should be embraced and advocated by me in my consultative capacity. Moreover, Webb et al. (2010) have reported that the therapist's adherence to evidence-based treatment manuals is not related to treatment outcome. In fact, 'loose compliance' that is tailored to the patient's individual needs may be the best treatment approach.

Such meta-analytic reviews have not gone without their critics, as highlighted by Ehlers et al. (2010). But, keep in mind that the clinicians that I am called upon to train still want to know specifically what to do with their challenging patients.

For the moment, let us assume that each of the acronym therapeutic approaches, does indeed, leads to favourable outcomes with patients diagnosed with PTSD and comorbid disorders. What are the common mechanisms that contribute to such patient improvements?

Another way to frame this question is to share an example of my supervisory role of clinical graduate students at the University of Waterloo in Ontario,

---

DBT: Dialectical Behaviour Therapy; CP: Counting Procedures; CMT: Compassion Mindfulness Training; IPT: Interpersonal Therapy; IRT: Imagery Rehearsal Therapy.

[2] SS: Seeking Safety Treatment; TARGET: Trauma Adaptive Recovery Education and Therapy; STAIR-MPE: Skills Training in Affective and Interpersonal Regulation Followed by Modified Prolonged Exposure.

Canada. In our clinic, we had several interview rooms side-by-side, each with one-way viewing mirrors. I would sit on a high-backed chair which had wheels and I could roll up and down the viewing corridor watching several students at one time. Okay, so imagine in each clinical interview room you could watch Edna Foa conducting Direct Therapy Exposure, Barbara Rothbaum using amplified Virtual Reality Exposure, Pat Resick conducting Cognitive Processing Therapy, Francine Shapiro conducting EMDR, Marsha Linehan teaching skills in Dialectical Behavior Therapy, and so forth. What makes these psychotherapists effective? What do 'expert' therapists do, and not do, that leads to positive treatment outcomes?

In answering this question, keep in mind that there is little or no evidence of the 'specificity' of treatment effects. Interventions that are designed to alter specific behavioural skill areas do not usually evidence changes in that domain. Moreover, when dismantling treatment studies are conducted, with the key treatment ingredients omitted or altered, favourable treatment results are still evident (see Rosen & Frueh, 2010).

Hopefully, you are beginning to appreciate the source of my challenge. What would you do? My solution has been to identify and enumerate the 'Core Tasks' of what underline treatment improvement. My list is gleaned from both the research literature and my 40 years of clinical work.

Core tasks of psychotherapy

What are the core tasks that characterize the performance of psychotherapists who achieve positive treatment outcomes? This question has been addressed from Carl Rogers' (1957) initial examination of the necessary and sufficient prerequisite conditions of psychotherapy to Jerome Frank's (Frank & Frank, 1991) analysis of common persuasive features of behaviour change to a search for the 'heart and soul' of change by Miller, Duncan and Wampold (2010).

In each instance, a set of common psychotherapeutic tasks have emerged. These tasks are dependent upon the quality and nature of the therapeutic relationship as being central to patient behavioural change. As highlighted by Ackerman and Hilsenroth (2003), Martin et al. (2000), Messer and Wampold (2002), Norcross (2002), Safran and Muran (2000) and Wampold (2001), the quality and nature of the therapeutic alliance accounts for a significantly larger proportion of treatment outcome variance than do therapist effects and the specific treatment interventions, or the specific form of acronym therapy that is being implemented. Approximately, one-third of treatment outcome is accounted for by the therapeutic relationship, significantly more than does specific type of therapy (Duncan et al., 2009). The therapeutic alliance relationship is the 'cornerstone' of effective therapy (Norcross, 2009). As Irvin Yalom (2002, p. 34) stated, 'the paramount task of psychotherapy is to build a relationship together that will become the agent of change'. Walsh (2011,

p. 585) observed that 'Ideally, therapeutic relationships then serve as bridges that enable patients to enhance life relationships with family, friends and community.'

The correlation between the quality of the therapeutic alliance and treatment outcome is approximately 0.26, which corresponds to a moderate effect size. The pattern of patient participation and the degree of patient therapeutic engagement in the first three therapy sessions is predictive of treatment outcome. Patients with weaker therapeutic alliance scores are more likely to drop out of psychotherapy (Sharf et al., 2010).

The relationship between the quality and nature of the therapeutic alliance and the treatment outcomes is further strengthened when psychotherapists assess and employ ongoing real-time patient feedback. Lambert and his colleagues (Lambert, 2010; Lambert et al., 2005; Shimokawa, Lambert, & Smart, 2010) and Miller et al. (2007) have demonstrated that measuring, monitoring and alerting psychotherapists to potential patient treatment failure on a session-by-session basis by soliciting patient feedback of treatment response maximizes treatment outcomes. Such feedback permits the psychotherapist to individually alter and tailor the intervention to the patient's needs, and thereby strengthens the therapeutic alliance.

The role of the therapeutic alliance in impacting treatment outcome has now been demonstrated with diverse clinical populations. For example, a meta-analysis of 24 studies of couple and family therapy using a variety of self-report alliance measures (Working Alliance Inventory, Couple Therapy Scale and Family Therapy Alliance Scale) found that the interplay of each family member's alliance with the therapist was related to treatment retention and outcomes. Patients who reported feeling 'safe' within therapy with the avoidance of excessive cross-blaming, hostility and sarcasm in sessions reported stronger therapeutic alliances and better treatment outcomes. Insofar as a shared sense of purpose and the establishment of overarching familial systemic goals were achieved, rather than individual goals, therapeutic alliance development and treatment outcome were enhanced (Escudero et al., 2011; Friedlander et al., 2011). McLeod (2011) conducted a similar meta-analysis of the relationship of therapeutic alliance and treatment outcome in youth psychotherapy and reported similar findings.

A different research approach to studying the role of therapeutic relationship in influencing treatment outcome has been to ask patients what they have found helpful and unhelpful on the part of their therapists. Hamilton and Coates (1993) interviewed abused women who offered the following observations of their psychotherapists.

Helpful psychotherapists

- 'Listened respectfully and took me seriously.'
- 'Believed my story.'

- 'Helped me see if I was still in danger and explored with me how I could deal with this situation.'
- 'Helped me see my strengths.'
- 'Helped me understand the impact of traumatic events on myself and on others.'
- 'Helped me plan for change.'

In contrast, unhelpful psychotherapists

- 'Did not listen and did not have an accepting attitude.'
- 'Questioned and doubted my story.'
- 'Dismissed or minimized the seriousness of my situation.'
- 'Gave advice that I did not wish to receive.'
- 'Blamed or criticized me.'

A similar profile of patient reactions was reported by Elliott (2008).

Whether one considers the findings of meta-analytic studies or the results of interview studies with patients, the degree to which the patient feels respected, heard, accepted, empathically understood, validated and hopeful enhances the likelihood of positive treatment outcomes. The felt sense of collaboration between the therapist and patient, including an emotional bond and negotiation of therapy tasks and goals has consistently predicted favourable treatment outcomes (Horvath et al., 2011).

The therapeutic alliance has come to be defined as the extent to which the patient and the psychotherapist jointly agree on the goals of treatment and the means or tasks by which to achieve these goals ('pathways thinking') and the quality of the affective bond that develops between them (Bordin, 1979; Horvath & Bedi, 2002; Norcross, 2002). McFarlane (1994) observes that trust is also an essential feature of the therapeutic relationship with traumatized patients. The patient must feel secure and confident that the therapist is genuine, empathetic and warm, and, moreover, that the therapist can cope with bearing witness to the patient's reported trauma and understand its significance. These various authors are highlighting that the therapeutic alliance is the primary 'vehicle', 'prerequisite', 'process', 'glue', that permits patients to develop the courage to avoid avoidance, reexpose themselves to traumatic events, reminders, cues and reengage life.

Additional core tasks of psychotherapy

If we now revisit the various trauma psychotherapists (Foa, Rothbaum, Shapiro, Linehan and the other acronym therapists), what do they have in common? Clearly, one thing is their ability to establish, maintain, monitor the therapist alliance and address any potential 'ruptures' accordingly. But they do much more within the relationship with their patient. They each:

- Assess for the patient's safety (conduct risk assessment) and ensure that basic patient needs are being met.
- Educate the patient about the nature and impact of trauma, PTSD and accompanying adjustment difficulties and discuss the nature of treatment.
- Address issues of confidentiality billing, logistics and the like, but always conveying a 'caring' attitude.
- Conduct assessments of the patient's presenting problems, as well as their strengths. What have the patient's done to 'survive' and 'cope'? They tap the 'rest of the patient's story'.
- Solicit the patient's implicit theory about his/her presenting problems and his/her implicit theory of change. The therapist provides a cogent rational for the treatment approach and assesses the patient's understanding. Makes the therapy process visible and transparent for the patient.
- Alter treatment in a patient-sensitive fashion, being responsive to cultural, developmental and gender differences.
- Nurture 'hope' by engaging in collaborative goal-setting, highlighting evidence of patient, family, cultural and community resilience.
- Teach intra- and interpersonal coping skills and build into such training efforts the ingredients needed to increase the likelihood of generalization and maintenance of treatment effects.
- The effective therapist does not merely 'train and hope' for generalization, but explicitly builds in such features as relapse prevention, attribution retraining, aftercare, putting patients in a consultative mode (or in the 'driver's seat'), so they become their own therapist.
- Provide interventions that result in symptom relief and address the impact of comorbid disorders.
- Encourage, challenge and cajole patients who have been avoidant to re-experience, reexpose themselves to trauma reminders, cues, situations and memories. Enlist the support of significant others in these reexposure activities.
- Teach patients a variety of direct-action problem-solving and emotionally palliative coping skills (for example, mindfulness activities), to the point of mastery, addressing issues of treatment non-adherence throughout.
- Help patients reduce the likelihood of revictimization.

Finally

- Engage patients in developing 'healing stories'.

In short, whatever the proposed acronym-based intervention (direct exposure, cognitive reprocessing, self-regulatory emotional controls, and the like), it is critical to remember that such specific interventions are embedded in a contextualized process. How much of the patient change that is achieved in trauma therapy should be attributed to each of these component steps and how much to 'manualized' treatment procedures?

I use the points above as a checklist in my psychotherapy consulting role. This checklist highlights how to make the so-called non-specifics of psychotherapy specific, trainable and measurable. It enumerates ways to enhance therapeutic alliance and treatment outcomes. The importance of these psychotherapeutic skills are highlighted by a better appreciation of the goals of trauma therapy from a Constructive Narrative Perspective.

Constructive Narrative Perspective

Most individuals (70–80%) who have experienced traumatic and victimizing experiences evidence resilience, and in some instances, post-traumatic growth (see Chapters 3 and 7 for fuller discussion of posttraumatic growth) (Bonanno, 2004; Meichenbaum 2006, 2007, 2009, 2011, 2012). The 20–30 per cent of the traumatized population who evidence adjustment difficulties and who are candidates for some form of trauma therapy evidence a cognitive emotional, behavioural and spiritual style that contributes to persistent PTSD. Patients who receive the diagnosis of PTSD are likely to engage in:

- Self-focused, mental defeating ruminative style of thinking;
- Avoidant thinking processes of deliberate suppressing thoughts, using distracting behaviours that inadvertently reinforce avoidant behaviours and PTSD symptoms;
- Overgeneralized memories and a recall style that intensifies hopelessness and impairs problem solving;
- Contra-factual thinking, repeatedly asking 'Why' and 'Only if' questions for which there are no readily acceptable answers;
- Engage in 'thinking traps' that reinforce hypervigilance, safety and emotionally distancing behaviours and that contribute to the avoidance of self-disclosing and help seeking;
- Negative spiritual coping responses (Having a 'spiritual struggle', anger responses, moral injuries, complicated grief, guilt, shame and the like).

The trauma patients tell others and themselves 'stories' that lead them to become stuck. One central goal of trauma therapy, no matter what form it may take, is to help patients develop and live a 'healing story'. There is a need for patients to integrate the trauma events into a coherent autobiographical account, so the traumatic events are landmarks, but not the defining elements of their accounts. Trauma patients need to develop 'redemptive' stories that bolster hope, strengthen self-confidence and indicate that their efforts will bear fruit. Changes in story telling provide access to new solutions.

The patient's ability to generate a coherent narrative helps to reduce distress and hypervigilance, increases a sense of control, reduces feelings of chaos and unpredictability, and helps the patient develop meaning. Narrative coherence conveys a sense of personal self-efficacy and helps the patient make sense of what happened and points a direction to the future. Trauma is only one part of an individual's life, rather than the determinant aspect. Effective trauma therapy helps the patient learn to let the 'past be the past'. Patients can learn to disentangle themselves from the influences and lingering impact of traumatic events. In trauma therapy, patients engage in a narrative healing process.

Trauma therapists, no matter which form of acronym therapy they employ, are in the business of helping traumatized patients become 'story-tellers' who can evidence resilience, moving from the 20–30 per cent group to the 70–80 per cent resilient group. The therapeutic alliance is the framework whereby trauma patients can share their trauma accounts, as well as what they did to survive and cope in the past (see Chapter 3 for linking alliance to outcome for trauma psychotherapy); bolster their courage to confront, rather than avoid trauma-related situations and remembrances; develop and strengthen coping strategies that foster hope; undertake meaning-making missions and reengage life. Move from being a 'victim', to a 'survivor', to a 'thriver'.

In my consultative capacity, I train trauma therapists to become 'exquisitive' listeners and help them become collaborators in their patient's journey to develop 'healing stories'. As Stephen Joseph (2011, p. 131) has observed: 'Human beings are story-tellers. We are immersed in stories.' The role of the trauma therapist is to help traumatized patients move along this journey of collecting data (results of personal experiments) that will 'unfreeze' their beliefs about themselves, others, the world and the future. The therapeutic alliance is the ground in which such growth develops and blossoms (Meichenbaum, 1996, 2007). Its importance to the change process needs to be highlighted, repeatedly.

Checklist of therapy behaviours to facilitate the therapeutic alliance

- Convey respect, warmth, compassion, support, empathy, a caring attitude and interest in helping. Be non-judgemental. Listen actively and attentively and let your patient know you are listening so he/she feels understood.
- Convey a relaxed confidence that help can be provided and a sense of realistic optimism, but not false hope. Communicate a positive expectancy of the possibility of change. Use phrases such as 'As yet', 'So far' and 'RE' verbs such as RE-frame, RE-author, RE-engage. Emphasize that your patient can be helped, but it will require effort on both of your parts.
- Validate and normalize the patient's feelings. ('Given what you have been through, I would be deeply concerned, if *at times* you were not feeling overwhelmed and depressed.')

- Use guided discovery and Socratic Questioning. Use 'How' and 'What' questions. Stimulate the patient's curiosity, so he/she can become his/her own 'therapist', 'emotional detective'.
- Enter the narrative text of the patient, using his/her metaphors. Assess the 'rest of the patient's story' and collaboratively discover what the patient did and was able to achieve *in spite of* traumatic/victimizing experiences.
- Explore the patient's lay explanations of his/her problems and his/her expectations concerning treatment. Collaboratively establish 'SMART' therapy goals (Specific/Measurable. Achievable, Realistic and Time-limited). Use motivational interviewing procedures.
- Model a style of thinking. Ask the patient, 'Do you ever find yourself in your day-to-day experiences, asking yourself the same kind of questions that we ask each other here in therapy?'
- Encourage the patient to self-monitor (collect data) so that he/she can better appreciate the interconnectedness between feelings, thoughts, behaviours and resultant consequences, and perhaps, inadvertently, unwittingly, and unknowingly behave in ways that may maintain and exacerbate presenting problems (e.g., avoidance behaviours reinforce PTSD symptoms).
- Conduct a pros and cons analysis and help the patient to break the behavioural 'vicious cycle'.
- Address any therapy interfering behaviours and potential barriers. Solicit patient commitment statements. Play 'devil's advocate'.
- Provide intermediate summaries and a summary at the end of each session. Over the course of treatment, have the patient generate this treatment summary. Highlight how the present session follows from previous sessions and is related to achieving treatment goals. Be specific. Have the patient generate the reasons why he/she should undertake behavioural changes.
- Help patients generate alternative 'healing' narratives that empower them to examine their dominant 'trauma' story and develop and live personal accounts that contribute to posttraumatic growth.
- Solicit feedback from the patient each session on how therapy is progressing and ways to improve treatment. Convey that you, the therapist, is always trying to improve and tailor treatment to the needs and strengths of each specific patient. Monitor the relationship for any alliance strains. Accept part of the responsibility for any difficulties in the relationship.

Conclusion

Much effort has been expended to develop evidence-based interventions with patients diagnosed with PTSD and comorbid disorders – what are called 'Acronym Therapies'.

Exposure-based interventions such as Direct Therapy Exposure and Cognitive Processing Therapy have been endorsed as being most effective. Meta-analytic studies of various so-called evidence-based therapies for PTSD patients *versus* bona-fide comparison groups that were intended to succeed have raised questions about the differential effectiveness of various treatments. Both dismantling and specificity-based studies have questioned the mechanisms of change on those interventions. Common to all these 'Acronym' therapies are a set of core psychotherapeutic tasks, with the most central being the nature and quality of the therapeutic relationship which accounts for the largest proportion of treatment outcome variance.

The impact of the therapeutic relationship on treatment outcome is strengthened when ongoing, real-time session-by-session feedback is solicited from patients and used by the psychotherapist to identify potential failures and dropout risk and to alter treatment accordingly. Other core psychotherapeutic tasks beside establishing, maintaining and monitoring therapeutic alliance include psychoeducation, nurturing hope by means of collaborative goal-setting and bolstering resilience, teaching coping skills and building in generalization procedures. Key ingredients in the development of a therapeutic alliance include empathy, trust, respect and a caring attitude. The check list above is a list of psychotherapeutic methods to enhance the therapeutic alliance and treatment outcomes.

A constructive narrative perspective of the therapeutic relationship highlights how to help traumatized/victimized patients develop 'healing stories' with redemptive endings that engender hope, self-efficacy and help move trauma patients (some 20–30% of victimized individuals) to the 70–80 per cent of resilient individuals. The therapeutic relationship provides patients with an opportunity to share, reframe and develop the courage to reexpose, re-experience, reengage and review their lives so traumatic events are incorporated into a coherent narrative and a personal account.

Summary points

- Meta-analytic studies have raised questions about the differential effectiveness of various treatments.
- The nature and quality of the therapeutic alliance accounts for the largest proportion of treatment outcome variance.
- Core relationship tasks include empathy, trust, respect and a caring attitude.
- A constructive narrative perspective of the therapeutic alliance highlights how to help traumatized/victimized patients develop 'healing stories' with redemptive endings that engender hope and self-efficacy.

Suggested reading

Duncan, B.L., Miller, S.D., Wampold, B.E., & Hubble, M.A. (Eds.). (2009). The heart and soul of change: Delivering what works in therapy (2nd ed). Washington, DC: American Psychological Association.

Meichenbaum, D. (2006). Resilience and posttraumatic growth: A constructive narrative perspective. In L.G. Calhoun & R.G. Tedeschi (Eds.). Handbook of posttraumatic growth: Research and practice (pp. 355–368). Mahwah, NJ: Erlbaum Associates.

Wamplod, B.E., Imel, Z.E., Laska, K.M., Benish, S., Miller, S.D., Fluckiger, C., Del Re, A.C., Baardseth, T.P., & Budge, S. (2010). Determining what works on the treatment of PTSD. Clinical Psychology Review, 30, 923–933.

References

Ackerman, S.J., & Hilsenroth, M.J. (2003). A review of therapist characteristics and techniques positively impacting the therapeutic alliance. Clinical Psychology Review, 23, 1–33.

Benish, S., Imel, Z.E., & Wampold, B.E. (2008). The relative efficacy of bona fide psychotherapies of post-traumatic stress disorder: A meta-analysis of direct comparisons. Clinical Psychology Review, 28, 746–758.

Bonanno, G.A. (2004). Loss, trauma and human resilience: How we understand the human capacity to thrive after extremely aversive events. American Psychologist, 59, 20–28.

Bordin, E.S. (1979). The generalizability of the psychoanalytic concept of the working alliance. Psychotherapy: Theory, Research and Practice, 16, 252–260.

Duncan, B.L., Miller, S.D., Wampold, B.E., & Hubble, M.A. (Eds.). (2009). The heart and soul of change: Delivering what works in therapy (2nd ed). Washington, DC: American Psychological Association.

Ehlers, A., Bisson, J., Clark, D.M., Creamer, M., Pilling, S., & Richards, A. (2010). Do all psychological treatments really work the same in posttraumatic stress disorder. Clinical Psychology Review, 30, 269–276.

Elliot, R. (2008). Research on the client experiences of therapy: Introduction to the special issue. Psychotherapy Research, 18, 239–242.

Escudero, V., Friedlander, M.L., & Heatherington, L. (2011). Using the e-SOFTA for video training and research on alliance-related behavior. Psychotherapy, 48, 138–147.

Frank, J.D., & Frank, J.B. (1991). Persuasion and healing: A comparative study of psychotherapy (3rd ed). Baltimore: John Hopkins University Press.

Friedlander, M.L., Escadero, V., Heatherington, L., & Diamond, G.M. (2011) Alliance in couple and family therapy. Psychotherapy, 48, 25–33.

Hamilton, B., & Coates, J. (1993). Perceived helpfulness and use of professional services by abused women. Journal of Family Violence, 8, 313–324.

Horvath, A.G., & Bedi, R.P. (2002). The alliance. In J.C. Norcross (Ed.). Psychotherapy relationships that work: Therapist contributions and responsiveness to patients (pp. 37–69). New York: Oxford Press.

Horvath, A.O., Del Re, C., Fluckiger, C., & Symonds, D. (2011). Alliance in individual psychotherapy. Psychotherapy, 48, 9–16.

Imel, Z.E., Wampold, B.E., Miller, S.D., & Fleming R.R. (2008). Distinctions without a difference. Direct comparisons of psychotherapies for alcohol use disorders. Psychology of Addictive Behaviors, 22, 533–543.

Institute of Medicine. (2008). Treatment of posttraumatic stress disorder: An assessment of evidence. Washington, DC: National Academic Press.

Joseph, S. (2011). What doesn't kill us: The new psychology of posttraumatic growth. New York: Basic Books.

Keijsers, G.P., Schaap, C., & Hoogduin, C.A. (2000). The impact of interpersonal patient therapists behavior on outcome in cognitive-behavior therapy. A review of empirical studies. Behavior Modification, 24, 264–297.

Lambert, M.J. (2010). Prevention of treatment failure: The art of measurement, monitoring and feedback in clinical practice. Washington, DC: American Psychological Association Press.

Lambert, M.J., Harmon, C., Slada, K., Whipple, J.L., & Hawkins, E.J. (2005). Providing feedback to psychotherapists in their patient's progress: Clinical results and practice suggestions. Journal of Clinical Psychology, 61, 165–174.

Martin, D.J., Garske, J.P., & Davis, M.K. (2000). Relation of the therapeutic alliance with outcome and other variables. A meta-analytic review. Journal of Consulting and Clinical Psychology, 68, 438–450.

McLeod, B.D. (2011). Relation of the alliance with outcomes in youth psychotherapy: A meta-analysis. Clinical Psychology Review, 31, 603–616.

McFarlane, A.C. (1994). Helping the victims of natural disasters. In J.R. Freedy & S.E. Hobfoll (Eds.). Traumatic stress: From theory to practice. New York: Plenum.

Meichenbaum, D. (1996). Forming alliances: Rescripting the narrative of trauma. Professional Counselor, June, 61–63.

Meichenbaum, D. (2006). Resilience and posttraumatic growth: A constructive narrative perspective. In L.G. Calhoun & R.G. Tedeschi (Eds.). Handbook of posttraumatic growth: Research and practice (pp. 355–368). Mahwah, NJ: Erlbaum Associates.

Meichenbaum, D. (2007). Stress inoculation training: A preventative and treatment approach. In P.M. Lehrer, R.L. Woolfolk, & W.E. Sime (Eds.). Principles and practice of stress management (pp. 497–518). New York: Guilford Press.

Meichenbaum, D. (2009). Core psychotherapeutic tasks with returning soldiers: A case conceptualization approach. In B. Morgillo Freeman, B.A. Moore, & A. Freeman (Eds.). Living and surviving in harm's way (pp. 193–210). New York: Routledge.

Meichenbaum, D. (2011). Resilience building as a means to prevent PTSD and related adjustment problems in military personnel. In B.A. Moore & W.E. Penk (Eds.). Treating PTSD in military personnel (pp. 325–355). New York: Guilford Press.

Meichenbaum, D. (2012). Roadmap to resilience. Clearwater, FL: Institute Press.

Messer, S.B., & Wampold, B.S. (2002). Let's face facts: Common factors are more potent than specific therapy ingredients. Clinical Psychology: Science and Practice, 9, 21–25.

Miller, S.D., Duncan, B.L., Brown, J., Sorrell, R., & Chalk, M.B. (2007). Using formal client feedback to improve outcome and retention. Journal of Brief Therapy, 5, 19–28.

Miller, S.D., Duncan, B.L., & Wampold, B.E. (Eds.). (2010). The heart and soul of change (2nd ed.). Washington, DC: American Psychological Association.

Muran, J.C., & Barber, J.P. (2010). The therapeutic alliance: An evidence-based guide to practice. New York: Guilford Press.

Norcross, J.C. (Ed.). (2002). Psychotherapy relationships that work: Therapist contributions and responsiveness in patients. New York: Oxford University Press.

Norcross, J. (2009). The therapeutic relationship. In B.L. Duncan, S.D. Miller, B.E. Wampold, & M.A. Hubble (Eds.). The heart and soul of change: Delivering what works in therapy (2nd ed., pp 113–142). Washington, DC: American Psychological Association.

Powers, M.B., Halpern, J.M., Ferenschak, M.P., Gillihan, S.J., & Foa, E.B. (2010). A meta- analytic review of prolonged exposure for posttraumatic stress disorder. Clinical Psychology Review, 30, 635–641.

Rogers, C.R. (1957). The necessary and sufficient conditions of therapeutic personality change. Journal of Consulting Psychology, 21, 95–103.

Rosen, G.R., & Frueh, B.C. (2010). Clinician's guide to PTSD. Hoboken, NJ: John Wiley & Sons.

Safran, J.D., & Muran, C. (2000). Negotiating the therapeutic. New York: Guilford Press.

Sharf, J., Primavera, L.H., & Diener, M.J. (2010). Dropout and the therapeutic alliance. Psychotherapy: Theory, Research and Practice, 47, 637–645.

Shimokawa, K., Lambert, M.J., & Smart, D.W. (2010). Enhancing treatment outcome of patients at risk of treatment failure: Meta-analytic and mega-analytic review of psychotherapy quality assurance system. Journal of Consulting and Clinical Psychology, 78, 298–311.

Walsh, R. (2011). Lifestyle and mental health. American Psychologist, 66, 579–592.

Wampold, B.E. (2001). The great psychotherapy debate: Models, methods and findings. Mahwah, NJ: Erlbaum.

Wampold, B.E., Imel, Z.E., Laska, K.M., Benish, S., Miller, S.D., Fluckiger, C., Del Re, A.C., Baardseth, T.P., & Budge, S. (2010). Determining what works on the treatment of PTSD. Clinical Psychology Review, 30, 923–933.

Wampold, B.E., Mondin, G.W., Moody, M., Stitch, F., Benson, K., & Ahn, H. (1997). A meta- analysis of outcome studies comparing bona-fide psychotherapies: Empirically 'All must have prizes'. Psychological Bulletin, 122, 203–215.

Webb, C.A., DeRubeis, R.J., & Barber, J.P. (2010). Therapist adherence/competence and treatment outcome: A meta-analytic review. Journal of Consulting and Clinical Psychology, 78, 200–211.

Yalom, I. (2002). The gift of therapy. New York, NY: Harper Collins.

3

Therapeutic Alliance in Working with Trauma Survivors

Janice L. Krupnick

Introduction

The therapeutic alliance, defined broadly as the collaborative bond between therapist and patient, has been conceptualized as that aspect of psychotherapy where emotional learning takes place (Scaturo, 2010). Consisting of the tasks, bonds and goals of the therapy that patient and therapist develop together (Bordin, 1976), it has been found to account for approximately twice as much of the variance in treatment outcome as specific technical interventions (Lambert, 2003; Wampold, 2001). Hence, the alliance is an important therapeutic variable for both practitioners and researchers to be familiar with within their chosen field of practice.

More than 30 years of research attests to the conclusion that the therapeutic alliance is an essential ingredient in the effectiveness of psychotherapy (as we saw in Chapter 2). This finding has been established across a range of psychosocial and pharmacological treatments (Krupnick et al., 1996), using a variety of measures to assess the strength of the alliance (Tichenor, 1989). The alliance has been studied in patients in long- and short-term psychotherapy (e.g., Bieschke et al., 1995; Eaton et al., 1988), as well as in inpatient and outpatient settings (e.g., Allen et al., 1985; Andreoli et al., 1993). Many studies have focused on patients with major depression (e.g., Feeley, 1993; Krupnick et al., 1994, 1996; Rounsaville et al., 1987), but the alliance has also been explored in the psychotherapy of drug-abusing patients (Tunis et al., 1995) and patients with borderline personality (Yeoman et al., 1994). Given the frequency of these diagnoses among patients who have experienced trauma, it is likely that at least some of the research participants in these studies were survivors of trauma. However, only a handful of studies have focused on thera-peutic alliance and outcome in patients who were specifically selected for study because they were trauma survivors. In these studies too, however, the central role played by the therapist and patient alliance has been affirmed (Cloitre et al., 2004; Keller et al., 2010; Smith et al., 2012). Indeed, not only is the therapeutic alliance important in the psychotherapeutic treatment of trauma survivors, but also the effect size of the association between therapeutic alliance and outcome may be much larger in psychotherapy with survivors of trauma than in more general samples of patients treated for depression and/or anx-iety who may or may not have experienced interpersonal violations (Cloitre et al., 2004).

This chapter will review some of the extant literature on the association between therapeutic alliance and treatment outcome, focusing on three studies in particular that explored this relationship in samples of women who suffered from either major depressive disorder, posttraumatic stress disorder (PTSD), or both following childhood sexual and/or physical abuse. In addition, it will explore some of the specific challenges that may be presented by trauma sur-vivors that can undermine or threaten the development of the therapeutic alliance. We will review insights and recommendations put forth by a number of researchers and clinicians about the development of the therapy relation-ship with trauma survivors (see also Chapter 6 of this volume for a single case example) as well as sharing some of their own clinical and research experience in working with this population.

Therapeutic alliance and treatment outcome

Two meta-analyses (Horvath and Symonds, 1991; Martin et al., 2000) have demonstrated that the therapeutic alliance was associated with treatment out-come not only across a number of investigations but also across different types of therapy. Further, it has been argued (Safran and Muran, 1995) that the quality of the alliance is even more important than the type of treatment in predicting therapeutic outcomes. Indeed, the relationship between the patient and therapist has been found to account for approximately twice as much of the variance in treatment outcome as specific technical interventions (Lambert, 2003; Wampold, 2001). Henry et al. (1994) asserted that the alliance may be therapeutic in and of itself. Given findings (e.g., DeFife and Hilsenroth, 2011; Tryon and Winograd, 2002) that early alliance is particularly important in terms of avoidance of premature termination of therapy, establishing a positive alliance is essential in predicting therapeutic success.

Yet establishing a positive therapeutic alliance, particularly in the early stages of treatment, may be difficult with survivors of trauma. This is especially likely if trauma occurred early and was prolonged, as in cases of childhood sexual and/or physical abuse. Gelso and Carter (1994) pointed out that alliance is formed in the complex transaction between therapist and patient, each of whom brings to therapy his or her own characteristics, personality and history. In the case of individuals who bring to therapy a trauma history, patients characteristically also bring a host of negative views of interpersonal interactions, given that their interpersonal experience has been exploitative and intrusive. As many clinicians who have worked with trauma survivors have discovered, patients who are survivors of interpersonal trauma typically have difficulty in tolerating the interpersonal nature of therapy, especially the need to trust another person with his or her pain (Turner et al., 1996). Cloitre and colleagues (2004) note that victims of childhood abuse show difficulties in emotion regulation (see Chapter 5 of this volume for a closer look at emotion regulation in the therapeutic relationship). Research demonstrates that childhood abuse victims have more difficulty managing anger, anxiety and depression (Browne & Finkelhor, 1986) and they report considerable problems in interpersonal functioning across a range of domains, including intimate relationships (Zlotnick et al., 1996).

Chemtob et al. (1997) reported that anger symptoms among those who had PTSD following trauma exposure caused ruptures in the therapeutic alliance that directly compromised treatment outcome, including premature termination of therapy. In Chemtob et al.'s (1997) cognitive behavioural approach to PTSD-related anger, they addressed these symptoms by focusing on three areas, problems with arousal, behaviour and beliefs. To help patients decrease arousal, they focused on teaching skills that could decrease overall arousal, such as relaxation skills, the use of self-hypnosis and the use of physical exercise to release tension. Focusing on behaviour, they recommend helping patients become more aware of how they typically feel when they feel threatened and helping them expand their range of possible responses, for example, by taking a time out or writing down thoughts when angry. Using their approach, therapists can help patients become more aware of the thoughts that lead up to anger and ask them to come up with more positive thoughts to replace the negative angry thoughts.

As noted above, most studies of therapeutic alliance and outcome have focused on broad categories of patients, such as those suffering from depression and/or anxiety, without specifying whether the patients are trauma survivors. Given that survivors of trauma typically present to treatment with major depression disorder and/or anxiety disorders, including PTSD, it is likely that at least a subset of patients in these studies are trauma survivors, but they may not constitute a majority or even a sizable minority of research participants. Only a few studies have looked at therapeutic alliance and outcome in samples comprised exclusively of trauma survivors and all of these studies focused on survivors of childhood sexual and/or physical abuse. Among these studies (Cloitre et al., 2002, 2004; Keller et al., 2010; Smith et al., 2012), however, all found that there was a significant relationship between the strength of the therapeutic alliance and outcome.

In their clinical trial of a two-phase treatment for childhood abuse-related PTSD, Cloitre and colleagues examined the relationship between therapeutic alliance and outcome among adult women who had experienced sexual or physical abuse as children. In this treatment, the first phase focused on stabilization and preparatory skills building. The second phase of the intervention was comprised mainly of imaginal exposure to traumatic memories of the abuse. Findings from this study indicated that the strength of the therapeutic alliance established during the first phase of treatment predicted successful reduction of PTSD symptoms during the treatment's second phase when exposure therapy was used (Cloitre et al., 2002).

In a subsequent study based on the randomized controlled trial described above, Cloitre et al. (2004) explored the related contributions of the therapeutic alliance and negative mood regulation to the outcome of their two-phase treatment for childhood abuse-related PTSD. Hierarchical regression analyses confirmed that the strength of the therapeutic alliance established early in treatment reliably predicted improvement in PTSD symptoms posttreatment. In this study, they also established that the therapy relationship was mediated by participants' improved capacity to regulate negative mood states in the context of the exposure therapy in the second phase. Based on these findings, the authors recommended that, at least for individuals who experienced trauma early in their emotional development, consideration should be given to a 'more complex theoretical model of treatment efficacy that incorporates the therapeutic alliance and related experiences such as social support as a means of resolving past psychological traumas and acquiring the specific regulatory skills to accomplish this goal' (Cloitre et al., 2004, p. 415). This recommendation encourages the approach that these authors have taken in working with survivors of early abuse. Their method uses techniques from Dialectical Behaviour Therapy (Linehan, 1993) to facilitate the patient's ability to regulate negative emotions in the first phase of treatment, followed by the use of prolonged exposure (Foa et al., 1999), a behavioural method, in the second phase. The role that they suggest is played by the therapeutic alliance is the creation of a firm foundation upon which the more disruptive process of prolonged exposure can take place. In other words, a strong therapeutic alliance helps to create the sense of trust and capacity to tolerate the strong emotion that can be evoked by the prolonged exposure method.

Keller and colleagues (2010) have noted that despite the potential importance of early alliance, we know very little about factors that impact its development in PTSD, a disorder specific to those who have experienced trauma. They note that several factors, such as avoidance and negative beliefs about others (Safran et al., 1990), may complicate the development of the alliance in psychotherapy involving patients with PTSD. In their examination of factors associated with early therapeutic alliance in PTSD treatment, they explored factors including treatment adherence, childhood sexual abuse history and social support. In this study of prolonged exposure for individuals with PTSD, they found that positive trauma-related social support was the sole predictor of a strong early alliance. A history of childhood sexual abuse was not predictive of a lower early alliance, a finding that is particularly interesting given that adults with abuse histories frequently have considerable difficulties with relationships (see Chapter 6 for clinical example of this phenomena). What this finding tells us is that while establishing relationships in the broad sense of the term might be problematic for these patients, establishing a therapeutic alliance might not suffer the same barriers. Of note was the finding that adults with histories of abuse were able to develop alliances with their therapists that were of the same quality of patients who had not been abused when they were children. Stronger early alliance scores were associated with completion of homework in the prolonged exposure treatment as well as total number of sessions completed. This last finding is of particular interest given Chemtob et al.'s (1997) finding that PTSD-related anger symptoms result in ruptures in the therapeutic relationship that directly compromised treatment outcome, including premature termination.

In a study of depressed women with sexual abuse histories who were randomly assigned to interpersonal psychotherapy or treatment as usual (defined as whatever type of intervention was customarily provided at the community mental health clinic at which the study was conducted), Smith et al. (2012) were interested in trying to determine why women with such histories tended to be less treatment responsive than depressed patients without such histories. They hypothesized that one contributor to poorer treatment outcomes might be the difficulty that women who had experienced childhood trauma of this nature would likely have in forming and maintaining secure relationships, such as the relationship between therapist and patient. They posited that these patients' relationship difficulties might be manifest in insecure attachment styles which could also impede the development of a positive therapeutic alliance. In this sample of depressed women, many of whom also met diagnostic criteria for comorbid PTSD and borderline personality disorder, a stronger working alliance was again associated with greater benefit from treatment. Each standard deviation increase in the rating of the therapeutic alliance corresponded to an average 4.32-point decrease in Beck Depression Inventory (Beck et al., 1996) scores over time. They had also hypothesized that the therapeutic alliance might be mediated by attachment anxiety and avoidance, but this hypothesis was not supported. In fact, attachment anxiety was not significantly associated with depressive symptom severity over time. Both attachment avoidance and the strength of the therapeutic alliance were independently associated with treatment outcome; attachment style did not mediate alliance. Greater attachment avoidance and weaker working alliance were each related to worse treatment outcomes, that is, worse depression symptoms, and these were independent effects. In addition, these effects were independent of the presence of comorbid borderline personality disorder and PTSD. In this study of interpersonal psychotherapy versus treatment as usual, the alliance played a stronger role in interpersonal psychotherapy, a relationship-focused intervention, than in treatment as usual.

In summary, there are relatively few studies of therapeutic alliance and outcome that have focused exclusively on trauma survivors. In spite of this, there is evidence that, in studies of adults with PTSD and/or major depression who experienced childhood sexual or physical abuse, the alliance can be successfully developed and the relationship between therapist and patient plays a significant role in treatment outcome. This has been found to be the case in cognitive behavioural treatment and in interpersonal psychotherapy, even though these treatments approach problems from very different perspectives. It has even been suggested that the importance of the relationship between therapist and patient may play a more important role in the treatment of trauma survivors, at least survivors of childhood interpersonal trauma, than in the treatment of other types of patients.

Given the fundamental role that is played by the therapeutic alliance in working with trauma survivors, it is essential that therapists working with this population know what to anticipate when beginning treatment. While the encouraging news is that it is possible to develop alliances that are just as strong with this population as with other patients (Keller et al., 2010), it is equally important to be aware of the particular challenges that working with such patients entails. Awareness of these challenges can help the clinician recognize and appropriately address alliance issues before they result in alliance ruptures and can help in building the alliance as the therapeutic dyad progresses in treatment. The next section will summarize some of the insights of experts with extensive experience in working with patients who have been subjected to interpersonal trauma.

Perspectives on the development of the therapeutic alliance

To date, studies of the therapeutic alliance and treatment outcome with trauma survivors have been based on investigations of cognitive behavioural treatments, including prolonged exposure and skills training in affective and interpersonal regulation followed by exposure, as well as interpersonal therapy and treatment as usual (as practised in community mental health). Explorations of the process of psychotherapy, including guidelines about how best to develop the therapeutic alliance with trauma survivors, however, have come primarily from theorists and researchers with humanistic/experiential or psychodynamic orientations. In Rogers' client-centred approach (1959), the focus of treatment is viewed as attunement in the therapy relationship as a means to change. Further, the Barrett-Lennard Relationship Inventory (Barrett-Lennard, 1962), based on measuring the degree to which the therapist offers empathy, regard and congruence to the patient, reflects one of the earliest attempts to measure the strength of therapist-offered conditions believed to contribute to the development of the therapeutic relationship. In the earliest writings about psychoanalytic theory and subsequently in the literature on psychodynamic psychotherapy, there has been extensive emphasis on the therapeutic relationship in its various manifestations. Indeed, gaining an understanding of potential transference and countertransference implications, as well as the importance of a strong therapeutic alliance, is at the heart of psychodynamic/psychoanalytic theory and practice.

General descriptions of the salient features of the therapeutic alliance have particular resonance when working with survivors of trauma. The important features of a strong alliance involve relationship capacities that are most likely to be undeveloped or seriously challenged among trauma survivors, especially those who have experienced early and prolonged abuse. Among those relationship challenges is the ability to trust, particularly those in positions of authority, as a therapist is likely to be perceived. Beauchamp and Childress (2001) and Tjeltveit (2006), in writing about the process of psychotherapy, have emphasized the importance of trust in the therapist and the therapeutic environment in helping the patient move forward in the therapeutic endeavour. To foster a sense of safety, the therapist must bring a high level of professional ethics and integrity to the situation. Attachment theorists conceptualize the therapy environment as analogous to the emotional and physical space within which a child experiences protection and safety in a healthy parental relationship (Winnicott, 1965). If an individual has not experienced this type of safety in earlier relationships with caretaking figures, however, as is the case with survivors of abuse, this trust must be earned and it is not likely to be earned easily.

Among those who have written about the therapy relationship with trauma survivors is Judith Herman, MD in her book *Trauma and Recovery* (1992). Herman has written that the core experiences in psychological trauma involve disempowerment and disconnection from others. In light of that, recovery must involve the empowerment of the patient and helping the individual develop new connections. Since, in the case of interpersonal traumas, that is, experiences that include physical and/or sexual assault, childhood abuse and domestic violence, violations took place in the context of relationships, recovery can take place only within the context of relationships as well. Recovery in these cases cannot occur in isolation. This perspective is an echo of much earlier work by psychoanalysts Alexander and French (1946), who wrote about the 'corrective emotional experience', defined basically as a way of re-parenting the individual who has been emotionally damaged by his or her relationships with others. It is also reflected in the work of Saakvitne and Pearlman (2000) whose treatment framework for working with survivors of childhood abuse is entitled 'Risking Connection'.

Herman's therapeutic stance in working with trauma survivors emphasizes paying attention to the areas in which such patients' psychological capacities have been damaged or deformed. These include patients' basic capacities for trust, autonomy, initiative, competence, identity and intimacy. The extent to which strengths in these areas have been damaged or perhaps never developed likely depends on the age at which interpersonal violations occurred and the frequency or duration of abuse. For example, in a sample of college-age women who had experienced single versus ongoing or multiple traumas, Krupnick and colleagues (Krupnick et al., 2004) found that those who had experienced multiple or ongoing traumas during their childhood or adolescence were likely to have more psychiatric diagnoses and more difficulty with interpersonal adjustment than those who had experienced only a single event. Using the same sample of young women, Briere et al. (2008) noted that individuals with greater cumulative trauma experienced greater symptom complexity. For those who experienced abuse during childhood, there is greater likelihood of more pervasive damage to psychological structures as they are in the process of being formed and more disruption to models of relationship that are being developed and internalized.

Despite the 'pull' that the therapist might feel to 'rescue' the survivor of horrendous exposure to trauma, as in the case of childhood sexual or physical abuse, it is imperative that the therapist resist such temptation. While the psychotherapist may have good intentions, wishing to help the person who has sought his or her help, efforts in this direction run counter to that which is actually therapeutic. As Herman (1992) points out, interventions that take power away from the trauma survivor cannot possibly foster recovery. The role of the therapist is to witness and validate the individual's experience. It is important that the patient be encouraged to take control of his or her own life and behaviour, developing a sense of competence and control.

The therapeutic relationship, by its very nature, is an unequal one in which the therapist, in his or her role as caretaker and helper, is in the dominant, superior position and the patient, by virtue of his or her needing help, is in the less powerful position. This power dynamic is not unlike that of parent and child, teacher and student, or older person with younger person. In cases of interpersonal abuse, the person who was in the more powerful position at an earlier time took advantage of that power by exploiting or overpowering the patient. Although this is the case in any psychotherapy situation, it is especially salient when working with trauma survivors that the therapist be aware of the dynamics of the relationship and its power implications. It is the therapist's role to use that power to foster the patient's recovery. Thus, the therapy relationship can provide a model of relationship counter to the one in which the patient was exploited or abused. It provides an opportunity for the patient to experience a relationship in which his or her autonomy, competence and power is encouraged and valued.

In some therapeutic approaches, for example, interpersonal psychotherapy or feminist therapy, the psychotherapist is encouraged to assume the role of patient advocate. Herman (1992), however, recommends the therapeutic stance of neutrality that is advanced in psychodynamic psychotherapy. She asserts that one can respect the patient's autonomy by remaining 'disinterested and neutral'. Herman (1992, p. 135) states that 'disinterested' means that the therapist abstains from using her power over the patient to gratify her personal needs. 'Neutral' means that the therapist does not take sides in the patient's inner conflicts or try to direct the patient's life decisions. By refusing to take sides in the patient's inner conflicts or directing the patient's life decisions, the therapist refrains from taking over or encouraging a sense of helplessness. This neutrality does not mean a stance of cool detachment or lack of caring. Rather, Herman writes, it involves understanding that the patient has experienced a fundamental injustice while conveying the message that, with the therapist's support and encouragement, he or she can find the right path for him or herself.

It can be helpful in formulating the therapeutic needs of the patient to anticipate what the difficulties are likely to be in terms of establishing a strong working alliance. Key among these difficulties is likely to be the sense of doubt and suspicion with which the trauma survivor enters psychotherapy. While the patient seeks and wants help from the therapist, it is not easy to trust another person because of his or her trauma history. Trauma survivors may need to repeatedly 'test' the therapist, especially in the early phase of treatment. Patients are likely to be very sensitive to therapist's reactions to their reports of their experiences. On the one hand, if the therapist recoils or changes the subject to less threatening topics, the patient may get the message that the therapist cannot bear to listen to his or her story. On the other hand, therapists who seem too interested may be suspected of being voyeuristic or exploitative. Given their prior experiences, it is likely that caretaking individuals may be perceived as uncaring or neglectful in some instances or opportunistic or exploitative in others. Patients may perceive the therapist as unable to listen to particularly gruesome or painful stories or interested mainly in exercising his or her power over the patient. Herman (1992) points out that, particularly if a patient has been subjected to chronic trauma, the dynamics of dominance and submission will be re-enacted in all subsequent relationships, including therapy.

Among the relationship potentials that might emerge in working with survivors of trauma is what Herman (1992) calls a 'traumatic transference'. She notes that patients often develop a particular view of the therapy relationship based on their earlier experience of terror while under the control of people in authority. Due to a fear of the victimizer who demanded submission and silence, the patient may need to keep the therapist under control. Since no one responded to cries for help, even if these were not overtly expressed, the patient may anticipate that no one will help in the therapy situation either. Such patients may be unusually sensitive to feelings of abandonment, creating particular anxieties around the time of therapist vacations and other separations.

Given the desire for rescue, a patient who has experienced trauma may develop rescue fantasies and may idealize the therapist as the omnipotent caretaker who will make everything better. When the therapist inevitably fails to live up to these expectations, the patient may be overcome with rage (Herman, 1992). Since the patient may feel that his or her life depends on the rescuer, there is a great need for the therapist to be perfect. As Herman (1992) points out, the helpless rage of the victim is a displacement of the rage from the perpetrator of the trauma to the current caretaker. This author goes on to suggest that the sense of humiliation and shame that patients experience as a consequence of feeling small and helpless can lead to the patient's wish to reduce the disappointing, envied therapist to the same condition of terror, helplessness and shame that she or he has suffered.

Working with survivors of incest, Courtois (1988) has emphasized the importance of maintaining a therapeutic stance of openness to and acceptance of the patient. Like Herman (1992), she advocates maintaining neutrality, but adds that it is advisable to be active and open in engaging the patient. The risk in being perceived as non-responsive or distant is that there may be a tendency to recreate or to be perceived as recreating dynamics of the past. If the therapist is viewed as unavailable, it is difficult for the patient to feel safe in disclosing what are likely to be shameful or frightening memories or feelings. Without what the attachment theorists describe as a 'holding' or 'facilitating' environment (Winnicott, 1965), the patient is likely to feel that it is unsafe to engage in deep self-exploration. Thus, a warm and caring, but not overindulgent, therapist provides the type of interpersonal environment that is conducive to self-disclosure and self-examination (Courtois, 1988).

Theorists who work with survivors of trauma invariably address issues of power and control since these are such central issues in psychotherapy with individuals who have experienced human-inflicted trauma. Thus, Courtois, in working with incest survivors; Herman (1992), in working with survivors of abuse; and Resick and Schnicke (1988), in discussing women who have experienced sexual assault, all write about these dynamics. Courtois (1988) recommends against being parental or authoritarian with abuse victims. She advocates creating a therapeutic environment in which the patient can feel powerful and efficacious. She points out that the patient is indeed the expert on her own experience, while the therapist serves as a supportive person who helps the patient explore that experience. The role of the therapist is to enable the patient to express thoughts and feelings that it was not possible to express during childhood and which are too overwhelming to explore and express alone at the present time. She reminds us that, because the patient has been betrayed in the context of an intimate relationship, other relationships are suspect. To counter the patient feeling alone and abandoned, worthless and undeserving, the therapist offers a model of a healthy, non-exploitative and growth-promoting relationship. As such, the alliance with a supportive, validating and consistent therapist offers special potential to heal the effects of incest. It serves as the foundation that permits the patient to do exploratory work.

When working with patients who have experienced the trauma of sexual assault, Resick and Schnicke (1988) advise therapists to examine their own beliefs about rape, for example, that women may unconsciously wish to be overpowered or that an individual cannot be raped by someone with whom he or she has previously had sexual relations. They suggest that any time a therapist asks 'why' a patient did or did not do something, there is an implication of blame and individuals who have experienced sexual assault are very sensitive to implications of this nature. They write that some therapists may feel uncomfortable hearing about the details of a sexual assault and, as a consequence, may avoid going after the details of a trauma survivor's story. It is easy to rationalize this type of avoidance, believing that they are protecting the patient because the individual will find delving too far into the details will prove overwhelming. What the therapist is overlooking in taking this perspective is that the patient has been living with these details and needs to know that the memory of her ordeal is not too horrifying for the therapist to hear or accept.

A number of clinicians and researchers who have specialized in the treatment of trauma survivors point out the link between trauma and the development of borderline personality disorder, especially among patients who have been subjected to repeated trauma over a considerable period of time. Briere and Runtz (1991) have written that borderline personality can be conceptualized as PTSD and Herman and van der Kolk (1987) have suggested that descriptions of borderline personality and PTSD are remarkably congruent. The descriptions of patients with what is referred to as 'complex PTSD' (Ford & Kidd, 1998) sound much the same as those who have been diagnosed with borderline personality. In both syndromes, major disturbances are found in the areas of affect regulation, impulse control, reality testing, interpersonal relationships and self-integration.

Horowitz et al. (1984) have described potential pitfalls in the development of a therapeutic alliance with a patient with borderline personality, particularly after a stressful life event. They note that the relationship with the therapist reflects the predispositions of the borderline patient in that the relationship is typically intense and unstable, marked by shifts in the patient's view of the therapy. They, like Herman (1992), warn therapists to expect that early idealizations of the therapist are likely to give way to painful disillusionments and rage, often after disappointments in the therapist that are objectively minor. They remind the reader that the therapist is often not attended to as a real person with strengths, vulnerabilities, imperfections and a personal existence outside the therapeutic setting. Wishing for a powerful rescuer, the patient with borderline personality is likely to perceive the therapist as a powerful force whose purpose is to help him or her navigate the patient's troubled world. When the therapist inevitably reveals his or her faulty human qualities, the defensive 'splitting' that is the hallmark of this type of personality

structure leads the patient to view the previously perceived 'all-good therapist' as 'all-bad'. The response to this perception is typically rage and can lead
to premature termination of treatment. Because of this, Horowitz and colleagues advise therapists, in working with this population of trauma survivors,
to clearly communicate the nature of the therapeutic alliance, putting what
might be seen as the 'obvious' into words. This may be especially important
when the patient reveals irritation, contempt, hostility or a lack of interest in
the therapist. At these times, it is especially important to convey to the patient
that the therapist's supportive and compassionate approach will remain in spite
of the patient's criticisms or reproaches. It may be useful in instances such as
these to remind the patient of previously helpful interchanges with the therapist to counter the loss of perspective that the patient is likely to experience
when she or he becomes disillusioned with the therapist.

Rather than allowing the transference to develop (in psychodynamic psychotherapy), as the therapist might be inclined to do with patient with more
stable self-concepts, the therapist would do well to promptly and repeatedly
conduct reality test with patients with borderline personality. This can counter
the progressive deepening of feelings that are based on transference reactions,
particularly of a negative and devaluing nature. It may be difficult to always
know when the patient is experiencing particularly negative views of the therapist because the patient may be too embarrassed to admit to between-session
thoughts of the therapist as bad. This may be evident to the therapist if the
patient's presentation has an 'as if' or contrived quality. At these times, it
can be helpful for the therapist to acknowledge the possibility of transitions
between 'good' and 'bad' images that the patient harbours of the therapist. The therapist's conveying compassionate acceptance and a willingness
to repeat previous episodes of work in order to help the patient re-establish
a sense of trust and engagement is another way to help the patient build a
stronger internal as well as interpersonal structure (Horowitz et al., 1984).

Remembering that the patient with borderline personality can shift from
views of the therapist as a benevolent caretaker or omnipotent rescuer to a
perception of this same therapist as an evil, malevolent figure should help the
therapist pay special attention to the nuances of the patient's internal states.
Even when the alliance seems secure, the risk of fearful expectation on the
patient's part is never far away. If the patient's fear and rage towards the therapist becomes too intense, his or her capacity for assessment of reality may
diminish. This may be countered by reviewing with the patient what the therapist actually said and what was actually meant by his or her intervention.
Emphasizing the therapist's goodwill despite the patient's affective storms can
help provide the 'holding environment' that allows the patient to feel safe
within the therapeutic context.

In Krupnick's recent work with low-income women with complex interpersonal trauma histories (Krupnick et al., 2008), she has explored relationship

patterns in this group that have implications for the therapeutic alliance. In this sample of primarily (75%) African American women, with a mean of almost seven different interpersonal traumas, typically beginning in childhood, a distinctive relational pattern emerged. In addition to high scores on interpersonal sensitivity, need for social approval and lack of sociability (subscales on the Inventory of Interpersonal Problems; Horowitz et al., 1988) at the outset of treatment, these research participants revealed a tendency to fall into one of two relational patterns. In one pattern, women had a tendency to re-enact patterns that put them at relational risk. Examples of this include their failing to establish appropriate boundaries with others, for example, family members having inappropriately high expectations of caretaking and the individual feeling unable to say 'no', or allowing men to make sexual demands that they felt they could not refuse. Others had a tendency to react to people with a 'chip on their shoulders', overreacting when they perceived a slight or misperceiving others as overly aggressive towards them. The other pattern involved the tendency to be socially withdrawn and avoidant. Krupnick and her colleagues (2008) saw both of these relational stances as problematic in that the one often put the woman at risk of further victimization while the other prevented her from establishing the types of relationships that might provide social support and corrective emotional experiences. For example, if a woman did not recognize what reasonable boundaries might be, based on her prior experience of having her boundaries violated and betrayed, she might unconsciously place herself in vulnerable positions with others, not protecting herself either physically or emotionally from dangerous others. If she was socially withdrawn and did not let others get too close, she was prevented from reworking relationship models that might be more growth enhancing.

In Krupnick's view (2001, 2008, 2012), the relational tendencies that were observed in women with complex assault and abuse histories presented expectable challenges in establishing a therapeutic alliance. For individuals who inadvertently placed themselves at relational risk because they had not developed the skills to determine whom they might reasonably trust, the goal might be to help them understand that they were worthy of compassionate treatment and that they were entitled to set boundaries that would allow them to feel safe. They might need help in understanding and clarifying what appropriate boundaries for them might be. This could present as a therapeutic challenge because a therapist might be inclined to delve into sensitive issues at a faster pace than is comfortable for the patient. If she is aware of feeling uncomfortable but doesn't perceive herself as having enough power in the therapy relationship to express her discomfort, she might terminate therapy or allow herself to become emotionally overwhelmed. Thus, it becomes important for the therapist to be sensitive to potential shifts in the patient's facial expressions or body posture that might express the discomfort she feels unable to articulate. The therapist might also indicate to the patient that he or she will not push the patient to go any faster or deeper into the issues than the pace at which the patient feels comfortable. Unlike the perpetrator of assault or abuse, the therapist will not force anything on the patient that she does not want or feel ready for. In other words, the patient's needs, wishes and state of readiness for personal exploration need to be considered, understood and respected.

There are a number of reasons why an individual who has been betrayed or violated might be wary of letting others, including the therapist, become emotionally close. One of these reasons is that the individual feels damaged and is reluctant to allow anyone to get close enough to perceive the ways in which she feels unworthy. For example, an individual who was in psychotherapy following a history of multiple sexual assaults said that she felt like she was 'damaged goods'. She questioned why anyone would want to be close to her because she had lost something essential that would warrant intimacy. Another reason to fear letting another person gain access to one's inner self is that it does not feel safe. If a person's expectation is that others will take advantage of that access to hurt her, it makes psychological sense that she would pull away. This could be played out in the therapy relationship in the patient's expectation that if the therapist really knew her, she would be scornful and judgemental. An example of the way in which this concern became evident in one of our (JLK's) treatments involved a patient who implied that she had an extensive abuse history but was reluctant to share the details because earlier caretaking figures had been untrustworthy. This reluctance was seen as impeding the development of the therapeutic alliance. To encourage the development of the alliance, I (JLK) explicitly acknowledged that given her history with people who were supposed to look after her best interests but who ultimately betrayed her, she might have some concerns about trusting me. This intervention allowed her to openly express her worries in this area and ultimately allowed her to let down her guard. Alternatively, the patient might fear that if she were to allow herself to become emotionally vulnerable, the therapist would exploit or harm her in some way. Because of this, she might well put up an emotional wall for self-protection. To demonstrate his or her good intentions, the therapist in these cases might put into words what the patient cannot or does not, for example, that it is understandable that the patient might be wary or uncertain of what to expect, given her history of relationships with others who were untrustworthy. It is only through continued interaction with the patient during which the therapist demonstrates that she or he is accepting, non-judgemental and in the patient's corner that trust can be acquired. 'Being in the patient's corner' does not suggest a disagreement with Herman's (1992) recommendation that the therapist remain 'disinterested' and 'neutral'. This stance is not meant to suggest taking sides. It suggests instead that therapists convey being on the side of helping the patient work out his or her own difficulties, encouraging autonomy and the development of a greater sense of control over one's own body and destiny (see also Chapters 4 and 7 for views on how to interpret these general principles of being on the client's side and Chapter 9 for the same principle applied in supervision). At the same time, however, the message is conveyed that the therapist strives for what is in the patient's interest, taking the side of helping the patient achieve her therapeutic goals. When working with those who have experienced extensive interpersonal trauma, the therapist needs to be patient in understanding that the development of trust is a process that takes time. Even when trust is established, there can be ruptures in the therapeutic alliance that occur because of therapeutic errors or misperceptions. An example of this involved the case of a patient with a history of abuse who alienated others with her confrontational style. When I (JLK) interpreted the likelihood that she scared others away with her 'chip on the shoulder style', she felt criticized and missed the following session. In the subsequent session after that, I addressed her feeling criticized and expressed understanding that this was her way to try to protect herself. By openly addressing the rift that had emerged between us, we were able to repair the patient's feeling of being misunderstood and assaulted by the prior interpretation. Thus, the development and maintenance of the therapeutic alliance is an ongoing process that requires therapeutic alertness and monitoring.

Conclusions

Working therapeutically with patients who have experienced trauma can present challenges and difficulties that may not be present in therapeutic endeavours with patients who lack trauma histories. At the same time, it can offer special rewards, for example, the satisfaction of helping individuals achieve the kind of loving and supportive relationships that they had not previously known. Identification of the particular relationship challenges that the trauma survivor faces can help guide the treatment, in terms of both the process of therapy and establishing therapeutic goals. Clarification of potential transference and countertransference reactions early in the therapy process can help the therapist navigate expectable ruptures in the alliance that can derail the course of intervention. Strong therapeutic alliances can be developed with patients who have experienced serious relationship violations, as long as the therapist can anticipate problems and can provide emotional safety.

Summary points

- Thirty years of process-outcome research has shown the value of the therapeutic alliance.
- The therapeutic alliance is a pan-theoretical construct that supports successful outcomes in trauma therapy.

> ▪ The therapeutic alliance can be facilitative in helping clients that have experienced a number of traumatic events.
> ▪ The therapeutic alliance can help the therapist to anticipate problems and can provide emotional safety.

Suggested reading

Cloitre, M., Stovall-McClough, K.C., Miranda, R., & Chemtob, C.M. (2004). Therapeutic alliance, negative mood regulation, and treatment outcome in child abuse-related posttraumatic stress disorder. *Journal of Consulting and Clinical Psychology, 72*(3): 411–416.

Wampold, B.E. (2001). *The Great Psychotherapy Debate: Models, Methods, and Findings.* Mahwah, NY: Lawrence Erlbaum.

References

Alexander, F., & French, T.M. (1946). *Psychoanalytic therapy: Principles and applications.* New York: Ronald Press.

Allen, J.G., Tarnoff, G., & Coyne, L. (1985). Therapeutic alliance and long-term hospital treatment out-come. *Comprehensive Psychiatry, 26,* 187–194.

Andreoli, A., Frances, A.J., Gex-Fabry, M., Aapro, N., Gerin, P., & Dazord, A. (1993). Crisis intervention in depressed patients with and without DSM-III-R personality disorders. *Journal of Nervous and Mental Disease, 181,* 732–737.

Barrett-Lennard, G.T. (1962). Dimensions of therapist response as causal factors in therapeutic change. *Psychological Monographs: General and Applied, 76*(43), 1–36.

Beauchamp, T., & Childress, J. (2001). *Principles of biomedical ethics* (5th ed.). New York: Oxford University Press.

Beck, A.T., Steer, R.A., & Brown, G.K. (1996). *Manual for the beck depression inventory-II.* San Antonio, TX: Psychological Corporation.

Bieschke, K.J., Bowman, G.D., Hopkins, M., Levine, H., & McFadden, K. (1995). Improvement and satisfaction with short-term therapy at a university counseling center. *Journal of College Student Development, 36,* 553–559.

Bordin, E.S. (1976). The generalizability of the psychoanalytic concept of the working alliance. *Psychotherapy: Theory, Research, and Practice, 16,* 252–260.

Briere, J., Kaltman, S., & Green, B.L. (2008). Accumulated childhood trauma and symptom complexity. *Journal of Traumatic Stress, 21*(2), 223–226.

Briere, J., & Runtz, M. (1991). The long-term effects of sexual abuse: A review and synthesis. In J. Briere (Ed.) *Treating Victims of Child Sexual Abuse. New Directions for Mental Health Services.* San Francisco: Jossey-Bass.

Browne, A., & Finkelhor, D. (1986). Impact of child sexual abuse. A review of the research. *Psychological Bulletin, 99,* 66–77.

Cloitre, M., Koenen, K., C., Cohen, L.R., & Han, H. (2002). Skills training in affective and interpersonal regulation followed by exposure: A phase-based treatment for

PTSD related to childhood abuse. *Journal of Consulting and Clinical Psychology, 70*(5), 1067–1074.

Cloitre, M., Stovall-McClough, K.C., Miranda, R., & Chemtob, C.M. (2004). Therapeutic alliance, negative mood regulation, and treatment outcome in child abuse-related posttraumatic stress disorder. *Journal of Consulting and Clinical Psychology, 72*(3), 411–416.

Chemtob, C.M., Novaro, R.N., Hamada, R.N., & Gross, D. (1997). Cognitive-behavioral treatment of severe anger in posttraumatic stress disorder. *Journal of Consulting and Clinical Psychology, 65*, 184–189.

Courtois, C.A. (1988). *Healing the incest wound: Adult survivors in therapy.* New York: W.W. Norton & Co.

Defife, J.A., & Hilsenroth, M.J. (2011). Starting off on the right foot: Common factor elements in early psychotherapy process. *Journal of Psychotherapy Integration, 21*(2), 172–191.

Eaton, T.T., Abeles, N., & Gutfreund, M.J. (1988). Therapeutic alliance and outcome: Impact of treatment length and pretreatment symptomatology. *Psychotherapy, 25*, 536–542.

Feeley, W.M. (1993). Treatment components of cognitive therapy for major depression: The good, the bad, and the inert. Unpublished doctoral dissertation. University of Pennsylvania, Philadelphia.

Foa, E.B., Dancu, C.V., Hembree, E.A., Jaycox, L.H., Meadows, E.A., & Street, G.P. (1999). A comparison of exposure therapy, stress inoculation training, and their combination for reducing posttraumatic stress disorder in female assault victims. *Journal of Consulting and Clinical Psychology, 67*(2), 194–200.

Ford, J.D., & Kidd, P. (1998). Early childhood trauma and disorders of extreme stress as predictors of treatment outcome with chronic posttraumatic stress disorder. *Journal of Traumatic Stress, 11*(4), 743–761.

Gelso, C.J., & Carter, J.A. (1994). Components of the psychotherapy relationship: Their interaction and unfolding during treatment. *Journal of Counseling Psychology, 41*, 296–306.

Henry, W.P., Strupp, H.H., Schacht, T.E., & Gaston, L. (1994). Psychodynamic approaches. In A.E. Bergin & S.L. Garfield (Eds.), *Handbook of psychotherapy and behavior change* (4th ed., pp. 467–508). New York: Wiley.

Herman, J. (1992). *Trauma and recovery.* New York: Basic Books.

Herman, J., & van der Kolk, B.A. (1987). Traumatic antecedents of borderline personality disorder. In B.A. van der Kolk (Ed.), *Psychological trauma* (pp. 111–126). Washington, DC: American Psychiatric Press.

Horvath, A.O., & Symonds, B.D. (1991). Relation between working alliance and outcome in psychotherapy: A meta-analysis. *Journal of Counseling Psychology, 38*, 139–149.

Horowitz, L.M, Rosenberg, S.E., Baer, B.A., Ureno, G., & Villesenor, V.S. (1988). Inventory of interpersonal problems: Psychometric properties and clinical applications. *Journal of Consulting and Clinical Psychology, 56*, 885–892.

Horowitz, M.J., Marmar, C., Krupnick, J., Wilner, N., Kaltreider, N., & Wallerstein, R. (1984). *Personality styles and brief psychotherapy.* New York: Basic Books.

Keller, S.M., Zoellner, L.A., & Feeney, N.C. (2010). Understanding factors associated with early therapeutic alliance in PTSD treatment: Adherence, childhood sexual abuse history, and social support. *Journal of Consulting and Clinical Psychology*, *78*(6), 974–979.

Krupnick, J.L. (2001). Interpersonal psychotherapy for PTSD after interpersonal trauma. *Directions in Psychiatry, 20*, 237–253.

Krupnick, J.L., Elkin, I., Collins, J., Simmens, S., Sotsky, S.M., Pilkonis, P.A., & Watkins, J.T. (1994). Therapeutic alliance and clinical outcome in the NIMH treatment of depression collaborative research program: Preliminary findings. *Psychotherapy, 31*, 28–35.

Krupnick, J.L., Green, B.L., Stockton, P., Goodman, L., Corcoran, C., & Petty, R. (2004). Mental health effects of adolescent trauma exposure in a female college sample: Exploring differential outcomes based on experiences of unique trauma types and dimensions. *Psychiatry: Interpersonal and Biological Processes, 67*, 264–279.

Krupnick, J.L., & Melnikoff, S.E. (2012). Psychotherapy with low-income patients: Lessons learned from treatment studies. *Journal of Contemporary Psychotherapy*, (Special Issue) *Working with financially impoverished clients*, 42(1): 7–15.

Krupnick, J.L., Green, B.L., Stockton, P., Miranda, J., Krause, E., & Mete, M. (2008). Group interpersonal psychotherapy for low-income women with posttraumatic stress disorder. *Psychotherapy Research, 18*(5), 497–507.

Krupnick, J.L, Sotsky, S.M., Elkin, I., Watkins, J., & Pilkonis, P.A. (1996). The role of the therapeutic alliance in psychotherapy and pharmacotherapy outcome: Findings in the National Institute of Mental Health Treatment of Depression Collaborative Research Program. *Journal of Consulting and Clinical Psychology, 64*(3), 532–539.

Lambert, M.J. (2003). The efficacy and effectiveness of psychotherapy. In M.J. Lambert (Ed.), *Bergin and Garfield's handbook of psychotherapy and behavior change* (5th ed., pp. 139–193). New York: Wiley.

Linehan, M.M. (1993). *Cognitive-behavioral treatment of borderline personality disorder*. New York: Guilford Press.

Martin, D.J., Garske, J.P., & David, M.K. (2000). Relation of the therapeutic alliance with outcome and other variables: A meta-analytic review. *Journal of Consulting and Clinical Psychology, 68*(3), 438–450.

Resick, P.A., & Schnicke, M.K. (1996). *Cognitive processing therapy for rape victims: A treatment manual*. Newbury Park, CA: Sage Publications.

Rogers, C.R. (1959). A theory of therapy, personality, and interpersonal relationships. In S. Koch (Ed.), *Psychology: A study of a Science, vol: III* (pp. 184–256). New York: McGraw Hill.

Rounsaville, B.J., Chevron, E.S., Prusoff, B.A., Elkin, I., Imber, S., Sotsky, S., & Watkins, J. (1987). The relation between specific and general dimensions of the psychotherapy process in interpersonal psychotherapy for depression. *Journal of Consulting and Clinical Psychology, 55*, 379–384.

Saakvitne, K.W., G amble, S.J., Pearlman, L.A., & Lev, B.T. (2000). *Risking connection: A training curriculum for work with survivors of childhood abuse*. Baltimore, MD: Sidran Institute Press.

Safran, J.D., Crocker, P., McMain, S., & Murray, P. (1990). Therapeutic alliance rupture as a therapy event for empirical investigation. *Psychotherapy: Theory, Research, Practice, Training, 27*, 154–165.

Safran, J.D., & Muran, J.C. (eds.) (1995). The therapeutic alliance (Special Issue). *In Session: Psychotherapy in Practice, 1*(1).

Scaturo, D.J. (2010). A tripartite learning conceptualization of psychotherapy: The therapeutic alliance, technical interventions, and relearning. *American Journal of Psychotherapy, 64,* 1–27.

Smith, P.N., Gamble, S.A., Cort, N.A., Ward, E.A., He, H., & Talbot, N.L. (2012). Attachment and alliance in the treatment of depressed, sexually abused women. *Depression and Anxiety, 29*(2), 123–130.

Tichenor, V., & Hill, C.E. (1989). A comparison of six measures of the working alliance. *Psychotherapy: Research and Practice, 26,* 195–199.

Tjeltveit, A.C. (2006). To what ends? Psychotherapy goals and outcomes, the good life, and the principle of beneficence. *Psychotherapy: Theory, Research, Practice, Training, 43,* 186–200.

Tryon, G.S., & Winograd, G. (2002). Goal consensus and collaboration. In J.C. Norcross (Ed.), *Psychotherapy relationships that work: Therapist contributions and responsiveness to patients* (pp. 109–135). New York: Oxford.

Tunis, S.L., Delucchi, K.L., Schwartz, KI., Banys, P., & Sees, K.L. (1995). The relationship of counselor and peer alliance to drug use and HIV risk behaviors in a six-month methadone detoxification program. *Addictive Behaviors, 20,* 395–405.

Turner, T.J., McFarlane, A.C., & van der Kolk, B.A. (1996). The therapeutic environment and new explorations in the treatment of post-traumatic stress disorder. In B.A. van der Kolk, A.C. McFarlane, & L. Weisaeth (Eds.), *Traumatic stress: The effects of overwhelming experience on mind, body, and society* (pp. 537–596). New York: Guilford Press.

Wampold, B.E. (2001). *The great psychotherapy debate: Models, methods, and findings.* Mahwah, NY: Lawrence Erlbaum.

Winnicott, D.W. (1965). *The maturational processes and the facilitative environment: Studies in the theory of emotional development.* London: Hogarth Press.

Yeoman, F.E., Gutfreund, J., Selzer, M.A., Clarkin, J.J., Hull, S.W., & Smith, T.E. (1994). Factors related to drop-outs by borderline patients: Treatment contract and therapeutic alliance. *Journal of Psychotherapy: Practice and Research, 3,* 16–24.

Zlotnick, C., Zakriski, A.L., Shea, M.T., & Costello, E. (1996). The long-term sequelae of sexual abuse: Support for a complex posttraumatic stress disorder. *Journal of Traumatic Stress, 9,* 195–205.

4

Affective–Cognitive Processing and Posttraumatic Growth

Stephen Joseph and David Murphy

Introduction

One of the findings from the psychotherapeutic literature on trauma is that different clients need to do different things in order to experience satisfactory levels of functioning following exposure to a traumatic event. As such we need to understand clients' needs in a broad and flexible way rather than through any one specific therapeutic technique. Building on the previous two chapters that considered the common factors and therapeutic alliance in trauma therapy, the aim of this chapter is to provide a framework within which we can consider the multiplicity of needs that clients may have and the role of the therapeutic relationship in responding to these needs. In the first section of this chapter, we will summarize the affective–cognitive processing model of posttraumatic growth. This is a broad-based framework that allows clinicians to enable clients to identify and formulate their difficulties in processing and thus what areas of therapeutic support may prove beneficial. In the second section of the chapter, we discuss the need for trauma therapists to consider their own philosophical stance to therapeutic change – and whether theirs is a medical or a growth-oriented approach. Taking the latter view ourselves, we consider the view that the therapeutic relationship is the vehicle of change because it creates the space for the self-determination of the client to unfold. Third, we offer a client-centred view of working with trauma in which the use of therapeutic techniques within non-directive practice is explored.

Affective–cognitive processing

Previously, we have proposed an affective–cognitive processing framework for understanding posttraumatic growth. The framework posits that posttraumatic stress reactions indicate the need for affective–cognitive processing and are a natural and normal state; people are intrinsically motivated to move towards psychologically growthful outcomes; and psychological and social-environmental factors either facilitate or thwart the intrinsic motivation towards growth (see, Joseph, Murphy, & Regel, 2012). This new reformulated model of affective–cognitive processing was based on Joseph, Williams and Yule's (1997) psychosocial model of posttraumatic stress. The psychosocial model was originally developed to understand how posttraumatic stress arises following trauma through a repetitive cycle of appraisal processes, negative emotional states and avoidant coping activity leading to reductions in social support, and how posttraumatic stress is further maintained by these factors once it has developed.

Although developed prior to the development of the field of posttraumatic growth, the model offered a perspective that proposed changes to the assumptive world and in ones understanding of the self could result (Joseph & Williams, 2005). As such we have developed the model to provide an explicit proposal of how successful affective–cognitive processing involves accommodation of new trauma-related information (see Figure 4.1).

The term now commonly used to describe such changes when they are of a positive psychological nature is posttraumatic growth. Posttraumatic growth is a wide-ranging concept that refers to three broad domains of positive change noted throughout the literature (Calhoun & Tedeschi, 2006; Tedeschi & Calhoun, 1996). First, interpersonal relationships are enhanced in some way. For example, people describe that they come to value their friends and family more, feel an increased sense of compassion for others and a longing for more intimate relationships. Second, people change their views of themselves in some way, for example, that they have a greater sense of personal resiliency, wisdom and strength, perhaps coupled with a greater acceptance of their vulnerabilities and limitations. Third, people describe changes in their life philosophy, for example, finding a fresh appreciation for each new day and reevaluating their understanding of what really matters in life.

Positive changes are widely reported by people following trauma. Studies have shown that growth is common for survivors of various traumatic events, including transportation accidents (shipping disasters, plane crashes, car accidents), natural disasters (hurricanes, earthquakes), interpersonal violence (combat, rape, sexual assault, child abuse), medical problems (cancer, heart attack, brain injury, spinal cord injury, HIV/AIDS, leukemia, rheumatoid arthritis, multiple sclerosis, illness) and other life experiences (relationship breakdown, parental divorce, bereavement, immigration). Typically 30–70

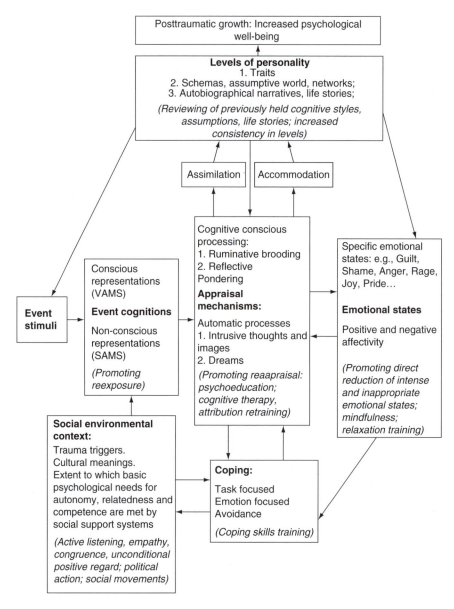

Figure 4.1 Posttraumatic affective–congnitive processing model

per cent of survivors will say that they have experienced positive changes of one form or another (Joseph & Butler, 2010).

The affective–cognitive processing framework offers a common factors approach useful to therapists from all orientations and allows for an understanding of the issues relevant to clients whether they present down-stream after serious problems have developed or upstream before problems arise.

To understand this framework, we begin with the traumatic event and read clockwise through event cognitions, appraisals, emotional states and coping, as a repetitive cyclic process, influenced by personality and social environmental conditions, which is ongoing until discrepancies between the pre-trauma assumptive world and the new trauma-related information are resolved.

Many practitioners first come into contact with survivors of trauma down-stream when psychological problems have developed to such an extent that they are interfering with everyday social and occupational functioning. There are several points at which intervention can be helpful. Points of intervention are marked in Figure 4.1 in italics involving:

1. *Identifying with the client those social support processes that may be impeding processing.* At different points in time, people have needs for emotional, practical and informational support. Emotional support refers to the provision of empathic understanding and reflective listening that is known to facilitate the emotional and cognitive processing of the other person. Practical support refers to the provision of helping behaviours that enable the person to cope with external problems and can take the form of assistance with paperwork, loan of money or dealing with a situation that the other person is not able to deal with. Informational support refers to the provision of advice or guidance about some aspect of the situation that the other person would benefit from. This can take the form of telling the person about psychological reactions or legal assistance that is available for example.

    Research has shown the importance of social support in buffering the effects of life events (Cohen & Wills, 1985) and more recent research shows that social support is related to posttraumatic growth (Prati & Pietrantoni, 2009). As such it may be helpful to discuss ways of obtaining other forms of support through family and friends outside the therapeutic setting and what is helpful and what is unhelpful. Often, however, people lack others who are able to provide the needed social support and the therapist becomes an important source of social support themselves. Therapists are not able to provide all aspects of social support but active empathic listening that communicates unconditional acceptance in the context of a genuine relationship can be sufficient in promoting the client's agency to make changes in their life.

2. *Therapeutic work that engages the client in regular and consistent exposure-related activities to promote reappraisal of the traumatic experience and its meanings.* By exposure, we mean any activities that allow for the client to confront the trauma-related information in a safe and contained environment. This includes talking and listening and/or structured exposure-based exercises. It may also involve actively engaging in the physical act of

accompanying the client in a feared situation and supporting them through the experience, helping them to reinterpret environmental stimuli they have learnt to be fearful of.

3. *Facilitating reappraisal of the emotional states to which appraisals give rise.* Clients may feel confused by their emotional states and feel that they are going crazy. As such explaining the nature of posttraumatic stress reactions may be helpful in creating a sense of unconditional acceptance of distressing emotional states. Helping clients make sense of their own experiences through empathic reflections that target both affective and cognitive aspects of experience will be useful.

4. *Facilitating helpful coping strategies.* It is recognized that often avoidance of trauma-related information is a feature of posttraumatic stress. Consequently, survivors of traumatic events may not seek help until their problems become so overwhelming that they eventually encounter support services due to the urgency of their situation. At this time, their use of avoidance as a way of coping may have become entrenched. As such supporting the development of new coping skills, strategies for seeking social support, safe place imagery and other ways of task-focused and emotional-focused coping will be useful.

5. *Reducing negative emotional states and supporting positive emotional states.* Teaching the client to use relaxation exercises, gratitude exercises, self-compassion, for example, may be helpful. For practitioners interested in working upstream and interested in early intervention, the reformulated model provides a theoretically grounded and evidence-based approach to identify blocks to processing at an earlier stage.

Within the affective–cognitive processing theory, the central theoretical premise, whether one is working upstream or downstream, is that people are intrinsically motivated towards posttraumatic growth. The therapist's task therefore is to facilitate more effective processing in the understanding that once this is achieved the client will automatically move in growthful directions. This view is based on Organismic Valuing Process (OVP) theory (Joseph & Linley, 2005). OVP refers to the process that orients the direction of the actualizing tendency that Rogers (1951, 1959, 1963) suggested is the basic motivation force within human organisms.

As such, as trauma therapists we are faced with the delicate balancing act between systematically supporting the client through reprocessing the trauma by using techniques commonly associated with trauma therapy; while also building a relationship in which there is a fundamental trust in the client's inherent capabilities to self-organize, self-direct and navigate their journey through therapy and the trauma-recovery process.

The client's struggle with affective–cognitive process following trauma in this model is considered to be their 'best current attempt' to resolve the conflicts between pre-existing cognitive schemas, distressing affective experiences and revising self schema to accommodate the new trauma-related information. At any one time, regardless of how distressed or dysfunctional they may appear, the client is seen as a person in the process of fulfilling their right to self-determination.

Traditionally, trauma therapists have looked upon the therapeutic relationship as utilitarian in the sense that it provides the backdrop that allows for the use of techniques that are decided on by the therapist considering their judgement of what the client needs. Such directive treatment methods are associated with the use of an illness ideology. In an illness ideology the treatment approach is specific to the problem requiring treatment. By definition, the illness ideology requires the therapist to take on the role of expert. As such it cannot be fully facilitative of the distressed person's self-determination.

In contrast, in non-directive therapy there is the recognition that the therapeutic relationship is more than the backdrop but is itself the vehicle of change in which self-determination of the client is paramount. Such a view is associated with the client-centred school of psychotherapy and what has been referred to as the growth metaphor for understanding psychological distress (Sanders, 2005). In this view, the person is considered to be always striving towards greater and more complex states of being – their striving is influenced by social and environmental factors. The required mix of ingredients that make up the ideal social environment for growth in each person will be distinctly unique to every therapeutic dyad. It is when the right social environment is present that growth following trauma can emerge.

It is our opinion, the second of these two views, the growth metaphor, which gives the fullest and most comprehensive account of the experience of both posttraumatic stress and posttraumatic growth. However, in adopting the theoretical stance of the growth metaphor one is also making other metatheoretical assumptions; for example, that the person is fundamentally always in the process of becoming, that this process is driven by the inherent motivational force that has been termed the actualizing tendency and that each person has the right to self-determination (Rogers, 1959, 1963).

The concept of posttraumatic growth, understood in this way, questions the assumption that traumatic stress reactions are inherently pathological. As such, there are a number of challenges which arise from the adoption of the affective–cognitive processing model (see Joseph & Linley, 2006). In the following, section we will discuss those challenges that relate directly to the practice of therapy with trauma survivors – most notably, therapeutic non-directivity.

Non-directive trauma therapy

The first such challenge is non-directivity. While growth might be a meta-level therapeutic outcome, in any given moment, as we will argue later, this is not

3 2783 00125 8790

PRAIRIE STATE COLLEGE
LIBRARY

the intention of the non-directive client-centred therapist. To fully respect the self-determination of the client, it is necessary that the therapist has no predetermined goals for the client – the only goal of the non-directive therapist is to respect the client's right to self-determination. Working as a non-directive therapist in the trauma field is a challenge, particularly because, for example, clinical guidance in the United Kingdom provided by the National Institute for Clinical Excellence (NICE; Guideline 26 for Post Traumatic Stress Disorder (2005)) supports the use of manualized forms of therapy. This approach is based on principles grounded in an illness ideology that treatments are designed specifically for the problem as it is formulated from the perspective of the treatment provider and not the person themselves. In the United Kingdom for instance, the two favoured manual-based therapies are trauma-focused cognitive behaviour therapy and eye movement desensitization and reprocessing (EMDR). These approaches have at their base a common core assumption that reduction of symptoms is the sole goal of therapy.

In line with the affective–cognitive processing model outlined above, we suggest that traumatic stress responses are the product of incomplete processing needs. It then follows, and in contrast to the currently recommended treatments, that there is no predetermined goal or specified intention in non-directive client-centred therapy. The only goal is to create the social-environmental support that the client needs to fulfil their right to self-determination – a part of which might be to continue to affectively cognitively process their experiences, in the understanding that by so doing the client will more effectively learn to manage and reduce their posttraumatic distress and change in ways that are psychologically growthful.

Non-directive client-centred therapy does not intend to influence the client in any specific direction or towards any predetermined therapeutic task, the goals that a therapist has are only goals for themselves. Brodley (2004, p. 37) suggested:

> [C]lient-centered therapy influences in a different way – by freeing the client to discover his or her own methods and processes of change while unopposed by therapist goals and expectations. Its non-directivity refers to the therapist's immediate non-directive intentions, not to the overall power of the therapy to influence by providing conditions for change.

It is apparent from this statement that non-directivity does not deny the potential for client-centred therapy to influence the trauma survivor; moreover, it refers to the moment-by-moment intention of the therapist not to direct the client in any specific direction, or towards any specific goals. In this sense, non-directivity refers to the positioning of the therapist in response to the client. Non-directivity is, however, a much-misunderstood concept. Grant (1990) suggested that two forms of non-directivity exist in psychotherapy. First, he describes *instrumental* non-directivity, in which the therapist is tied to the task of promoting growth in the client, and states '[I]f being nondirective facilitates growth for a client in a particular instance, then it is valuable; if it does not, then the therapist decides whether continuing to be nondirective or adopting a different approach would be more effective' (ibid., p. 371). In the instrumental version, the link between taking up the non-directive approach as a technique and promoting growth is explicit. In contrast, Grant suggests the *principled* version of non-directivity:

> [T]he therapist does not attempt or intend to make anything happen – growth, insight, self acceptance – in the client, but rather provides the therapeutic conditions in the belief that they are expressions of respect and with the hope that the client will make use of them (p. 371).

So, this means that for the trauma therapist, creating the right social relational environment conditions and placing trust in the client to self-organize and to respect their right to self-determination, the client is empowered to direct themselves towards the most relevant aspects of their traumatic experience in need of processing. The therapist does not need to diagnose, tailor their techniques or to have them aimed towards the alleviation of symptoms. This is because, when the relationship conditions are right, the client will use the therapy in the most effective way and meet their personal, emotional and psychological needs following a trauma. In short, the client is able to resume the cycle of affective–cognitive processing as shown in Figure 4.1 which may have previously become impeded.

The proposal suggests that clients have the capability to self-organize and direct the therapy and the therapist's task is to create the relationship conditions in which this becomes constructively possible. In a non-directive client-centred approach to trauma therapy, the therapist has only goals for herself. Out of respect for the unique presentation of the client and for each individual client's unique combination of 'posttraumatic stress reactions', the therapist is concerned with the relationship as an end in itself. Whereas in other therapeutic approaches, the therapeutic relationship is regarded as the context or container in which the 'real' therapeutic work is done, here the therapeutic relationship 'is' the therapeutic work. This seems to us to not only be the logical stance to adopt in response to the theoretical proposal that posttraumatic stress responses are adaptive and the clients best attempt to affectively cognitively process experience, but also is an ethical stance to do least harm based on the principle of respecting the client's right to self-determination.

Techniques in non-directive trauma therapy

In the sections above, we have highlighted a number of areas in which client and therapist can work collaboratively to facilitate affective–cognitive processing of trauma-related information. Some of those suggestions involved the therapist engaging in techniques to facilitate client processing. This raises an important issue for non-directive client-centred therapists working in the field of trauma. There are many technique-driven therapies in the field of trauma that specifically aim to lead the client towards a predefined outcome. However, it is an unhelpful oversimplification to conflate the notion of thera-peutic techniques with directive therapies. It is possible for there to be a place for the use of techniques in non-directive client-centred therapy. For example, exposure is often helpful but can it ever be considered non-directive therapy if the therapist uses therapeutic strategies to explicitly direct the client towards exposure? The simple answer is 'no', not if the exposure technique is selected by therapist and applied to the client on the basis that the therapist believes this is the most appropriate technique for the treatment of a specific problem based on their judgement that the symptom itself is the problem.

The non-directive client-centred approach would not assume the responsi-bility of making the assessment of what is best for the client. In this model, it is the client who is considered to know what she needs, or at least to know what it is that most needs to be worked on at any given moment. The ther-apist is there not to diagnose the client or to organize a strategic approach for treating the client's symptoms; rather they are concerned with communi-cating their empathic understanding and unconditional regard for the client and their expression of distress and to be attuned to the client's need. As such the client will develop a fuller understanding of their experience, to know for themselves what the true nature of the problem is and achieve this by find-ing meaning in their experiences. Through this dialogue between client and therapist, the client shows the therapist what needs to be worked on and the therapist empathically responds to this.

Many non-directive client-centred therapists will at times use techniques in therapy, such as exposure, with clients in trauma-focused work. However, the use of techniques in these circumstances is not driven towards specific out-comes and remains a non-directive approach. As Joseph and Linley (2006) argue, the issue is not about *what* the therapist does, but about *how* they do it. How then does the therapist incorporate techniques when the rela-tionship is an end in itself? To answer this, we will expand the discussion of principled non-directivity and explore what it might mean in practice; we will then consider the view of Brodley and Brody (1996), who provide a rationale for techniques within non-directive client-centred therapy and that we have applied within our trauma-focused work.

We noted above the distinction made by Grant (1990) between instru-mental and principled non-directivity. Grant argued that in instrumental non-directivity there is inherent within the approach a specified aim or goal in being non-directive. The goal is ultimately to make growth occur in the client. Non-directivity in this sense is another technique just like behavioural expo-sure following trauma. Non-directivity, in the instrumental version, is used intentionally by the therapist, is under the control of the therapist and aims to make something else happen. According to Grant (1990), instrumental non-directivity is linked to the efficacy of counselling. He suggests this is the case because the therapist primarily asks whether non-directivity is the best approach to facilitate growth. Implicit in this statement is that, to determine efficacy, the therapist must also have some basic assumptions about what constitutes growth for the client. Instrumental non-directivity is deployed as a strategic intervention to make something specific, whether it be symptom reduction or psychological growth, happen.

In principled non-directivity, the therapist does not totally disregard the idea of efficacy. Grant (1990) points out that for responsible ethical practitioners, offering a service makes it essential to be mindful that what we offer is helpful to the client. However, before considering efficacy, Grant (1990) suggested that the primary question for the principled non-directive stance is more closely related to asking 'do the therapist's actions respect the client'? That is, principled non-directivity is not at the root of client-centred therapy because it works and makes the client grow, it is, rather, adopted as a stance to create the space into which the client can grow and in a climate where their voice is respected. Principled non-directivity also requires that the therapist is open to the expressions and requests from clients. The principled non-directive client-centred therapist is active and responsive and is engaged with the client. Grant (1990) notes that answering questions is seen as a requirement as it directly responds to the client's voice which is the only available expression of the client's growth at any given moment. It is the genuine meeting of people in an encounter that is the process of growth for the client.

In the context of trauma therapy, growth for clients does not refer merely to the outcome or the changes in levels of avoidance or intrusion that can be observed afterwards, rather it refers to the moment-by-moment process that the client is immediately engaged in and that the therapist is witness to. In this sense, the ethical and moral duty of the therapist is to respect the client's self-directed movements regardless of whether they are immediately oriented towards the therapeutic strategies of exposure or confrontation. It would seem from Grant's (1990) thesis that it is necessary for the principled non-directive client-centred therapist to respond to the client in a variety of ways that will be most respectful to their needs. This fits well with the affective–cognitive processing model as it highlights the range of possible points at which a client might require a response from their therapist yet does not suggest the need to diagnose the client or prescriptively select techniques.

How can this incorporate the non-directive client-centred therapist's use of the techniques that have been shown to be efficacious and remain true to the non-directive attitude? Brodley and Brody (1996; reprinted in Moon, Witty, Grant, & Rice, 2011) have argued that being client-centred does not necessarily mean that techniques will never be used:

> It is consistent with, and actually an implication of, client-centered theory for the therapist to address client's questions and accommodate his or her

requests, if doing so is within the therapist's capabilities. Answering questions and honouring client's requests for information, ideas, guidance, *or techniques* follows from the nondirective attitude.

(italics added p. 254)

This statement might at first seem to contradict the sentiment expressed above regarding non-directivity. However, a closer examination of Brodley and Body's (1996) thesis shows us that this statement is not to be taken out of the context of principled non-directivity. It is *not* a licence to do what one wants. For example, the use of techniques that might be considered helpful by the client, in principled non-directive client-centred therapy, are so when they are provided by the therapist because they are a *response* to the client and not because they have some predetermined, specific, objective, goal-oriented effect on the client's process.

In short, techniques are not consistent with client-centred therapy when they are diagnostically determined by the therapist but may well be appropriate when a technique is a genuine response to a question or request from the client, and its use is integrated into the therapist's expression of the therapeutic attitudes of empathic understanding, unconditional positive regard and congruence. Thus, we can return to the description of threats that may impede affective–cognitive processing in clients' and the various therapeutic techniques that may be useful, as shown in Figure 4.1, in the understanding that such a description of process is not intended as instructions for practice except insofar as it helps to heighten the therapists' empathic understanding of their clients' needs and their ability to be genuine in the relationship and responsive to clients' requests.

Conclusion

There are many approaches to psychotherapy (see Chapter 2) and in the field of trauma these are often presented as very highly specific treatments for the problem called Posttraumatic Stress Disorder. These 'Trademarked' therapies are usually little more than a constellation of therapeutic techniques that are put together to make an apparently coherent whole. However, Trademarked therapies seem to be rarely based on a clearly articulated meta-theory; rather, they seem implicitly grounded in an illness ideology for understanding psychological distress. In contrast, what we have outlined here is an approach to working therapeutically with trauma clients that is based on the meta-theory of the human organism as continually striving towards enhancing or maintaining itself. Posttraumatic stress response is the person's expression of their striving at that moment for psychological congruence. After a trauma, each person has within them the capacity to grow and as therapists it is our job to help remove the blocks to the potential for growth. We can remove blocks to growth by helping to create with the client the kind of social environment that is required for growth to occur. We have argued above that in doing this we are respecting the client's right to self-determination and that the logical stance to adopt as a therapist to this is principled non-directivity. It is the living of an ethical stance in response to a traumatized client, creating with them social relational environment suitable for them to grow into, that we see as the raison d'être of the trauma therapist who is concerned about the therapeutic relationship as the primary vehicle for therapeutic change.

Summary points

- There are two modes of non-directivity within the therapeutic relationship.
- The relational stance of the therapist can be either principled or instrumental.
- The principled stance is based on a meta-theoretical perspective of intrinsic motivation towards growth.
- People move through the process of growth by affective–cognitive processing.

Suggested reading

Grant, B. (1990). Principled and instrumental nondirectiveness in person-centered and client-centered therapy. *Person-Centered Review, 5*, 77–88.
Joseph, S. (2011). *What doesn't kill us: The new psychology of posttraumatic growth.* New York: Basic Books.
Joseph, S., Murphy, D., & Regel, S. (2012). An affective–cognitive process model of post traumatic growth. *Clinical Psychology and Psychotherapy*, DOI: 10.1002/cpp.1798.

References

American Psychological Association (2005). *Diagnostic and statistical manual: 4th edition, text revision.* Washington: American Psychological Association.
Brodley, B. T. (2004). Non-directivity in client-centered therapy. *Person-Centered and Experiential Psychotherapies, 5*, 36–52.
Brodely, B. T., & Brody, A. F. (1996). Can one use techniques and still be client-centered? In R. Hutterer, G. Pawlowsky, P. F. Schmid, & R. Stipsits (Eds.), *Client-centered and experiential psychotherapy: A paradigm in motion* (pp. 396–374). Frankfurt am Main, Berlin, Bern, New York, Paris, Wien: Peter Lang. Reproduced in

K. A. Moon, M. Witty, B. Grant, & B. Rice (Eds.), *Practicing client-centered therapy: Selected writings of Barbara Temenar Brodley.* Ross-on-wye: PCCS Books.

Calhoun, L. G., & Tedeschi, R. G. (Eds.). (2006). *Handbook of posttraumatic growth: Research and practice.* Mahwah: NJ: Lawrence Erlbaum.

Cohen, S., & Wills, T. A. (1985). Stress, social support, and the buffering hypothesis. *Psychological Bulletin, 2,* 310–357.

Grant, B. (1990). Principled and instrumental nondirectiveness in person-centered and client-centered therapy. *Person-Centered Review, 5,* 77–88.

Grant, B. (2005). Taking only what is given: Self-determination and empathy in non-directive client-centered therapy. In, B. E. Levitt (Ed.), *Embracing non-directivity: Reassessing person-centered theory and practice in the 21st century.* Ross-on-Wye: PCCS Books.

Joseph, S. (2004). Client centred therapy, post traumatic stress disorder and post traumatic growth: Theory and practice. *Psychology and Psychotherapy: Theory, Research and Practice, 77,* 101–120.

Joseph, S., & Butler, L. D. (2010). Positive changes following adversity. *PTSD Research Quarterly, 21/3,* 1–8.

Joseph, S., & Linley, A. (2005). Positive adjustment to threatening events: An organismic valuing theory of growth through adversity. *Review of General Psychology, 9,* 262–280.

Joseph, S., & Linley, P. A. (2006). *Positive therapy: A meta-theory for positive psychological practice.* London: Routledge.

Joseph, S., Murphy, D., & Regel, S. (2012). An affective–cognitive process model of post traumatic growth. *Clinical Psychology and Psychotherapy,* DOI:10.1002/cpp.1798.

Joseph, S., & Williams, R. (2005). Understanding posttraumatic stress: Theory, reflections, context, and future. *Behavioural and Cognitive Psychotherapy, 33,* 423–441.

Joseph, S., Williams, R., & Yule, W. (1997). *Post-traumatic stress: Psychosocial perspectives on PTSD and treatment.* Chichester: Wiley.

Maddux, J. E., Snyder, C. R., & Lopez, S. J. (2004). Toward a positive clinical psychology: Deconstructing the illness ideology and constructing an ideology of human strengths and potential. In P. A. Linley & S. Joseph (Eds.), *Positive psychology in practice* (pp. 320–334). Hoboken, NJ: Wiley.

Murphy, D. (2009). Client-centred therapy for severe childhood abuse: A case study. *Counselling and Psychotherapy Research, 9,* 3–10.

National Institute for Health and Clinical Excellence (2005). Guideline 26 for Post Traumatic Stress Disorder.

Prati, G., & Pietrantoni, L. (2009). Optimism, social support, and coping strategies as factors contributing to posttraumatic growth: A meta-analysis. *Journal of Loss and Trauma, 14,* 364–388.

Rogers, C. R. (1951). *Client-centered therapy: Its current practice, implications and theory.* London: Constable.

Rogers, C. R. (1957). The necessary and sufficient conditions of therapeutic personality change. *Journal of Consulting Psychology, 21,* 95–103.

Rogers, C. R. (1959). A theory of therapy, personality, and interpersonal relationships as developed in the client-centred framework. In S. Koch (Ed.), *Psychology: A study of a Science, Vol. 3: Formulations of the person and the social context* (pp.184–256). New York: McGraw-Hill.

Rogers, C. R. (1963). The actualizing tendency in relation to 'motives' and to consciousness. In M. R. Jones (Ed.), *Nebraska Symposium on Motivation, 11,* 1–24. Lincoln, NE: University of Nebraska Press.

Sanders, P. (2005). Principled and strategic opposition to the medicalisation of distress and all of its apparatus. In S. Joseph and R. Worsley (Eds.), *Person-centered psychopathology: A positive psychology of mental health.* Ross-on-Wye: PCCS Books.

Sommerbeck, L. (2005). Non-directive therapy with clients diagnosed with a mental illness. In B. E. Levitt (Ed.), *Embracing non-directivity: Reassessing person-centered theory and practice in the 21st century.* Ross-on-Wye: PCCS Books.

Tedeschi, R. G., & Calhoun, L. G. (1996). The posttraumatic growth inventory: Measuring the positive legacy of trauma. *Journal of Traumatic Stress, 9,* 455–471.

Witty, M. (2005). Non-directiveness and the problem of influence. In B. E. Levitt (Ed.), *Embracing non-directivity: Reassessing person-centered theory and practice in the 21st century.* Ross-on-Wye: PCCS Books.

5

Enhancing Emotional Regulation with Complex Trauma Survivors

Julian D. Ford

Introduction

Enhanced affect regulation is a central goal across a wide variety of psychotherapy models and theories (Berking et al., 2008; Cameron & Jago, 2008; Cloitre et al., 2010; Ford et al., 2012; Greenberg & Pascual-Leone, 2006; Hannesdottir & Ollendick, 2007; Hayes et al., 2006; Higginson et al., 2011; Kohut & Wolfe, 1978; Lynch et al., 2007). As we saw in the previous chapter, the focus on affective as well as cognitive components of trauma processing is central to therapeutic work in non-directive approaches. In this chapter, I will discuss how enhancing affect regulation competences can be considered as a core therapeutic goal with clients with complex trauma histories prior to or concurrently with evidence-based PTSD treatment. I will describe three empirically supported psychotherapy models for trauma survivors that specifically target affect regulation skills. Finally, I will suggest two complementary strategies for enhancing affect regulation when clients do not respond favourably to trauma- or skills-focused therapy.

Affect dysregulation

Greenberg and Pascual-Leone (2006) describe four ways in which psychotherapy can enhance client's abilities to process emotions: 'emotional awareness and arousal, emotional regulation, active reflection on emotion (meaning making), and emotional transformation' (p. 611). Recognizing emotions and learning to regulate the intensity of arousal and the positive–negative valence associated with them provides the foundation and scaffolding clients need to be able to identify and find meaning in emotion states, and to transform mal-adaptive ones (e.g., chronic anxiety, dysphoria, grief or anger) into adaptive ones (e.g., curiosity, pride, hope).

Affect regulation encompasses not only these forms of emotion processing, but also a wider range of self-regulation processes. Affect has a motivational aspect in addition to the hedonic state of emotions, and therefore affect regulation includes being able to use emotions to set goals and to identify actions that can achieve emotion-guided goals (Watkins, 2011), as well as to actually engage in behaviour in a manner that enhances both emotion regulation and goal attainment (Jucksch et al., 2011). Thus, affect regulation requires a variety of sophisticated self-regulation competences that translate emotion into goals, intentions and goal-directed action. Affect regulation adds a unique focus to our understanding of self-regulation because it brings into focus how other forms of self-regulation (e.g., arousal modulation, behavioural activation and inhibition, cognitive appraisals; interpersonal engagement or withdrawal) are influenced by a crucial meta-goal: achieving (or regaining) and sustaining tolerable and desirable emotions.

When interpersonal psychological trauma (e.g., life-threatening violence or maltreatment; loss of a primary caregiver or exposure to emotionally abusive caregiving) occurs in sensitive developmental epochs (e.g., infancy or early childhood) or transitions (e.g., from childhood to adolescence to adulthood), the resultant survival reactions/adaptations (Ford, 2009) by the victim may lead to a complex array of biopsychosocial problems (D'Andrea et al., 2012; Ford, 2011; Kaffman, 2009), including persistent anxiety, dysthymia, eating disorders, substance use disorders, aggression, antisocial behaviour, risk-taking, self-harm and suicidality. This combination of traumatic stress and developmental disruption have been described as 'complex trauma' (Cook et al., 2005), or 'developmental' (van der Kolk, 2005) or 'developmentally adverse interpersonal' (Ford, 2005) trauma. All of the sequelae of complex trauma have a common feature: impaired affect regulation (Ford, 2005).

Affect regulation depends upon both the psychobiological attributes of the individual (e.g., genetic proneness to, or social learning of, anxiety vs. adaptability (Rutter, 2006)) and the reliable supportive availability by primary caregivers or the ability to access cognitive/affective schema ('internal working models') that confer a sense of secure attachment (Bowlby, 1982). Complex trauma often occurs in a relational context that is chaotic and fraught with danger, such as in violent or abusive families or communities. As a result, survival can become a lifelong theme around which the individual organizes their identity and relationships (Ford, 2009). This can promote reactive tendencies and weaken adaptive strengths, while also imprinting a sense of emotional insecurity and cognitive disorganization in relationship to primary attachments (Koenen, 2006) that undermines the development of affect regulation. For example, Maughan and Cicchetti's (2002a) study of children with and without histories of maltreatment found that the maltreated children were twice as likely (80% vs. 37%) to exhibit dysregulated emotions (under-controlled/ambivalent or over-controlled/unresponsive types); in addition, emotional dysregulation was associated with problems across a range of affects (e.g., depression and anxiety), and it mediated the relationship between maltreatment and depression/anxiety. Abused children tend to selectively attend and react to stimuli that signal potential threat (Ayoub et al., 2006) as do children with anxiety disorders (Pine, 2007), and this survival-based hypervigilance is fundamentally incompatible with affect regulation.

Consistent with this view that the development of affect regulation can be profoundly impaired by exposure to traumatic stressors early in life, in a sample of toddlers from an urban low-income population, exposure to potential traumatic events was related to problems with affect regulation, social functioning and internalizing and externalizing symptoms, especially for those whose mothers observed dramatic behaviour changes afterwards (Mongillo et al., 2009). When those children had been exposed to violence as infants or toddlers, they were at risk of developing internalizing and externalizing symptoms and having poorer social competence several years later in elementary school (Briggs-Gowan, Ford, & Carter, 2012). Violence-exposed young children were more likely than others to develop PTSD symptoms specifically related to affect dysregulation (i.e., avoidance/emotional numbing and hyperarousal), and those symptoms mediated the relationship between early-life violence exposure and school-age problems. The key role of early-life violence exposure was highlighted by the additional finding that these relationships were independent of sociodemographic risk (living in poverty or in troubled/impoverished communities) and recent (i.e., in the past year) violence exposure. Studies with community (Ford et al., 2010), clinical (Ford et al., 2009) and criminal justice (Ford et al., 2008) samples of older children and adolescents provide further evidence that exposure to violence and maltreatment in early childhood are associated with persistent affect regulation problems which take the form of PTSD, other psychiatric disorders and serious behavioural problems.

Case vignette: Laura

Laura ("Laura" is a composite of several clients and not the name of any actual client, in order to preserve their privacy), a 38-year-old mixed race (Caucasian mother, Black Caribbean-American father) woman, has been married for 15 years and is the mother of an adolescent daughter and son. Laura grew up as the only daughter and oldest child (with two younger brothers) in a very religious (Catholic) household, with parents who were socially and occupationally successful leaders in their neighbourhood and community. The family's secret life behind closed doors was entirely different – 'every kind of hell you can imagine', in Laura's words. Both parents engaged in incestuous sexual activities with all of the children, threatening to kill Laura as the oldest and therefore responsible child if anyone ever found out. Her parents were violently abusive towards Laura and her brothers, and towards each other, when they used mind-altering drugs (which her mother procured through her work in the healthcare field) and forced the children to do so in order to engage in bizarre pseudo-religious rituals that usually required humiliation and rape.

Laura said that she knew from a very young age, before beginning elementary school that she 'would have to be the one sane person' in order to 'keep them from killing us and each other'. She became very skilled at monitoring her parents' emotional states and deciding when to intervene to get them to re-direct the psychological, physical and sexual violence away from her brothers or from each other towards her.

> My parents pretended they were omnipotent and totally in control, but they really were very weak and took turns being victimizer and victim, as they taught my brothers and me to be their victims and also to comfort and soothe them. If one or the other of them was heading toward an explosion or a melt-down, I would intentionally do something to infuriate or placate them, and then they'd forget about everyone else and take it out on me or make me gratify them. I could do this because I would completely detach myself. I'd be there physically but I'd go away completely in my mind, so I often had no awareness or memory of what happened until I'd wake up hours or days later in terrible pain, but still alive!

Laura's tragic description poignantly illustrates her resilience and the extreme adaptations that she had to make – some intentionally (for example, learning to strategically read and react to her parents' emotion dysregulation), but most on an automatic biological survival basis (for example, profound dissociation, somatoform displacement and self-perception as a machine-like observer, interventionist and object of abuse). Initially in therapy she was able to describe a sense of horror and sadness about the violence and violation to which she and her brothers had been subjected. It took much longer for her to recognize and acknowledge that she had come to regard herself – body, emotions, mind – with loathing similar to that to which she had been subjected by her parents, and to that which she felt towards her parents and brothers.

> I tried for years to have no feelings at all about my family, the sick things my parents did and the equally sick things I did to survive and keep everyone alive, and even about my brothers and myself. But secretly I was looking down on and despising all of us for being so disgustingly weak and despicable. But I also felt special because of our secret, and because I was the strong one.

Thus, Laura had learnt to survive by detaching herself from her body, emotions and mind, while using those parts of herself to strategically influence the course of the deadly dangerous family rituals so as to preserve their secrecy and to modulate everyone's emotions and arousal. She purposefully chose to leave the family at the age of 15 when she could see that her mother was becoming so threatened by her father's attraction to her that she feared her mother would kill one or both of them. She ran away to the streets of a distant city, where she survived by allowing a pimp to prostitute her, but not before she informed her parents that she would keep in contact with her brothers and if there was any further abuse of them she would either come back and kill them herself or expose them. She knew this probably would limit but not stop the abuse of her brothers, and she felt deeply ashamed for abandoning them. Laura proceeded to extricate herself from the streets, graduate from college and marry a college classmate who 'was as unlike my parents as any living human being'. She was successful and enjoyed raising her children, and then developed a career when they were in school. It wasn't until years later, when her son was approaching the age that her brothers had been when she left, that she began to have excruciating physical pain and fatigue, and terrifying nightmares of faceless monsters ripping her body to shreds. Only then did Laura consider seeking help.

Affect regulation

The therapy models with the strongest research evidence base for the treatment of adults (Cahill et al., 2009) and children (Saxe, McDonald, & Ellis, 2007) with posttraumatic stress disorder (PTSD) – that is, prolonged exposure, Cognitive Processing Therapy, Trauma Focused Cognitive Behaviour Therapy, and Eye Movement Desensitization and Reprocessing – are designed to help clients to process trauma memories in order to reduce avoidance and associated re-experiencing, emotional numbing and hyperarousal symptoms. Although children and adults with complex trauma histories have been shown to benefit from these therapies, high levels of anger, guilt or shame (Jaycox & Foa, 1996) or aggression and conduct problems (Cohen et al., 2010) suggestive of affect dysregulation have been found to be associated with poor outcomes. Also, high drop-out rates from trauma memory processing therapies have been reported by studies of women with PTSD secondary to histories of child abuse (Cloitre et al., 2010; McDonagh-Coyle et al., 2005).

A recent meta-analysis of therapy outcome studies with adult survivors of childhood sexual abuse found that cognitive behaviour therapy was superior to other modalities for anxiety, depression and other internalizing problems, but not for problems associated with more severe affect dysregulation (e.g., externalizing or interpersonal problems) (Taylor & Harvey, 2010). Thus, some adult clients with trauma histories, especially those who experienced violence or maltreatment in childhood, may respond best to therapy if affect regulation problems are directly addressed. Indeed, some therapy models that have not traditionally emphasized the therapeutic relationship increasingly are addressing relational factors in the client–therapist interaction (e.g., Cook et al., 2004;

Zoellner et al., 2011). And therapies are emerging for PTSD which explicitly focus on affect regulation and the therapeutic relationship (Courtois & Ford, 2009; also see Chapter 4), as I will next discuss.

Three manualized PTSD cognitive behaviour therapy models that do not require trauma memory processing have been designed to enhance skills for affect regulation, anxiety management and interpersonal functioning: Seeking Safety (Najavits et al., 2006; Zlotnick et al., 2009), Skills Training for Affect and Interpersonal Regulation (STAIR; Cloitre et al., 2010), and Trauma Affect Regulation: Guide for Education and Therapy (TARGET; Ford et al., 2011, 2012). These psychotherapies have shown promise in clinical and field trial studies with adult and adolescent survivors of complex trauma. They were designed to systematically help clients understand the impact that trauma has on affect regulation and to enhance skills and resources to maintain or regain emotional balance and hope even when confronted with feelings of severe distress and related cognitions and behaviours (for example, rage, helplessness, dissociation or impulses to self-harm).

Clients who have severe difficulties with affect regulation and their therapists may prefer not to engage in trauma memory processing, or to not do so until clients have solid affect regulation skills. If the clinical picture is complicated by the presence of comorbid disorders – particularly addictive (Ford et al., 2007), dissociative (Nijenhuis & Van der Hart, 2011), somatoform (Van Dijke et al., 2010b) or Axis II personality (Van Dijke et al., 2010b) disorders or severe mental illness (e.g., psychotic or bipolar disorders; Ford & Fournier, 2007) – affect regulation skills tend to be at best quite limited, and typically are severely impaired. Therefore, even with a client who is willing or actively seeking to therapeutically work through trauma memories, building competence in affect regulation is often recommended as a first step (Cohen et al., 2010; Cook et al., 2004). The evidence-based therapies cited above therefore have incorporated psychoeducation and behavioural exercises designed to enhance adaptive emotion recognition and expression, cognitive reappraisal of emotion-related beliefs and arousal modulation prior to and during their trauma memory interventions. As clients gain in their affect regulation capacities, they and their therapists may be more likely to consider trauma memory processing therapy even if they were initially reluctant to do so. Thus, the availability of affect regulation-focused therapies can broaden the repertoire of real-world clinicians and enable them to better deploy a full range of evidence-based treatments (including those that involve trauma memory narrative work) with complex trauma survivors. In addition, when therapy helps clients to experience a fuller range of emotion and to reduce emotional distortions or imbalance, this can enhance their engagement in the therapeutic relationship as a result of greater trust and confidence in themselves and in their therapist.

However, the crucial challenge for clinicians is to know what to do when clients are so severely affectively dysregulated that they cannot learn or consistently effectively utilize these emotion regulation skills – or when a client's apparently solid affect regulation competences seem to dissolve or disappear when the client experiences severe stress reactions in therapy (e.g., during trauma memory processing; when crises occur). Several lines of evidence suggest two strategies to addressing profound posttraumatic affective dysregulation when highly effective approaches to distress tolerance, mindfulness and emotion regulation skills or other empirically supported therapies that do not focus on traumatic stress but address affect dysregulation, for example, dialectical behaviour therapy (Lynch et al., 2007), acceptance and commitment therapy (Hayes et al., 2006) or mindfulness approaches to cognitive behaviour therapy (Berking et al., 2008), are not sufficient.

Mentalization

A first additional strategy for enhancing affect regulation with extremely dysregulated complex trauma survivors is based on the core process of self-examination in psychotherapy. 'Mentalizing' has been described as the self-reflective observation of one's own and others' mental processes – 'keeping mind in mind' (Allen et al., 2008, p. 312). Mental processes are largely opaque, evident primarily from their downstream results (e.g., thoughts, emotions, attitudes or motivations which are communicated through overt behaviour). Thus, mentalizing requires inference and imagination in addition to observation. This involves the central activity in every approach to psychotherapy: the development of hypotheses about why and how people, including oneself, think the way they think, feel the way they feel, want what they want, and ultimately as a result of these mental processes, do what they do. From this perspective, psychotherapy can be understood as teaching clients a way of thinking that is fundamentally empowering: not just what to think or feel, or how to behave, but how to make sense of (and therefore potentially be able to influence) the inner workings of people's mental processes – how the mind actually works, including both universal processes and idiosyncratic variations on those mental processes that distinguish each unique person, including oneself.

Mentalizing is particularly relevant for psychotherapy with complex trauma survivors. As Allen, Fonagy, and Bateman (2008) describe, mentalizing is particularly difficult to do when a person is experiencing states of hyperarousal or hypoarousal that are hallmarks of complex traumatic stress disorders (Ford, 2009; Lanius et al., 2010):

> Developing the ability to mentalize is one thing; using it consistently is another.... Mentalizing goes best when your level of emotional arousal is neither too high nor too low. You need to feel relatively safe to mentalize. If you're feeling threatened – angry or frightened – you'll be more concerned with self-protection than with taking the time and effort to

mentalize.... In states of high emotional arousal...[y]ou can feel so panicky or infuriated that you can't think straight, much less consider what someone else is thinking of feeling.... mentalizing is most difficult when you most need to do it.

(p. 316, italics in original)

Neuroimaging studies suggest that mentalizing, that is, thinking with a focus on 'the subjective nature and the intentional content (what they are "about" from a first-person perspective) of mental processes (e.g., thoughts, feelings, beliefs, volition) significantly influence[s] [all] levels of brain functioning (e.g., molecular, cellular, neural circuit) and brain plasticity' (Beauregard, 2007, p. 218). These studies suggest that when psychotherapy simultaneously evokes intense emotion states and self-referential cognitive processing (see Joseph and Murphy chapter four for a similar proposal), this may enhance cortical (prefrontal) inhibition of limbic (amygdala) activation (Beauregard, 2007) and connectivity in other brain areas which constitute what has been described as a 'default mode network' (Daniels et al., 2010). This neural network is activated when people adopt a meditative or self-reflective (e.g., 'what does this mean to me?') mindset, and is notably impaired in persons with childhood trauma histories (Daniels et al., 2011) and PTSD (Lanius et al., 2010).

Mentalizing also is consistent with 'perceptual control theory' (Higginson et al., 2011), which posits that,

at the heart of living organisms is the process of control −...a continual process of making our experience 'just right' or how we want it to be...[by] comparing how things are with how we want things to be and if they do not match, doing something to get closer to how we want things to be (p. 250).

From this theory's perspective, psychological problems occur when a person cannot achieve the psychological sense of security and control that involves both self-reflection − 'How do I want to feel, think, act?' − and error monitoring − 'What is not right for me?' Intriguingly, areas in the brain associated with error monitoring are closely connected with areas in the default mode network (i.e., the anterior and posterior portions, respectively, of the cortex; Daniels et al., 2011). Thus, mentalizing may provide a basis for therapeutically addressing the biological and psychological impairment experienced by a wide range of psychiatric disorders, and particularly in complex PTSD.

Moreover, mentalizing provides a vehicle for therapists to help clients actively engage in the therapeutic relationship. What therapists 'do' when teaching and guiding their clients in mentalizing is to model and encourage the client to join them in observing and describing how the client's mind 'works' (e.g., what is important to the client when noticing, reflecting on, and finding meaning in life experiences). This is a paradigmatic shift from the traditional medical model focused on pathology (i.e., what's wrong with the client's mind) to a strengths-based approach (i.e., what's right about how the client perceives, feels, thinks, and acts) that is transtheoretical and inherently relational (Fosha et al., 2010; Kohut & Wolf, 1978). When the therapist focuses on respectfully understanding – rather than correcting – the client's way of mental processing, the client experiences this as validating (Gendlin & Rychlak, 1970) and as an invitation to collaborate as a full partner. Mentalizing thus provides a relational base of acceptance and discovery, from which clients are able to rigorously address key problems faced by trauma survivors (e.g., avoidance of troubling memories, anxiety, or conflict; demoralizing or self-defeating beliefs). The therapist uses the respectful and reflective approach of mentalizing to join with the client in a relationship based upon mutual learning rather than adopting a hierarchical and pedagogical (corrective) distance from the client.

Clients with complex trauma histories often want to be able to think about their thoughts, feelings and memories with the clarity provided by mentalizing, that is, by adopting a participant–observer perspective and understanding rather than being confused and overwhelmed by their thoughts, feelings or memories. Allen et al. (2008) provide an illustrative case of a client who had apparently resolved several trauma memories in psychotherapy but still felt tortured by guilt due to having had an abortion (pp. 225–228). When the therapist helped her to 're-consider her view that she had been "selfish" in having the abortion' the client, 'now able to reflect, . . . concluded that she had been in no position to raise a child [and] no longer thought of herself as a selfish murderer'. A reflective mentalizing perspective made all the difference for this client, but the key question for psychotherapists treating other clients with complex trauma histories is, was there something that the therapist did in this case that made it possible for this client to regulate her affect sufficiently to be able to adopt the mentalizing perspective? Allen and colleagues (2008) attribute this to the therapist providing 'containment' via a secure therapeutic relationship that includes a trustworthy alliance, psychoeducation, encouragement of healthy relationships and teaching emotion regulation skills. However, they define mentalizing itself as the 'ultimate means of containment', hypothesizing a synergistic relationship between the two. What the therapist did to enable the client to achieve the sense of security necessary to be able to mentalize (rather than staying trapped in intrusive memories, avoidance and dissociation) remains a mystery.

Therapist affect regulation

One possible solution to this conundrum is to apply affect regulation bidirectionally rather than unidirectionally. This second, and complementary, strategy is an extension of a core psychodynamic precept derived from the Biblical proverb (Luke 4:23 – Physician, heal thyself) that is endorsed in some form by virtually every school of psychotherapy. Therapists must be aware of and able to regulate their own affective responses to clients. With the advent of the interpersonal framework for psychoanalysis championed by Sullivan, clinicians became attuned to the impact that their affect states and defences – technically, countertransference – could have on the client and the therapeutic interaction. As Fromm-Reichmann (1950) cautioned:

> Where there is lack of security, there is anxiety; where there is anxiety, there is fear of the anxieties in others. The insecure psychiatrist is, therefore, liable to be afraid of his clients' anxiety...[and] may not want to hear about their anxiety and their anxiety-provoking experiences...[and] is liable to obstruct his clients' verbalizations and the investigation of important emotional material. Moreover, to the client the psychiatrist's anxiety represents a measuring rod for his own anxiety-provoking qualities. If the therapist is very anxious, the client may take that as a confirmation of his own fear of being... 'bad'.
>
> (1950, pp. 24–25)

As psychotherapy models evolved and incorporated ego strength, personal actualization and relational security as important mechanisms of change, in addition to the classical analytic and psychiatric emphases on the management or resolution of conflict and deficits, it became apparent that the therapist's positive emotion states also may influence the client. Meta-models of psychotherapy correspondingly have gone beyond cautioning therapists to attempt to prevent their negative affect from contaminating the therapeutic process. Instead, as Lamagna and Gleiser (2007) describe, emotion can be deployed therapeutically to:

> (1) foster...capacities for self-regulation through shared states of affective resonance between therapist, client, and dissociated self-states; (2) facilitate...authentic, open internal dialogue between self-states which can alter engrained patterns of intra-psychic conflict and self-punishment; (3) develop...abilities for self-reflection and emotional processing by co-mingling previously disowned affect and emotional memories with here and now experience; and (4) attend...to positive affects evoked through experiences of transformation, self-compassion, and self-affirmation (p. 25).

Fosha (2001) highlighted the potential for therapists to not only facilitate clients' emotion awareness and expression by developing emotional resonance with their clients, but also to enable clients to regulate their affect states 'through coordinated emotional interchanges between client and therapist...in an emotionally alive therapeutic relationship'(p. 227). In order to orchestrate such complex 'emotional interchanges', psychotherapists must first regulate their own affect – both in order to have the ability to purposefully adjust the tone and intensity of the emotions they bring to the interaction and to understand and track clients' often initially dysregulated affect states. Consistent with this view, Dales and Jerry (2008) emphasized the necessity for therapists to develop 'self-integration and awareness in order to help increase their client's capacity for the same' (p. 283, italics added). This approach derives from the client-centred (Gendlin & Rychlak, 1970), psychodynamic (Kohut & Wolf, 1978) and experiential (Fosha et al., 2010) models which have highlighted the essential role that therapist self-awareness and affect regulation play in achieving both a therapeutic relationship and effective psychotherapy.

Complex trauma survivors' severe affect dysregulation can elicit strong emotional reactions from therapists which range from sympathy, sorrow, fear and guilt to frustration, impatience, anger and disgust or contempt – particularly from therapists who value being emotionally engaged with, and responsive and attuned to, each client (Courtois & Ford, 2013). In addition, no therapist is free from personal and professional stressors that may result in physical or emotional exhaustion, stress/worry or irritation/frustration filtering into the foreground rather than the background of the therapist's awareness. Here too, even seasoned and well-trained therapists may either avoid or be overly drawn toward clients whose personal characteristics or disabilities are 'triggers' for the therapist personally (Fromm-Reichmann, 1950). In such cases, the therapist may become overly prescriptive or indifferent due to feeling impatience or boredom with complex trauma survivors. The client's impairments may seem unresolvable not because this is factually true but because therapists experience their own affect dysregulation. This is particularly true with complex trauma survivors for whom wordless, implicit, dissociated and somatosensory forms of affective distress have become a dominant form of experiencing. Therapists often experience intense countertransference reactions based upon misperceiving these clients as 'wilfully' blocking the therapy or being too emotionally 'blocked', 'fragile', 'impaired', or 'hostile' to interact in ways that are emotionally reassuring for the therapist. Needless to say, when the therapist becomes trapped in these distress-based pejorative beliefs about a client, the therapeutic relationship is almost certain to be undermined by the therapist's unintentional communication of frustration, impotence and hopelessness.

Therapist affect regulation thus may be crucial to developing and sustaining a genuinely therapeutic relationship based on co-regulation with clients who have complex trauma histories. I therefore hypothesize that when therapists treating complex trauma survivors are able to regulate affect sufficiently to be a 'good enough' caregiver (Winnicott, 1971), clients first co-regulate (Bowlby, 1982), and then develop the capacity to independently regulate, their affect. Therapists who sustain affect regulation with severely dysregulated clients could be thought of as having a kind of 'wisdom' which seems magical but actually is the biological, psychological and relational outcome of affect regulation (Meeks & Jeste, 2009). Thus, we need to take our own medicine, or practice what we preach. Conventionally understood, this is a prescription for therapists to confront and resolve personal conflicts, maladaptive beliefs and coping patterns and dysregulated emotions in their own psychotherapy (Fromm-Reichmann et al., 1950). Yet, this agenda, like psychoanalysis, is potentially interminable. Moreover, there is no guarantee that even the most therapeutically mature, self-aware and self-regulated therapist can reliably generalize the insights and behaviour change from their own therapy to doing therapy with very dysregulated complex trauma survivors. Where can therapists find a protocol to guide them in moment-to-moment affect regulation while interacting with complex trauma survivor clients?

No such protocol exists, but an approach to begin the process of developing and validating one can be suggested. This begins with the development of practical templates to deconstruct the complex nuances of affect regulation. The conceptual model in the TARGET psychotherapy may serve as a useful example. A sequential set of steps is taught to clients in TARGET, using the acronym 'FREEDOM' as a mnemonic (see below). While the ostensible agenda in TARGET is to teach the client to use this sequence to better understand and accomplish affect regulation, in training therapists to use the intervention it is apparent that they must understand – and also personally use – the affect regulation sequence in order to not only teach it as a set of skills but moreover to provide the client with the direct experience of affect regulation via co-regulation.

- FOCUS – *slow down, orient, self-check*
- RECOGNISE – *Stress triggers*
- EMOTION – *One main emotion*
- EVALUATE – *One main thought*
- DEFINE – *One main personal goal*
- OPTIONS – *Build on your positive choices*
- MAKE A CONTRIBUTION – *Make the world a better place*

Case vignette: Laura

Laura's most pressing concern from the outset of therapy was to be able to anticipate and prevent or manage dissociative flashbacks

> If you can't help me stop replaying the torture I went through growing up in my family, this therapy is worthless. I've re-lived those memories more times than I can count with therapists who told me that I just had to stick with it, or make it into a story, or move my eyes back and forth, or get

different parts of me to help each other, or re-write the nightmares like movie scripts, or pay attention to what my body is trying to tell me – it all sounded great but here I am, still in hell with the flashbacks and nightmares.

Adopting a mentalizing approach, the therapist asked if Laura had ever been given an explanation of what was happening in her brain and mind when flashbacks or nightmares occurred. She replied that she'd been told she had PTSD which was caused when trauma made her so scared and hypervigilant that her body pumped out adrenaline all the time and she had become addicted to the 'fight-flight' syndrome and the adrenaline 'rush'. The therapist asked if she knew about the alarm in her brain that can get stuck in the 'on' position by trauma, and how it was designed to help her stay alert and protect her rather than to cause flashbacks. Laura had heard that PTSD might involve some kind of brain damage, but it was a revelation to her to learn that trauma didn't damage the brain but instead could over-activate a perfectly healthy and useful part of her brain. 'So why does this alarm keep going off in my brain, when I'm not in any danger anymore and I don't want to be dragged back through that mess all over again?' The therapist showed Laura that the brain's alarm centre was connected to a memory filing and retrieval centre right next to it in the brain, and explained how those centres worked with a third area at the front of the brain (the 'thinking centre') to figure out how to handle stress – and how this teamwork resulted in the alarm centre being re-set so it wouldn't keep going off.

> 'Well if it's that simple', Laura replied, 'why does my @#$%&@& brain's alarm stay stuck on and make my memory centre keep pulling up those horrible flashbacks and nightmares?'

The therapist explained that survival threats like those Laura had experienced could cause a perfectly functioning alarm to get out of alignment and stuck in the 'red zone' because it was necessary for her to be super-alert to handle the traumas. Laura realized that was exactly how she had felt as a child, constantly alert for the next threat to herself or her brothers. Logically, she asked, 'Okay, so if my brain's alarm got stuck in the high alert position, what do I do to re-set it now? Don't tell me I have to just think happy safe thoughts because that only makes me feel more tense, unhappy, and crazy! Is there a pill I can take to shut down this damn alarm?!'

Laura's paradoxical feeling of hope and hopelessness, having the opportunity to see anew how her brain, mind, and body had adapted in healthy but problematic ways to survival threats, led to an outburst of anger ('Why didn't anyone explain this to me before, why have I had to suffer for years when all I needed was to know what happened to me?!') followed by suspicion ('You're making this sound too simple, why should I trust you?, you can't know what I've been through! You can't imagine how horrible my life has been, and you tell me it's just a little mal-function in my brain! You can't possibly help me, you're a fraud and a liar!') and then suicidality ('I'm not going through this all over again, this was my last hope and I have nothing to live for now. I'll make one of those phony no-suicide contracts, but you can't stop me when I leave!').

The therapist recognized these reactions as entirely understandable affect dysregulation by a person who had experienced many prior incidents of hope followed by devastating betrayals, in the traumatic circumstances in her family throughout her childhood. While carefully tracking Laura's rapid fluctuations of arousal and emotion, the therapist applied mentalizing and the FREEDOM framework by reflecting back to Laura both her 'alarm' reactions ('I hear you and you're making perfect sense: you've had too many betrayals in the past to not be cautious, or downright suspicious and infuriated, with anyone who seems to be offering you a solution') and the less obvious but more fundamental feelings and wishes that she was implying but not directly articulating ('And I see how you've somehow had the determination and found the strength to keep searching for a real solution, and for relationships that aren't exploitive or abusive but truly sustaining'). This re-framing of the client's posttraumatic difficulties as an admirable attempt to escape the vicious cycle of exploitation and abuse implies a degree of intimacy on the part of the therapist that must be 'earned' rather than simply assumed. If this statement is made at a point when the client is just beginning to test the waters to determine if the therapist is genuinely trustworthy and able to help, the client may perceive it as a seduction designed to lure the client into a false sense of trust and self-esteem – or as an obligatory and impersonal comment that the therapist 'has to say' to try to boost the client's morale. On the other hand, if said in the context of an emerging or well-developed therapeutic relationship, this statement can provide the client with hope and an impetus for deeper self-reflection.

Simultaneously, the therapist monitored his own 'alarm' reactions (e.g., adrenaline surges; feeling shocked and fearful; thoughts of self-doubt – 'Do I really know what I'm doing here, why should I think I can help this woman when other better therapists haven't been able to? What if she does try to kill herself, it will be my fault!') and the more fundamental and sustaining feelings in his body (breathing calmly, relaxed facial muscles) and emotions (compassion, hope, determination) as well as complementary thoughts and goals ('I know that my ability to stay calm and take everything she says seriously will help her to regain a sense of trust and hope. I don't have to have all the answers, just the strength and security to see her through this understandable crisis – which will show her more about how to regulate her emotions than anything I or anyone else could teach from a textbook').

Through this interaction, and in numerous similar episodes of spiking affect dysregulation, Laura and her therapist were able to develop a shared approach to helping her to build an inner foundation of understanding and hope as she was able to envision how her brain and mind had had to adapt to survive but could newly adapt in order to enable her to think rather than react. This required many repetitions of co-regulation when Laura found herself again in the state of despair and rage that she had lived with but been unable to consciously recognize or articulate as a child. At those times, whether occurring when processing a troubling childhood memory or a current experience of intrusive re-experiencing, Laura would seem to lose her capacity to mentalize until she was able to regain a balanced level of arousal and a sense of safety with the therapist's own affect regulation serving as a co-regulator and role model for affect regulation.

Conclusion

Affect regulation is both a fundamental problem and a potential basis for recovery for complex trauma survivors. Although it is beyond the scope of this chapter to discuss in detail, it is worth noting that affect regulation also is both a prerequisite for and a positive outcome of psychotherapies that engage clients in trauma memory processing – including cognitive, behavioural, experiential and somatic-focused therapies for PTSD and complex traumatic stress disorders (Courtois & Ford, 2012). Equally importantly, an affect regulation perspective reminds therapists that helping clients develop their ability to observe their own mental processes and create a theory of mind that enhances their actual and perceived sense of control – that is, to mentalize – is a crucial foundation for all therapeutic work and for life. And this perspective also can alert therapists to the potential importance of tending to their (our) own minds and affect, by systematically applying mentalization and affect regulation to oneself while doing therapy. When treating complex trauma survivors, this 'walking the walk' may be of particular value, because it may be the most authentic way to demonstrate to these clients that it is possible to achieve what trauma has denied them: genuine help from a trustworthy guide who can show, in action as well as in words, the way to (re)gaining the capacity to regulate affect.

Summary points

- Acquisition of emotion regulation competences is the core therapeutic goal with clients with complex trauma histories and emotion regulation by therapists provides a consistent 'good enough' (Winnicott, 1971) behavioral model and interactional scaffolding for the traumatized client to be able to gradually acquire parallel emotion regulation capacities.
- The therapist's emotion regulation plays a crucial role in developing/sustaining the therapeutic working alliance, that is, the client's and therapist's felt sense and associated attributions (beliefs,

expectations, attitudes) of a trustworthy collaborative relation-ship in which the client's safety, well-being and actualization are a primary shared goal.

▪ Traumatized clients initially rely upon the therapist's emotion regulation in order to gain (or regain) the capacity to increas-ingly autonomously self-regulate: 'co-regulation' of emotional experiencing precedes and provides a foundation for client self-regulation.

▪ Mentalizing (self-reflective examination of mental processes) pro-vides a framework for enabling clients to move from co-regulation to autonomous emotion regulation.

Suggested reading

Allen, J., Fonagy, P., & Bateman, A. (2008). *Mentalizing in clinical practice.* Washington, DC: American Psychiatric Association.

Courtois, C. A., & Ford, J. D. (2012). *Clinician's guide to treatment of complex traumatic stress disorders.* New York: Guilford.

D'Andrea, W., Ford, J. D., Stolbach, B., Spinazzola, J., & van der Kolk, B. (2012). Phenomenology of symptoms following interpersonal trauma exposure in chil-dren: An empirically-based rationale for enhancing diagnostic parsimony. *American Journal of Orthopsychiatry, 82,* 187–200.

Ford, J. D. (2009). Neurobiological and developmental research: Clinical implications. In C. A. Courtois & J. D. Ford (2013), *Treating complex traumatic stress disorders: An evidence-based guide* (pp. 31–58). New York: Guilford Press.

Fromm-Reichmann, F. (1950). *Principles of intensive psychotherapy.* Chicago: Univer-sity of Chicago Press.

Greenberg, L. S., & Pascual-Leone, A. (2006). Emotion in psychotherapy: A practice-friendly research review. *Journal of Clinical Psychology, 62*(5), 611–630.

Herman, J. L. (1992). *Trauma and recovery.* New York: Basic Books.

Pine, D. S. (2007). Research Review: A neuroscience framework for pediatric anxiety disorders. *Journal of Child Psychology and Psychiatry, 48*(7), 631–648.

References

Ayoub, C. C., O'Connor, E., Rappolt-Schlichtmann, G., Fischer, K. W., Rogosch, F. A., Toth, S. L., et al. (2006). Cognitive and emotional differences in young mal-treated children: A translational application of dynamic skill theory. *Development and Psychopathology, 18*(3), 679–706.

Beauregard, M. (2007). Mind does really matter: Evidence from neuroimaging stud-ies of emotional self-regulation, psychotherapy, and placebo effect. *Progress in Neurobiology, 81,* 218–236.

Berking, M., Wupperman, P., Reichardt, A., Pejic, T., Dippel, A., & Znoj, H. (2008). Emotion-regulation skills as a treatment target in psychotherapy. *Behaviour Research and Therapy, 46*, 1230–1237.

Bowlby, J. (1982). Attachment and loss: Retrospect and prospect. *American Journal of Orthopsychiatry, 52*(4), 664–678.

Briggs-Gowan, M. J., Carter, A. S., & Ford, J. D. (2012). Parsing the effects violence exposure in early childhood: Modeling developmental pathways. [Research Support, N.I.H., Extramural]. *Journal of Pediatric Psychology, 37*, 11–22. doi:10.1093/jpepsy/jsr063.

Cahill, S. P., Rothbaum, B. O., Resick, P., & Follette, V. (2009). Cognitive behavior therapy for adults. In E. B. Foa, T. M. Keane, M. J. Friedman, & J. A. Cohen (Eds.), *Effective treatments for PTSD* (2nd ed., pp. 139–222). New York: Guilford.

Cameron, L. D., & Jago, L. (2008). Emotion regulation interventions: A common-sense model approach. *British Journal of Health Psychology, 13*(Pt 2), 215–221.

Cloitre, M., Stovall-McClough, K. C., Nooner, K., Zorbas, P., Cherry, S., Jackson, C. L., et al. (2010). Treatment for PTSD related to childhood abuse: A randomized controlled trial. *American Journal of Psychiatry, 167*(8), 915–924.

Cohen, J. A., Berliner, L., & Mannarino, A. (2010). Trauma focused CBT for children with co-occurring trauma and behavior problems. *Child Abuse and Neglect, 34*(4), 215–224.

Cook, A., Spinazzola, J., Ford, J. D., Lanktree, C., Blaustein, M., Cloitre, M., DeRosa, R., Hubbard, R., Kagan, R., Liataud, J., Mallah, K., Olafson, E., & Van der Kolk, B. (2005). Complex trauma in children and adolescents. *Psychiatric Annals, 35*, 390–398.

Cook, J., Schnurr, P. P., & Foa, E. B. (2004). Bridging the gap between posttraumatic stress disorder research and clinical practice: The example of exposure therapy. *Psychotherapy: Theory, Research, Practice, Training, 41*(4), 374–387.

Courtois, C. A., & Ford, J. D. (2013). *Treatment of complex trauma: A sequenced, relationship-based approach.* New York: Guilford Press.

Dalgleish, T. (2004). Cognitive approaches to posttraumatic stress disorder: The evolution of multirepresentational theorizing. *Psychological Bulletin, 130*, 228–260.

Dales, S., & Jerry, P. (2008). Attachment, affect regulation and mutual synchrony in adult psychotherapy. *American Journal of Psychotherapy, 62*(3), 283–312.

Daniels, J. K., Frewen, P., McKinnon, M. C., & Lanius, R. A. (2011). Default mode alterations in posttraumatic stress disorder related to early-life trauma: A developmental perspective. *Journal of Psychiatry and Neuroscience, 36*(1), 56–59.

Daniels, J. K., McFarlane, A. C., Bluhm, R. L., Moores, K. A., Clark, C. R., Shaw, M. E., et al. (2010). Switching between executive and default mode networks in posttraumatic stress disorder: Alterations in functional connectivity. *Journal Psychiatry Neuroscience, 35*(4), 258–266.

Duquette, P. (2011). Reality matters: attachment, the real relationship, and change in psychotherapy. *American Journal of Psychotherapy, 64*(2), 127–151.

Ford, J. D. (2005). Treatment implications of altered neurobiology, affect regulation and information processing following child maltreatment: *Psychiatric Annals, 35*, 410–419.

Ford, J. D., Connor, D. F., & Hawke, J. (2009). Complex trauma among psychiatrically impaired children. *Journal of Clinical Psychiatry, 70*, 1155–1163.

Ford, J. D., Elhai, J. D., Connor, D. F., & Frueh, B. C. (2010). Poly-victimization and risk of posttraumatic, depressive, and substance use disorders and involvement in delinquency in a national sample of adolescents. *Journal of Adolescent Health, 46,* 545–552.

Ford, J. D., & Fournier, D. (2007). Psychological trauma and post-traumatic stress disorder among women in community mental health aftercare following psychiatric intensive care. *Journal of Psychiatric Intensive Care, 3,* 27–34.

Ford, J. D., Hartman, J. K., Hawke, J., & Chapman, J. (2008). Traumatic victimization, posttraumatic stress disorder, suicidal ideation, and substance abuse risk among juvenile justice-involved youths. *Journal of Child and Adolescent Trauma, 1,* 75–92.

Ford, J. D., & Russo, E. (2006). Trauma-focused, present-centered, emotional self-regulation approach to integrated treatment for posttraumatic stress and addiction: TARGET. *American Journal of Psychotherapy, 60,* 335–355.

Ford, J. D., Russo, E., & Mallon, S. (2007). Integrating treatment of posttraumatic stress disorder and substance use disorder. *Journal of Counseling and Development, 85,* 475–489.

Ford, J. D., Steinberg, K., Hawke, J., Levine, J., & Zhang, W. (2012). Randomized trial comparison of emotion regulation and relational psychotherapies for PTSD with girls involved in delinquency. *Journal of Child and Adolescent Clinical Psychology, 41,* 1–12.

Ford, J. D., Steinberg, K., & Zhang, W. (2011). Affect regulation and social problem-solving psychotherapies for high-risk mothers with PTSD. *Behavior Therapy, 42,* 561–578.

Fosha, D. (2001). The dyadic regulation of affect. *Journal of Clinical Psychology, 57,* 227–242.

Fosha, D., Siegel, D., & Solomon, M. (2010). *Healing power of emotion.* New York: Norton.

Frewen, P. A., Dozois, D. J., & Lanius, R. A. (2008). Neuroimaging studies of psychological interventions for mood and anxiety disorders: empirical and methodological review. *Clinical Psychology Review, 28,* 228–246.

Gendlin, E. T., & Rychlak, J. F. (1970). Psychotherapeutic processes. *Annual Review of Psychology, 21,* 155–190.

Hannesdottir, D. K., & Ollendick, T. H. (2007). The role of emotion regulation in the treatment of child anxiety disorders. *Clinical Child and Family Psychology Review, 10,* 275–293.

Harvey, M. (1996). An ecological view of psychological trauma and trauma recovery. *Journal of Traumatic Stress, 9,* 3–23.

Hayes, S. C., Luoma, J. B., Bond, F. W., Masuda, A., & Lillis, J. (2006). Acceptance and commitment therapy. *Behaviour Research and Therapy, 44*(1), 1–25.

Higginson, S., Mansell, W., & Wood, A. M. (2011). An integrative mechanistic account of psychological distress, therapeutic change and recovery: The Perceptual Control Theory approach. *Clinical Psychology Review, 31*(2), 249–259.

Jaycox, L. H., & Foa, E. B. (1996). Obstacles in implementing exposure therapy for PTSD: Case discussions and practical solutions. *Clinical Psychology and Psychotherapy, 3,* 176–184. doi: 10.1002/(SICI)1099-0879(199609)3:3<176::AID-CPP100>3.0.CO;2-1.

Jucksch, V., Salbach-Andrae, H., Lenz, K., Goth, K., Dopfner, M., Poustka, F., et al. (2011). Severe affective and behavioural dysregulation is associated with significant psychosocial adversity and impairment. *Journal of Child Psychology and Psychiatry,* 52(6), 686–695.

Kaffman, A. (2009). The silent epidemic of neurodevelopmental injuries. *Biological Psychiatry, 66*(7), 624–626.

Koenen, K. C. (2006). Developmental epidemiology of PTSD. *Annals of the New York Academy of Sciences, 1071,* 255–266. doi: 10.1196/annals.1364.020.

Kohut, H., & Wolf, E. (1978). The disorders of the self and their treatment. *International Journal of Psycho-Analysis, 59,* 413–425.

Lamagna, J., & Gleiser, K. A. (2007). Building a secure internal attachment: An intra-relational approach to ego strengthening and emotional processing with chronically traumatized clients. *Journal of Trauma and Dissociation, 8*(1), 25–52.

Lanius, R. A., Bluhm, R. L., Coupland, N. J., Hegadoren, K. M., Rowe, B., Theberge, J., et al. (2009). Default mode network connectivity as a predictor of post-traumatic stress disorder symptom severity in acutely traumatized subjects. *Acta Psychiatrica Scandinavica, 121,* 33–40.

Lanius, R. A., Vermetten, E., Loewenstein, R. J., Brand, B., Schmahl, C., Bremner, J. D., et al. (2010). Emotion modulation in PTSD: Clinical and neurobiological evidence for a dissociative subtype. *American Journal of Psychiatry, 167*(6), 640–647.

Lanius, R. A., Williamson, P. C., Hopper, J., Densmore, M., Boksman, K., Gupta, M. A., et al. (2003). Recall of emotional states in posttraumatic stress disorder: An fMRI investigation. *Biological Psychiatry, 53*(3), 204–210.

Lynch, T. R., Trost, W. T., Salsman, N., & Linehan, M. M. (2007). Dialectical behavior therapy for borderline personality disorder. *Annual Review of Clinical Psychology, 3,* 181–205.

Maughan, A., & Cicchetti, D. (2002). Impact of child maltreatment and interadult violence on children's emotion regulation abilities and socioemotional adjustment. *Child Development, 73*(5), 1525–1542.

McDonagh-Coyle, A., Friedman, M., McHugo, G., Ford, J.D., Mueser, K., Descamps, M., et al. (2005). Psychometric outcomes of a randomized clinical trial of psychotherapies for PTSD-SA. *Journal of Consulting and Clinical Psychology, 73,* 515–524.

Meeks, T. W., & Jeste, D. V. (2009). Neurobiology of wisdom: A literature overview. *Archives of General Psychiatry, 66*(4), 355–365.

Mongillo, E.A., Briggs-Gowan, M., Ford, J.D., & Carter, A.S. (2009). Impact of traumatic life events in a community sample of toddlers. *Journal of Abnormal Child Psychology, 37*(4), 455–468.

Najavits, L. M., Gallop, R. J., & Weiss, R. D. (2006). Seeking safety therapy for adolescent girls with PTSD and substance use disorder: A randomized controlled trial. *Journal of Behavioral Health Services & Research, 33*(4), 453–463.

Nijenhuis, E., & Van der Hart, O. (2011). Dissociation in trauma. *Journal of Trauma and Dissociation, 12,* 416–445.

Paivio, S., & Pascual-Leone, E. (2010). *Emotion-focused trauma therapy.* Washington, DC: American Psychological Association.

Pearlman, L. A., & Caringhi, J. (2009). Living and working reflectively to address vicarious trauma. In C. A. Courtois & J. D. Ford (Eds.), *Treating complex traumatic stress disorders: An evidence-based guide* (pp. 202–224). New York: Guilford Press.

Rottenberg, J., & Gross, J. (2007). Emotion and emotion regulation: A map for psychotherapy researchers. *Clinical Psychology: Science & Practice, 14,* 323–328.

Rutter, M. (2006). Implications of resilience concepts for scientific understanding. *Annals of the New York Academy of Sciences, 1094,* 1–12.

Saxe, G., MacDonald, H., & Ellis, H. (2007). Psychosocial approaches for children with PTSD. In E. B. Foa, M. J. Friedman, T. M. Keane & P. Resick (Eds.), *Handbook of PTSD: Science and practice* (pp. 359–375). New York: Guilford.

Sloan, D. M., & Kring, A. M. (2007). Measuring changes in emotion during psychotherapy: Conceptual and methodological issues. *Clinical Psychology: Science and Practice, 14,* 307–322.

Smyth, J. M., & Arigo, D. (2009). Recent evidence supports emotion-regulation interventions for improving health in at-risk and clinical populations. *Current Opinion in Psychiatry, 22,* 205–210.

Taylor, S. T., & Harvey, J. E. (2010). A meta-analysis of the effects of psychotherapy with sexually abused children and adolescents. *Clinical Psychology Review 30,* 517–535.

Tee, J., & Kazantzis, N. (2011). Collaborative empiricism in cognitive therapy. *Clinical Psychology: Science and Practice, 18,* 47–61.

Trosper, S. E., Buzzella, B. A., Bennett, S. M., & Ehrenreich, J. T. (2009). Emotion regulation in youth with emotional disorders: Implications for a unified treatment approach. *Clinical Child and Family Psychology Review, 12,* 234–254.

Van de Kolk, B. (2005). Developmental trauma disorder: Towards a relational diagnosis for children with complex histories. *Psychiatric Annals, 35*(5), 401–408.

Van Dijke, A., Ford, J. D., Van der Hart, Van Son, M., van der Heijden, P., & Bühring, M. (2010a). Affect dysregulation in borderline personality disorder and somatoform disorder: Differentiating under- and over-regulation. *Journal of Personality Disorders, 24,* 296–311.

Van Dijke, A., Van der Hart, O., Ford, J. D., Van Son, M., Van der Heijden, P., & Bühring, M. (2010b). Affect dysregulation and dissociation in borderline personality disorder and somatoform disorder: Differentiating inhibitory and excitatory experiencing states. *Journal of Trauma and Dissociation, 11,* 424–443.

Watkins, E. (2011). Dysregulation in level of goal and action identification across psychological disorders. *Clinical Psychology Review, 31*(2), 260–278.

Winnicott, D. W. (1971). *Playing and reality.* London: Tavistock.

Zlotnick, C., Johnson, J., & Najavits, L. M. (2009). Randomized controlled pilot study of cognitive-behavioral therapy in a sample of incarcerated women with substance use disorder and PTSD. *Behavior Therapy, 40*(4), 325–336.

Zoellner, L. A., Feeny, N. C., Bittinger, J. N., Bedard-Gilligan, M. A., Slagle, D. M., Post, L. M., et al. (2011). Teaching trauma-focused exposure therapy for PTSD: Critical clinical lessons for novice exposure therapists. *Psychological Trauma, 3*(3), 300–308.

6

Chronic Traumatization and Internal Retreats: The Impact on the Therapist

Martin J. Dorahy

Introduction

As we have seen in the previous two chapters, the effect of trauma within interpersonal relations can have a significant and profound impact on the survivor's affective processing capacities. Difficulties in affective processing present therapists with a challenge in meeting the client in order to do the necessary therapeutic work while not pushing their often fragile process too far. Mr G was 28 years old when he presented for psychological therapy following a referral from his psychiatrist. Approximately six years before therapy, he had been beaten almost to the point of death in a random gang attack. Two years prior to this event he lost all access to, and contact with, his young daughter following a particularly vitriolic court battle with his ex-partner in which he found it very difficult to represent himself effectively but refused legal support. Around this time, he became aware that the man he believed was his father, and who had been aggressive, violent and emotionally abusive towards him as a child was not his father. Rather than liberate him, this revelation had a constricting effect, as he felt intense shame about being the only one in the family who had not been aware of this 'secret'. He also assumed responsibility for his natural father leaving shortly before his birth. He began to steadily 'close down' to family members, having less contact with them and not making them aware of his feelings and thoughts. He began to perceive himself as quite unsafe in their presence, believing he could not trust them, nor share anything of his life with them; it was not safe to 'let them in'. He presented for therapy in a similar fashion. The therapist represented a figure that would presently or eventually deceive and hurt, and therefore it was safest not to open up to the therapist and allow him to see some of Mr G's world. He also worked to keep painful memories from the past at bay, finding almost unbearable any thought or discussion of the events that had impacted so heavily on him. Several attempts using various psychological techniques to stabilize Mr G and assist his fear and anxiety appeared to push him further into himself and away from the therapist. It was clear that therapy with Mr G would need to progress steadily and at a pace that would allow him to move safely out of the psychological isolation he used to protect himself, so he could connect at a level with the therapist that would foster therapeutic change. Despite this understanding, the therapist began to notice after many months of work that he (the therapist) was starting to become quite anxious around Mr G, fearing that Mr G was so fragile he could easily break into many pieces that would be impossible to bring back together. This heightened and near debilitating anxiety from the therapist seemed to coincide with glimpses of therapeutic progress and times when Mr G was beginning to edge out of his psychological hibernation.

This chapter seeks to explore a particular dynamic in the relationship between a traumatized client and a therapist that is captured in the above vignette. This dynamic has been observed particularly in male clients exposed to child and adult traumas in familial (family of origin) and social (political violence) contexts. The clients under consideration have tended to have the following characteristics when they presented for therapy and one or more of these characteristics have lasted months or sometimes years into the work:

1. A reluctance to attend therapy.
2. A belief that therapy will not work for them.
3. Attending therapy to satisfy, or at the behest of, someone else (e.g., psychiatrist, partner, or the therapist themselves).
4. A deep fear of the therapist and what s/he is capable of doing.
5. Verbal and non-verbal actions that make it clear they cannot commit to therapy and could leave at any time.
6. They have socially and psychologically isolated themselves so as not to rely on anybody. They make it clear to the therapist they will never become reliant on or connected with them. The realization that they have forged an important relationship (maybe years into therapy) evokes considerable fear and a sense at some level that they have betrayed their dictum to never 'get involved with anyone'.
7. Any effort by the therapist to 'do' anything with the client (e.g., eye movement desensitization and reprocessing, emotion-focused therapy, cognitive behaviour therapy, hypnosis, etc.) is either resisted actively (missing the next session, or closing down any communication by the therapist) or passively (e.g., 'entertaining' the therapist by going along with them and 'playing the part').
8. The notion of therapy being a cooperative endeavour is unable to be contemplated. The frame of reference is one where the client reluctantly comes

to therapy NOT to change or be assisted (i.e., their current psychological organization feels too safe to alter, regardless of its costs).
9. The psychological place they have created for themselves, while at times disadvantageous and tenuous, is firmly held onto.

Overview

Relational trauma and psychological therapy share an important characteristic: both involve an individual whose experience is to a greater or lesser extent influenced by the actions of another. That is, from the individual's (victim/clients) point of view there is a subject (themselves) and an object (the other), thus both victimization and therapy occur in the context of a two-person psychology (i.e., the motivations, actions and responses of two individuals are accountable for understanding what has occurred and its after-effects). In therapy, we hope the actions of the other/s (e.g., the frame, the use of silence, particular interventions and their timing) will facilitate psychological growth. In relational trauma, the actions of the other/s stunt psychological growth.

Complex, relational trauma characterized by interpersonal assault and betrayal from a trusted other often results in an internal retreat where the individual attempts to protectively wrap themselves up in themselves as a way to manage the fear now posed by relating to others. Therapy by its very nature brings the client into contact with another who seeks to begin a relationship with them. This new person/object is to a greater or lesser extent perceived by the client as having the same capacity, at least at the level of fear and fantasy, to violate and harm psychologically and physically, and the internal retreat is resorted to as a protective strategy. This internal retreat is experienced by the therapist as the client being hypersensitive to and terrified of engaging in any form of relating that goes beyond the exchange of pleasantries and intellectualized, factual information. The client seems difficult to impact, as something of an immoveable object. Yet instead of responding with therapeutic force to 'free' the client, the therapist begins to see this immoveable client object as wrapped in a fragile shell that requires sensitive handling. This perception of the client increases anxiety in the therapist.

In this chapter, I explore this dynamic. It begins by examining the client's 'retreat' (i.e., 'turning inwards') and finishes with the therapist's 'egg shell' perception, along with two inlets for the anxiety it evokes; fear that the shell around the client will be broken by the therapist, leaving (1) the client vulnerable, damaged and alone, or (2) the therapist vulnerable to psychological attack by the client. Thus, the therapist fears they will 'break' the client or be 'broken' by them (i.e., they are experiencing a countertransference response). These are examples of two different manifestations of concordant countertransference (Racker, 1988), where the therapist connects with (1) the vulnerability of the client and (2) their intense fear of (psychological) annihilation. Words, sentences and therapeutic directions become filled with anxiety to avoid one or the other of these feared outcomes.

It is hoped that therapists from different orientations can make use of this chapter and determine if it stands up to their clinical experience and scrutiny. Despite it being rooted in observations from therapy, where appropriate these observations will be bedded in theoretical formulations to provide a more clinically relevant framework for understanding the dynamic under examination. It should be made clear that the term 'retreat' is being used at different times as a verb and a noun. The verb refers to a withdrawal or recoiling. Such an action may create a psychological haven or refuge (noun) for an individual (Steiner, 2003), and thus in this chapter the verb 'retreat' (e.g., to recoil) may lead to the noun 'retreat' (e.g., a haven).

Steiner (2003) has coined the term 'psychic retreat' to refer to a defensive operation and organization which 'provides the [client] with an area of relative peace and protection from strain when meaningful contact with the [therapist] is experienced as threatening... In some [individuals] a more or less permanent residence in the retreat may be taken up and it is then that obstacles to development and growth arise' (p. 1). From a descriptive perspective, Steiner's definition reflects how the word 'retreat' is being used in this chapter; as a defensive recoiling away from the external world and threatening aspects of the internal world in order to protect from further harm. This retreat may become a habitualized safe haven from which the world and relationships are perceived and understood.

Trauma and the retreat inwards

One way that traumatized individuals respond in the aftermath of violation, betrayal and victimization is to attempt to mimic in some way and in an ongoing manner their immediate defensive strategy during the trauma; to close themselves off to the other person, to withdraw into their own mind while attempting to keep at bay their own disturbing thoughts, actions and internal processes. As Chu (1998) notes, there is a delicate balance between withdrawing inwards and also avoiding thoughts, feelings and other internal stimuli that may trigger intrusive thoughts and reliving episodes, which make the internal world unsafe. Thus, the internal retreat of trauma survivors must necessarily be restrictive and finely tuned so that the danger of others and the danger of psychological material are both managed and avoided; 'the retreat then serves as an area of the mind where reality does not have to be faced' (Steiner, 2003, p. 3). Drawing on his clinical experience, Symington (2007) theorizes that for individuals who have retreated into themselves as a result of trauma, self-preoccupation is at the heart of their psychological experience and as a result they are operating with a 'restricted view of the self. It is not the whole self, but only one aspect of the self' (p. 224). Such individuals 'wrap' themselves up so that much of their external and internal worlds are ignored, disavowed or dissociated. This strategy of turning their focus inward and retreating into the internal world where the self becomes the central frame of reference allows trauma survivors a certain degree of perceived protection against further threat because their contact with and reliance on others is wilfully constrained. But because the sense of self has become so restricted it comes at quite a cost in terms of how the individual (1) explains their life experiences and the reasons for their victimization, (2) manages their life, and (3) relates to others.

Reliance solely upon the self may provide some degree of protection against further feelings of betrayal, disappointment and harm (Janoff-Bulman, 1979). It also may provide some sense of control over one's environment and internal world, as a way to overcompensate for strong feelings of helplessness in these domains (Lisak, 1994). However, reliance solely upon the self also means that the trauma survivor has difficulty entertaining the role of others, as the self is the central figure in any reasoning regarding the culpability for trauma, because their orientation and ideology has become so tightly organized around themselves. Kinsler, Courtois and Frankel (2009) note that '[b]y virtue of their repeated experiences of abuse and neglect, [survivors of relational maltreatment] come to "know," in the deepest sense of internal knowing, that they are somehow to blame and deserving of the abuse' (p. 184). Clinical researchers and therapists working with traumatized individuals have continually noted the dynamic where the mental representation the victim has of the perpetrators is positively preserved, while the image they have of themselves is sullied (e.g., Chu, 1998; Frawley-O'Dea, 1997). Chu (1998) points out that this allows the victim the illusion of control (see also Filipas & Ullman, 2006; Janoff-Bulman, 1979); that they were not helpless victims in their own traumatization, unable to do anything to stop it, but were rather responsible for it, and therefore had control over it. In addition, this conclusion is fostered by the subtle and/or explicit information given by the perpetrator during and after the victimization (e.g., the perpetrator promoting consensuality by saying 'you're enjoying this, aren't you'). Seeing the self as responsible also provides a defence against the fear of attachment loss. For example, one client came to realize that 'I protected him [the perpetrator] from any responsibility for what happened because I feared he wouldn't love me anymore if I didn't.'

Retaining images of the self as bad, rotten and responsible are inevitable consequences of the internal retreat. The restricted view of the mechanics of interactions, with the self at the centre, does not allow others to be entered into the explanatory equation. Janoff-Bulman (1979), among others, has noted the difference between 'behavioural' self-blame, where the person perceives their actions as responsible for traumatic events, and 'characterological' self-blame, where the person perceives themselves, their character (and faults in it) as responsible. The clients discussed here appear to engage in both behavioural and characterological self-blame to explain their traumatic history: 'My actions and something about me lead these things to happen because I'm a useless, worthless person.' Thus, the individual simplifies a two-person scenario/psychology (i.e., the motivations and actions of the perpetrator and the actions and responses of the victim) to a one-person scenario/psychology (i.e., the motivations, actions and responses of the victim alone, with the other person omitted). This frame of reference maintains the devalued self.

In the case of Mr G, he could experience a dampened down degree of hatred and blame towards those who had perpetrated against him in adulthood. But he had a solid image of himself as worthless and at fault for his childhood victimization, despite at times moving between demeaning and exulting his abusive parental figure. The function of the retreat inwards in these cases is not only to protect the self from others and to feel a sense of some control over life, but to protect the image of the perpetrator as loving and caring (i.e., defending against attachment loss). This outcome is assured from the restricted operating space of the retreat. While other people may be perceived as harmful and untrustworthy, the person believes they are responsible for the treatment they receive from others, including their caregivers.

A theoretical foundation for the internal retreat

In expanding on psychoanalytic, developmental, cognitive and personality theorists, Blatt (2006, 2008) has elucidated a model of personality and psychological distress based on the development and interaction of two opposing psychological forces; the drive to connect with others and the drive to be autonomous and self-directed. The biologically derived compulsion to connect with another is evident from the first moments of life when the baby seeks out a caregiving object (e.g., Fairbairn, 1946; See Trevanthen & Aitken, 2004, for review of this complex issue). As the baby develops, the move towards greater independence and autonomy begins to become evident with exploration away from the caregiver and moves towards a psychological self-directedness that is evident with resistance to parental demands (e.g., the 'terrible 2s'). Healthy development allows the streams of interpersonal relatedness and autonomy to develop relatively independently but with some degree of reciprocity. As Blatt (2006, 2008) notes, a child who has not developed trust in the caregiver (interpersonal relatedness) will have grave difficulty developing a more autonomous and individuated sense of self. These streams continue throughout life to exert some degree of tension between each other as desires to connect with others are tapered by the desire to be self-directed (e.g., personally achieve).

Blatt (2006, 2008) suggests that individuals whose personality style is organized with a greater emphasis on connecting with others (what he calls an anaclitic orientation) are 'primarily field dependent', such that their psychological functioning is significantly regulated and influenced by environmental factors (e.g., other people; Blatt, 2006, p. 500). Those more focused on self-direction and autonomy (what he calls introjectively oriented) tend to be 'predominantly field independent', such that their psychological experiences and judgements are largely influenced by internal, rather than environmental, factors.

Blatt (2006, 2008) argues that biological variables (e.g., innate capacity for self-regulation – including variations in alertness and attention, and capacity for emotional expression, as evident in the neonatal period) interact with highly distressing environmental circumstances to disrupt the separate and integrative development of the two streams, '[leading] to defensive, markedly exaggerated emphasis on one developmental dimension at the expense of the other' (Blatt, 2006, pp. 504–505). Traumatizing events in a relational context, especially early in life, seemingly are the type of events that would lead to a defensive emphasis on self-direction, autonomy and inward focus, to keep at bay the risk of further hurt which may come from connecting with others (see Chapter 4 of this volume and client self-determination). Thus, an introjective focus to defensively manage the drive towards others provides a model for the internal retreat that can result from relational trauma and is evident in the therapeutic context. This framework helps understand how the retreat operates to minimize potential present and future harm. The retreat also operates to reduce reactivation in the present of painful memories (e.g., feelings, thoughts, images) from the past.

Memory retrieval cues and the internal retreat

Therapy and the therapeutic relationship are founded and rely upon memory processes. Human memory, especially related to experiences from one's personal life (i.e., autobiographical memory) is a process largely reliant upon cues to trigger retrieval of stored information (Baddeley, 1999; Schacter, 1996). This is experientially evident, for example, when a visit from an old friend provides many visual and verbal cues for the retrieval of distant experiences vaguely remembered or long forgotten. These may reflect among many other things shared experiences related to specific incidences or a general sense of the times, spaces and places spent together; strong feelings that were experienced between the two; and memories of others present at the time. Memories of past relational experiences are ripe for cuing when one human being begins a relationship with another, as the cues to memory retrieval need only approximate the original experience. It is this cognitive fact (that cues need only approximate the original experience) that permits transference in the therapeutic relationship and allows it to be by its nature pervasive: for example, 'Not everything is transference, but transference exists in everything, which is not the same thing' (Etchegoyen, 2005, p. 83). As such, these cues and the memories they evoke need not be conscious, but can strongly influence actions, thoughts and feelings in the present moment. Cognitive psychologists speak of 'implicit' retrieval when a past experience unbeknown to the individual influences their current functioning (e.g., language, behaviour, thoughts, feelings; see Schacter. 1987, 1996; Tulving, 2000 for reviews; or Dorahy & Huntjens, 2007, in the context of complex trauma presentations). Consequently the therapeutic context provides unassuming retrieval cues for past relational experiences. As Stern (2004, p. 198) summarizes,

> memory is viewed as a collection of fragments of experiences. These get turned into a whole remembering experience in the following way. Events and experiences going on at the present time act as a context (a present remembering context) that selects, assembles, and organizes the fragments into a memory.

The more entrenched patterns of relating that a client engages in will often be implicit (outside their awareness) until, perhaps with the help of therapy, that non-aware content enters awareness. The therapeutic context implicitly, if not explicitly, activates in the present, painful past relational memories. In other words, the relational context of therapy cues, selects, assembles and organizes past experiences in relationships such that the therapeutic relationship and the therapist are imbued with the characteristics and qualities of past relationships and others in them. As Bromberg (1998) succinctly states, the past is relived 'as a frozen replica that structures the person's image of the future and of the present. Instead of being able to deal with 'what happened to me', the person enters therapy in order to deal with 'what he is sure *will* happen to him and what is happening to him now'' (p. 259, italics in original; see also Garland (1998) for an elucidation of the process of 'binding' in which overwhelming and relationally painful remnants of the past get bound with more recent traumatic material).

However, one of the principles underlying the effectiveness of retrieval cues to evoke previous memories is distinctiveness (Roediger & Guynn, 1996). Cues which distinctively distinguish specific past events from the myriad events occurring in a person's life are more likely to act as effective retrieval cues. The internal retreat, by keeping others, including the therapist, at bay, reduces the distinctiveness of the therapist and therapeutic relationship, to act as cues for past relational pain. If all people are kept 'at arm's length', they cannot come to be characterized with the same importance and emotional intensity as the relationship/s which produced betrayal and pain. Once the therapist and therapeutic relationship begins to be trusted, cared for and of value, they start to reflect more closely the original objects of pain and therefore act as more powerful memory cues for that pain.

As the therapeutic relationship intensifies, the past becomes more alive in the present (Stern, 2004). The therapist and the therapeutic relationship become more effective cues for the retrieval of a collage of emotional (not

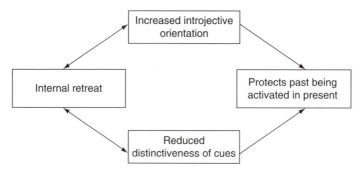

Figure 6.1 Internal retreat

simply intellectual) memory fragments associated with being wounded in relationships, which in turn shines a particularly frightening light back on the relationship with the therapist and the perceived pain they have the potential to cause (e.g., Mr G said approximately 12 months into therapy, 'I am just waiting for you to let me down'). Thus in the client's mind the present is a reflection of the past, such that the therapist will invariably dismiss, disappoint, betray and reject, if allowed into the client's psychological world. In this situation, the internal retreat as the default safe-haven position provides a dual protection strategy. Firstly, by attenuating or weakening the emotional link with the therapist, and thereby the effectiveness of the therapy to offer potent retrieval cues, the internal retreat allows some safety from the reactivation of past memories in the present moment. Secondly, if the present is less coloured by the past, the betrayal, rejection and despair that the client expects from the therapist is perceived to be less unbearable (i.e., the illusion that the past will not fuel present pain). Thus, by weakening the degree to which the therapy offers effective cues to the past, the internal retreat provides protection against the painful past and also the potential of a painful present.

Bringing together introjective style and reduced retrieval cue discrimination, the internal retreat can be schematically depicted (Figure 6.1).

Movement from the internal retreat

The psychological organization (including defensive strategies) which characterizes the internal retreat was initially created in a traumatic relational context, and is believed to be flexible enough to be reshaped by new relational experiences (Kinsler et al., 2009). Therapy provides a relational opportunity for containing and reparative emotional experiences. But the client needs to move from the internal retreat that they have fled to and through which all experiences and encounters with others are filtered. Thus, they have to move from a place of safety which is also psychologically stagnating, to a place of uncertainty and fear which provides a path to psychological growth (Steiner, 2003). For the traumatized clients under consideration here, moving from the internal retreat is hard fought for both them and the therapist. Gaining some ground on the anaclitic/attachment side means giving up some ground and a sense of perceived safety on the introjective (retreat) side. This means the client giving up some control over activities in their mental space, so the therapist can act as a more effective retrieval cue for past painful memories and can have some influence in helping to contain and understand that past. Up until that moment, the client has been the sole dweller in their mental space and regulated alone the restricted activities within it. Allowing a change to the psychological status quo evokes significant all-or-none fears of losing control of the mental space (i.e., coming out of the internal retreat) and/or allowing another to control it. The client is required to adopt a diametrically opposed attitude to themselves and the therapist than the one evident in the retreat, such that the pair is seen as collaborators rather than competitors (Blatt, 2008). The therapeutic relationship needs to be reconstructed as based on cooperation not competition. Thus, helping clients make moves from their internal retreat takes time, patience and sensitive handling, with all efforts focused on developing the relational connection with the client through cultivating safety, containment and familiarity (e.g., Herman, 1992; Steiner, 2003; Van der Hart et al., 2006). This allows the past to be cued by the present and thereby allows the present (the containing therapeutic relationship and trusted therapist) to influence the past (Foa & Kodak, 1986; Stern, 2004).

Until some degree of emotional connection (anaclitic functioning) can be achieved, the traumatized client will struggle to see other perspectives or be able to look at their history and current experience through other lenses (this can be linked here to the idea of mentalizing referred to previously by Ford in Chapter 5). That is, until some degree of trust and connection can be developed in the therapist, with an attitude of cooperation not competition, other perspectives, other people and other relational outcomes than hurt and betrayal cannot be contemplated in the client's mind; the client at this stage has few alternative representations of themselves, others and relationships. As the emotional connection between client and therapist develops and some introjective (retreat; competition) functioning is given up for some increases in anaclitic (attachment; cooperation) functioning, the client starts to get an 'intellectual' appreciation of the roles of others in their life, especially those that harmed them. For example, after approximately 12 months of weekly therapy, one client began to become more attached to the therapist and the therapy, and noted that he could see that his father treated him violently and that it was not his [the client's] fault. However, he did not as yet *feel* that was true. Some movement out of his retreat to allow the therapist to be entertained in his world freed up a space to allow an alternative model of his father and their relationship to be intellectually entertained. The anaclitic/attachment orientation of the client needed to further develop in the therapeutic relationship (i.e., he needed to continue to move out of his introjective retreat) before he would be able to emotionally feel that he was not responsible for his father's behaviour. This took a further 18 months of therapy and various forays to and from his internal retreat.

In their Interacting Cognitive Subsystems model, Teasdale and Barnard (e.g., 1993, Teasdale, 1993, 1999) suggest that the cognitive system has two different ways in which meaning for events can be represented. The first, propositional meaning, is the specific meaning of an event which is based on language and can be objectively communicated to others in an understandable manner. The second, implicational meaning, relates to the thematic aspects of an event experienced as the 'felt sense' of what the event means for the person (Teasdale, 1999). This model proposes that only the thematic, non-language based, implicational level of meaning is directly related to emotions. Thus, in the example outlined above, the client could entertain at a propositional/intellectual level that he had not been responsible for his father's violence, but he needed to further move from his introjective retreat and connect more emotionally with the therapist before changes could be made at the thematic level of meaning to change the feelings and deeper meaning associated with his father's behaviour and himself.

If the client remains in the internal retreat, the therapist's input, in the form of challenging or alternative perspectives, cannot be meaningfully and therapeutically taken in because the retreat is organized around a single explanation of events with the client himself at the centre. Some degree of attachment to the therapist (which allows movement from the retreat, and others to be entertained) brings more meaningful contemplation of this information, even at a propositional (intellectual) level. The client in their retreat is more often than not unable to 'hear' the therapist. During sessions, the therapist is a non-influential part of the client's environment in terms of changing both propositional and implicational meaning. In other words, the client's psychological world is not malleable at such points, because the therapist is not part of it.

Movement from the internal retreat and anxiety in the therapist

From the therapist's perspective, the client firmly entrenched in an internal retreat, and seemingly unmoveable, is experienced at different times with degrees of irritation, frustration, helplessness and relief. The work is arduous and at times stopped or blocked. The client attends sessions which at some level indicates to the therapist a desire to change, but progress is slow or non-existent as the retreat acts as a familiar haven too safe to vacate. On some days and some moments, the retreated client offers relief to the therapist as the painful feelings paving the way to change and growth need not be faced. Yet, often frustration and helplessness descend on the therapy as the thoughtful and reflective therapist struggles to understand what might break the impasse, and is worn by the seemingly competitive endeavours of the fearful client. Helplessness may be fuelled by an unwitting engagement in a transference re-enactment (Sandler, 1976) where the therapist mirrors the client and retreats into themselves (Steiner, 2003), citing their own professional and personal limitations as the impediment. If such a position can be tolerated and understood, it can offer not only valuable therapeutic insight, but also protect against reactive blaming of the client. Frustration in the therapist (complimentary countertransference) may act to keep at bay feelings of incompetence or inadequacy (concordant countertransference), stirred by the client's feelings, and to a greater or lesser extent reflect the therapist's own material (Symington, 2007).

Yet, helplessness, relief and frustration quickly turn to an urgent 'felt-sense' of anxiety as the client begins to leave the retreat. It is helping traumatized clients leave their internal retreat that is anxiety provoking. Before this, both the client and therapist are safe from agonizing feelings and the struggle of psychological growth (Steiner, 2003). When the therapist starts to feel the anxiety brought about by perceiving the client as wrapped in an egg shell, rather than a 'concrete suit', and starts fearing the client's or their own fragility, they are in the arena of drawing the person out of their internal retreat. This brings with it the potential for a destabilization of safety as the client begins to experience the therapist and the therapeutic context as potent retrieval cues for past relational pain. At this point they also begins to entertain in a meaningful way the role and importance (positive and negative) of other people in their past and present experiences, including the therapist.

The 'fragile' anxiety of the therapist signals the possibility and fear of moving out of the internal retreat. It seems to be evoked when the immovable (client) object starts to become potentially moveable. At this point, the 'egg shell' perception develops because there is some degree of uncertainty about how the person will respond as they start to leave the retreat and face the reality they have attempted to shield themselves from. The therapist is confronted with many anxiety-provoking considerations: is the client ready and psychologically strong enough for this next phase of work (i.e., the dilemma between 'exercising clinical judgement' and 'trusting the process') or how will the client manage the feelings and thoughts evoked – by acting out, by de-compensating, by facing, grieving and giving up their old understandings of themselves, others and the world. These moments in therapy represent moments of risk where the therapist, working to safely assist the clients from their retreat, holds a degree of uncertainty about the outcome.

The client is perceived as more psychologically delicate at this time and the therapist becomes fearful that movement from the retreat may be destabilizing and may start to doubt their ability to therapeutically manage the client's fragility. The therapist fears being overwhelmed if the client 'breaks'. The therapist's annihilatory fears for the client may mirror those of the client, who see themselves as unsafe, vulnerable and terrified of irreparable fragmentation as they leave their 'fortress'.

This dynamic and the interplay of feelings associated with it have not been limited to those who were victims of violence. They have also been experienced in individuals who have routinely used violence in adult life as a means of defending against internal and external threat or used sadistic attacks in an attempt to destroy the threat (e.g., Perelberg, 1995). Yet another dynamic has also been experienced with greater frequency and intensity in this group. This group of individuals have come to utilize violence to buffer against psychological destruction and this default defensive position is experienced by the therapist and feared by the client as they begin to contemplate movement from the retreat. Thus, fear of the client being damaged is usurped by fear of the therapist being damaged. This fear may be driven by the client identifying with the person/s who perpetrated against them and the therapist identifying with the client during this perpetration (e.g., Chu, 1998; Ferenczi, 1933). This dynamic has been experienced to a far lesser extent in those who have not utilized violence and sadistic attacks as psychological survival strategies. In these individuals, the shared anxiety of the client and therapist as the retreat begins to be moved from is destabilization and fragmentation, as aggression directed at others has not become a means of managing psychological threat.

In the traumatized clients under investigation here, the urgent and 'felt' anxiety of the therapist is brought about by perceiving the client as wrapped in a fragile shell and fearing the consequences (to the client or themselves) of the brittle shell breaking. Yet this experience in the therapist is a necessary step in therapy and a sign of progression, despite the disconcertion it brings for both parties. If it can be tolerated and managed, it has the capacity to allow the client freedom from the retreat, which increases the possibility of psychological growth.

Consequently, countertransference as communicated in the therapist's moment-to-moment feelings in the therapy becomes a salient, meaningful tool for monitoring the progress and stage at which the client is at. Yet this 'tool' is not only sensitive to the projective identifications of the client (i.e., the therapist responding emotionally, physically and intellectually to the client's material and unconscious correspondence) but is sensitive to the therapist's own history of experience. Countertransference responses are an amalgam of the therapist's material and the client's material (Symington, 2007). The more the therapist can be aware of their own triggers for, and defences to, vulnerability, uncertainty, weakness, risk and control, along with their own relational and intra-psychic history, the more they will be able to use the countertransference as an empathic communicative connection that the client has with them. This will allow some gauging of the nature and intensity of the client's current psychological space and promote holding and containing of the painful material the client is finding unmanageable (Casement, 1999). It therefore has the capacity to operate as a compass when negotiating movement from the retreat. For example, the 'fragile' anxiety ('egg shell' perception) felt by the therapist as the retreat is moved from can be held and understood as therapeutic progress rather than defended against or withdrawn from to reduce the discomforting feeling (e.g., by asking impulsive, reactive, therapeutically unhelpful questions or subtly taking the client in a different direction).

One facet of the multifactorial process of moving from 'concrete suit' to 'egg shell' is a growing awareness of hope rather than fear that things may be different. As the therapist begins to be entertained and the single version of events (the client at fault and responsible) that characterizes the retreat begins to be challenged, other alternative explanations for the client's life and future become possible. Hope for other possibilities allows movement from the retreat, and hope is consciously possible when other possibilities become evident. Casement (1999) suggests that underpinning the subtle and unaware communications that clients engage in, which are picked up in the therapist's countertransference, is hope that things can be different. It is important for the therapist to convey and instil the hope that such clients are likely to be quite unaware of, even if only keeping in mind the notion of holding the hope for both parties when it feels non-existent in the client (McWilliams, 1999). This may come as much from actions as from words.

As the 'egg shell' perception began to be experienced and endured with Mr G, the content of one session led the therapist to reflect, 'you wouldn't like to think you are starting to feel more connected and trusting of me'. Mr G pensively dropped his gaze to the floor and with a quiet, muffled intonation, noted 'no, I never wanted that to happen, but it has'. Later in the session, he stated that he never 'lets anyone in, it's safest that way. But you have become important in my life and I never thought that would happen, I've worked hard to make sure it wouldn't'. Before this point in the work, such thoughts could not be entertained by Mr G. He took respite in his internal retreat, where he, and only he, existed as the central reference point in his life, and the therapist was perceived as a competitor rather than an ally. This point in therapy was the start of much painful work, which ultimately allowed Mr G to give up his (traumatic) attachment and firm idealized/positive view of his abusive caregiver.

Conclusion

In orienting towards themselves, traumatized individuals, such as Mr G discussed here, often work to sever any reliance on, or emotional contact with, others. They themselves become the centre of their world (Symington, 2007) and as a result come to see and interpret their histories through the only lens available; themselves as the sole and driving force – writer, director and protagonist. Other figures are in minor supporting roles, if present at all. Just as they work to protectively cut off others from their external world, individuals hole-up in their internal (introjective) retreats, attempt to cut others from, and their own access to, their internal world (Steiner, 2003). The internal retreat therefore is characterized by a severing of objects externally (i.e., other people) and internally (i.e., altering or distorting accurate mental representations of dyadic relationships between themselves and others, especially those from their traumatic past). This severing process brings about the situation in which the individual themselves takes responsibility for the distressing events inflicted upon them. This allows them to have some sense of control and understanding of the motivations of others (e.g., 'I caused them to do that'), and helps keep these others free of blame (i.e., protects the mental representation of the other).

By keeping others, including the therapist, at an emotional distance, the retreat operates to reduce retrieval cues that activate past painful relational memories. In attempting to handle the past in this way, the present is perceived as more manageable and safer. Thus, the retreat becomes an integral part of psychological life. It is not only the place the traumatized individual has cocooned themselves at the beginning of the therapeutic relationship, but the place they withdraw to during therapeutic dangers (i.e., incidents which signal previous relational breaches; e.g., vacation breaks; being 'encouraged' to step too far beyond their comfort zone in therapy). Yet, the protection it offers is somewhat illusionary as the past continues to pervade the client's life (making the retreat necessary), including their view and expectation of the therapist and the therapeutic relationship.

It is only when the present relational situation (the therapeutic relationship) is able to have a greater impact on the present moment than past relational experiences that tentative steps can be taken to leave the retreat. This is a point of contact in the therapy where the client and therapist begin to connect more emotionally (the possibility for cooperation rather than competition is entertained; the client begins to relinquish some control of their psychological space and allows another in) and this evokes anxious fragility in the therapist, regarding either the client or themselves. Providing a present context that can heal past relational experiences requires not only therapeutic skill, technique and containment, but also patience. If attempts are made to 'fast-track' the shift from past to present (e.g., by offering reassurance and explanation rather than, or in the absence of, curiosity and exploration) in order to lure complex trauma clients from their retreat, the therapist risks swiftly reinforcing the dominance of the past over the present as they become the figure controlling and cajoling the client's life. The therapist then becomes in the client's mind a living, breathing contemporary replication of those from their past who could control and inflict damage. At best at this stage, the client may stop therapy. At worst, they may feel re-traumatized and reinforce the defences and psychological operations that make-up their internal retreat.

Summary points

- Chronic relational traumatization may lead to an internal retreat designed to protect from threatening external stimuli and painful psychological material. Wherein the internal retreat, the self becomes the central frame of reference for explaining events of the past and protecting from past, present and future threat.
- The retreat is supported by introjective functioning and a dilution of distinctive retrieval cues for past relational trauma.
- Movement from the retreat is needed for the entertainment of alternative explanations and understandings of self and past relational experiences.
- Movement from the retreat evokes anxiety in the therapist about the client's or their own fragility ('egg shell' perception) and the 'egg shell' perception is an important aspect and indicator of therapeutic progress.

Acknowledgements

The author would like to thank Dr Fiona J. Bailey, Matthew Warwick and Prof. Warwick Middleton for comments on earlier drafts of this manuscript.

Suggested reading

Blatt, S. J. (2008). *Polarities of experience: Relatedness and self-definition in personality development, psychopathology and the therapeutic process.* Washington, DC: American Psychological Association.
Chu, J. A. (1998). *Rebuilding shattered lives: The responsible treatment of complex post-traumatic and dissociative disorders.* New York: Wiley.
Courtois, C. A., & Ford, J. D. (Eds.) (2009). *Treating complex traumatic stress disorder: An evidence-based guide.* New York: Guilford Press.

References

Baddeley, A. D. (1999). *Essentials of human memory.* Hove: Psychology Press.
Blatt, S. J. (2006). A fundamental polarity in psychoanalysis: Implications for personality development, psychopathology, and the therapeutic process. *Psychoanalytic Inquiry, 26,* 494–520.
Blatt, S. J. (2008). *Polarities of experience: Relatedness and self-definition in personality development, psychopathology and the therapeutic process.* Washington, DC: American Psychological Association.

Bromberg, P. M. (1998). *Standing in the spaces: Essays on clinical process, trauma and dissociation.* Hillsdale, NJ: The Analytic Press.

Casement, P. (1999). *On learning from the patient.* London: Routledge.

Chu, J. A. (1998). *Rebuilding shattered lives: The responsible treatment of complex post-traumatic and dissociative disorders.* New York: Wiley.

Dorahy, M. J., & Huntjens, R. J. C. (2007). Memory and attentional processes in dissociative identity disorder: A review of the empirical literature. In E. Vermetten, M. J. Dorahy, & D. Spiegel (Eds.), *Traumatic dissociation: Neurobiology and treatment* (pp. 55–75). Arlington, VA: American Psychiatric Press.

Etchegoyen, R. H. (2005). *Fundamentals of psychoanalytic technique.* London: Karnac.

Fairbairn, W. R. D. (1946). Object-relationships and dynamic structure. *International Journal of Psychoanalysis, 27,* 30–37.

Ferenczi, S. (1933/1949). Confusion of tongues between the adult and the child. *International Journal of Psychoanalysis, 30,* 225–230.

Filipas, H. H., & Ullman, S. E. (2006). Child sexual abuse, coping responses, self-blame, posttraumatic stress disorder, and sexual revictimization. *Journal of Interpersonal Violence, 21,* 652–672.

Foa, E. B., & Kodak, M. J. (1986). Emotional processing of fear: Exposure to corrective information. *Psychological Bulletin, 99,* 20–35.

Frawley-O'Dea, M. G. (1997). Transference paradigms at play in psychoanalytically oriented group therapy with female adult survivors of childhood sexual abuse. *International Journal of Group Psychotherapy, 47,* 427–441.

Garland, C. (1998). Thinking about trauma. In C. Garland (Ed.), *Understanding trauma: A psychoanalytical approach* (pp. 9–31). London: Karnac.

Herman, J. L. (1992). *Trauma and recovery.* New York: Basic Books.

Janoff-Bulman, R. (1979). Characterological versus behavioural self-blame: Inquiries into depression and rape. *Journal of Personality and Social Psychology, 37,* 1798–1809.

Kinsler, P. J., Courtois, C. A., & Frankel, A. S. (2009). Therapeutic alliance and risk management. In C. A. Courtois & J. D. Ford (Eds.), *Treating complex traumatic stress disorder: An evidence-based guide* (pp. 183–201). New York: Guilford Press.

Lisak, D. (1994). The psychological impact of sexual abuse: Content analysis of interviews with males survivors. *Journal of Traumatic Stress, 7,* 525–548.

McWilliams, N. (1999). *Psychoanalytic case formulation.* New York: Guilford Press.

Perelberg, R. J. (1995). A core phantasy in violence. *International Journal of Psychoanalysis, 76,* 1215–1231.

Racker, H. (1988). *Transference and countertransference.* London: Hogarth Press.

Roediger, H. L. III, & Guynn, M. J. (1996). Retrieval processes. In E. L. Bjork & R. A. Bjork (Eds.), *Memory* (pp. 197–236). New York: Academic Press.

Sandler, J. (1976). Countertransference and role responsiveness. *International Review of Psychoanalysis, 3,* 43–47.

Schacter, D. L. (1987). Implicit memory: History and current status. *Journal of Experimental Psychology: Learning, Memory and Cognition, 13,* 501–518.

Schacter, D. L. (1996). *Searching for memory: The brain, the mind and the past.* New York: Basic books.

Steiner, J. (2003). *Psychic retreats: Pathological organizations in psychotic, neurotic and borderline patients.* London: Routledge.

Stern, D. N. (2004). *Present moments in psychotherapy and everyday life.* New York: Norton.

Symington, N. (2007). Narcissism as trauma preserved. In N. Symington (Ed.), *Becoming a person through psychoanalysis* (pp. 215–226). London: Karnac.

Teasdale, J. D., & Barnard, P. J. (1993). *Affect, cognition and change: Re-modelling depressive thought*. Hove: Lawrence Erlbaum Associates.

Teasdale, J. D. (1993). Emotion and two kinds of meaning: Cognitive therapy and applied cognitive science. *Behaviour Research and Therapy, 31*, 339–354.

Teasdale, J. D. (1999). Emotional processing, three modes of mind and the prevention of relapse in depression. *Behaviour Research and Therapy, 37*, S53–S77.

Trevanthen, C., & Aitken, K. J. (2004). Infant intersubjectivity: Research, theory, and clinical applications. *Journal of Child Psychology and Psychiatry, 42*, 3–48.

Tulving, E. (2000). Introduction: Memory. In M. S. Gazzaniga (Ed.), *The new cognitive neurosciences* (pp. 727–732). Cambridge, MA: MIT Press.

Van der Hart, O., Nijenhuis, E. R. S., Steele, K., 2006. *The haunted self: Structural dissociation and the treatment of chronic Traumatization*. New York: Norton.

7

Working as an Expert Companion to Facilitate Posttraumatic Growth

Richard G. Tedeschi and Lawrence G. Calhoun

Introduction

Recent years have seen an increase of focus on empirically supported psychological treatments for a variety of psychological disorders (American Psychological Association, 2006). This is a salutary development, as it directs practitioners to focus their efforts on interventions that are most likely to yield improvements for their clients in an efficient manner, and can help clinicians avoid unsupported methods (see Chapter 2 for a critical review of empirically supported treatments in trauma therapy). At the same time, factors associated with the therapeutic alliance and other ways clinicians develop a therapeutic relationship with clients have been demonstrated to be at least as important in therapy outcome as the technical aspects of treatments emphasized in much of the research on particular therapy approaches (Norcross, 2004; Norcross & Wampold, 2011). This chapter will focus on the therapeutic relationship in the context of work with survivors of traumatic events. We use the terms 'trauma', 'crisis', 'major stressor' and related terms as generally synonymous expressions to describe circumstances that significantly challenge or invalidate important components of the individual's assumptive world. We will provide a very brief introduction to the concept of posttraumatic growth (PTG), a term we introduced in 1995, describing its main features and some of the elements that appear to be connected to its development. We will also provide a general description of the approach to clinical work that we have called expert companionship, by focusing on one client's experience to illustrate the approach, and how the perspective may be used to positively influence the therapeutic relationship.

It will become clear that we see trauma treatment as an opportunity to not only decrease symptoms and alleviate suffering but also to enable survivors of highly stressful events to engage in a process of personal transformation that can leave them recognizing that they may have changed for the better as a result of struggling with the aftermath of their trauma.

Posttraumatic growth

Let us begin by first considering the concept of PTG. The terminology comes from efforts to provide a theoretical basis for, and quantification of, reports that have been evident for centuries of how the struggle with traumatic events can be a catalyst for change (Tedeschi & Calhoun, 1995, 1996). The inventory to assess PTG that we devised, the Posttraumatic Growth Inventory (PTGI), was based on previous qualitative work and on an examination of published reports of changes experienced as a result of the encounter with major life crises. The PTGI assesses change on five domains of growth: increased sense of personal strength, improved relationships, spiritual change, a greater appreciation of life and the development of new life opportunities or priorities. These changes arise out of a process that has been described in various iterations, most recently in Calhoun, Cann, and Tedeschi (2010). The latest modelling of this process emphasizes the importance of such factors as the pre-trauma personal characteristics and beliefs of the trauma survivor, ability to manage emotional distress in order to help convert automatic rumination into more deliberate, reflective patterns of thinking and the influence of the proximal and distal social environment, so that trauma survivors can reconstruct challenged core beliefs and personal narratives. (See also Chapter 4 for another model based on affective–cognitive aspects of processing needs.) Ultimately, the process of PTG involves cognitive changes to the assumptive world (Janoff-Bulman, 1992) in the context of highly emotional experiences of loss and personal disorientation. What is therefore defined as 'traumatic' is dependent on the degree to which there is a challenge to core beliefs or the assumptive world, not dependent on particular events, which for some might be quite traumatic and others not.

The changes that arise in the context of trauma survivorship occur most often in natural settings of social support. But by understanding the process, we have made suggestions about how to facilitate it (Calhoun & Tedeschi, 1999) in clinical work. These suggestions rely heavily on qualities of therapeutic relating, and evolved into the expert companionship model (Calhoun & Tedeschi, 2006). In this approach, we emphasize companionship rather than expertise, even though we are trying to describe a way for clinicians to be more expert in their attempts to help trauma survivors. In a way, this model comes out of our early research on trauma survivorship when we were conducting very open, non-structured interviews with bereaved persons or with persons who had been seriously injured and become disabled in adulthood (Calhoun & Tedeschi, 1989–1990; Tedeschi & Calhoun, 1988).

In those early interviews, we originally set out to understand wisdom, but by being open listeners, we ended up learning about the process we would come to call PTG. The basic approach was to learn from the people we were listening to, and this is a basic tenet of expert companionship. The clinicians who are expert companions approach trauma survivors as people who have much to offer in terms of describing their personal experience, their attempts to cope, what they need in a relationship that will be helpful and what personal changes may be emerging. By paying close attention to these descriptions, clinicians can learn where in the process of recovery and PTG the survivor may be, and what the clinician can provide. In *listening without necessarily trying to solve* the problems the trauma survivor faces, companionship assumes a central role.

Expert companions

Expert companionship is certainly related to traditional descriptions of effective therapeutic relating, including Rogers' (1957) concepts of client-centeredness, and the common factors of psychotherapy (Weinberger, 1995). But in the context of trauma therapy, and in attempting to facilitate PTG as part of the therapy outcome, there are certain emphases. First is the somewhat paradoxical stance of learning from the client rather than seeking to change the client. As suggested above, this can be seen as the stance of the qualitative researcher, who is looking to understand the psychological constructions of the person being studied. Although the emphasis at the start is on learning about the survivor's experience, it becomes even more crucial to understand what the trauma has done to the survivor's core beliefs or *assumptive world* (Janoff-Bulman, 1992). It is more crucial because in attempting to reconsider these core beliefs, trauma survivors often begin to change in significant ways that become PTG. The expert companion must stay psychologically close through this process, and cultivate a somewhat more active role in pointing out the nuances of change and PTG.

But well-trained clinicians must also be experts in the most effective and efficient ways to help clients with certain kinds of difficulties. Although the expert companion perspective does not focus exclusively, or perhaps even primarily, on the expertise of the clinician, it is important for clinicians to seamlessly blend companionship with the use of approaches that have been proven effective for particular kinds of client difficulties.

Consider an excerpt from this initial therapy session with 30-year-old Clint, and how the clinician helps set the stage for PTG by becoming an expert companion.

Clint: I am embarrassed to even talk about this. I was rehearsing in the car coming over, trying to figure out how to put it. I've never been in therapy before, so I'm a little nervous.

Therapist: Any way you want to say it is OK. This is anxiety-arousing at first for most people. You met me a few minutes ago, and now you are getting ready to talk about very personal things.

C: Yeah, pretty strange.

T: I think you'll find it easier as we go along.

C: Well, anyway, I had an emotional affair with this woman. I'm married, and have three kids. I've really messed up.

T: Tell me what happened.

C: Well, to make it worse, she lives next door. Our kids play together.

T: It does sound pretty messy.

C: And I told her I loved her, and I wrote all these emails to her saying pretty bad things about my wife, and when she got hold of them, well, as you can imagine she was just crushed. I can't believe I did that to her. So, now we are kind of separated in the same house.

T: How long ago did this happen?

C: She, my wife, I mean, found the emails three weeks ago. But we haven't been getting along so well for the past couple years. And last year I started texting with Chrissy, my neighbour, and her husband saw it and got on me about it, and we stopped, and then about a month later it kind of started up again, and my wife saw it and we stopped, and then started again, and now it's really blown up with those emails. And her husband is threatening me, and I am just trying to lay low. But their house is like ten feet away from ours. And our youngest is six months, so I was doing this while she was pregnant you know, and I guess that's pretty bad.

T: You said she was crushed.

C: Yeah, she got angry, but mostly just can't believe I did this to her. I betrayed her. She's shocked at me. I'm shocked at myself.

T: You had these red flags on at least two occasions that this was not a good idea.

C: I didn't really mean to do it. I didn't want to hurt anyone.

T: You said it was an emotional affair.

C: Yeah, I told her I loved her, but now I don't really think so.

T: Did you have sex with her?

C: Yeah.

T: And you said some pretty bad things about your wife in the emails?

C: Yeah, but I don't see things that way now. I can see more clearly that I wasn't being fair to her.

T: How so?

C: I thought I do a lot. I do laundry, cook, clean, help with the kids, I take them to school and such, make breakfast.

T: Didn't feel appreciated?

C: Exactly. So when she asked me to do things I just felt not appreciated. But I see that we both have it hard. She works, too. And three kids. I shouldn't be carrying grudges. I should know better, I was brought up different.

T: In what way?

C: We had a strong faith. My grandfather was a preacher, and was a huge influence on me. My father was a trucker so he was gone a lot. I grew up with my grandfather, and he taught me how to live right. That's the other thing. (Long pause)

T: The other thing?

C: He died yesterday.

T: Oh, I'm sorry.

C: Yeah.

T: Did he know about all this?

C: He does now (points upward).

T: You failed your wife and failed him?

C: Failed myself. Failed God. Just failed.

T: Not who you thought you were.

C: Not at all. I've got to figure out why I did this. I can't let this happen again. She's got a foot and a half out the door.

T: You are a disappointment to yourself, and need to know how you let that happen.

C: And not let it happen again.

T: Never again.

C: Right.

T: And repair the damage.

C: I love my wife – I don't want to lose her. But she doesn't know who I am anymore.

T: Maybe you're not sure either?

C: I wish I hadn't done this. I shouldn't have gotten so involved, and paid attention to the signs I should stop. Julie and Johnny were both willing to be forgiving at a couple points, and I just went back. Man, was that stupid? I could have avoided this whole mess. I'm not a bad guy. I just want peace. I don't like conflict.

T: And then you created a bunch.

C: Imagine that. I don't like to hurt anyone. Like Johnny, Chrissy's husband, he came over and confronted me. Grabbed me and threw me down. He's a big guy, former Marine. I don't get into fights. I'm a sensitive guy.

T: How would you like me to help?

C: I need to figure myself out, why I did this. And then be better.

T: Be a better man?

C: Absolutely.

T: Live out your principles?

C: Right.

T: Like your grandfather taught you. Honour him.

C: I'm so ashamed of myself. I take responsibility. I'm the cause of it all. Guilty.

T: That's a good start – feeling guilty and responsible. If you come here and you are honest with yourself like that, we can figure out how you deceived yourself and justified all this.

C: Sacrificed my principles, and granddad's.

T: And reclaim them now. Figure out what you really believe and what you will live out.

C: Be a much better husband.

T: Maybe your marriage will be better than before.

C: It's almost over now, so I don't know.

T: If you are going to stay married, it has to be better, or this kind of thing could happen again.

C: Yeah, I've got to be better and my marriage has to be better.

T: That's up to you, but I can help you figure it out.

C: That would be really good, because I don't have anyone to talk to about this, or anyone I want to talk to about this.

T: It's embarrassing.

C: It is, so it is pretty much just me and Julie talking about it, and I have to work on myself – she can't do that.

T: Well, we can, so I'm glad you're here.

C: Me, too.

Note how the therapist relates to this new client in very direct ways and stays close to his concerns, asking very few questions for information, but instead invites the client to talk about his experience and how it is affecting his core beliefs. Although these beliefs are not articulated in this first session, it is implied that they are certainly counter to having an affair with the neighbour. This becomes even more poignant because the source of many of these beliefs, grandfather, has just died. The therapist is an expert companion by helping Clint reflect on his major emotional experience – the embarrassment he remarks upon at the very start, his feeling of shame and sense of failure, and his desire to live up to his principles. In doing so, the therapist also remarks that these negative feelings are a good starting point for honest discussion, and that it is possible, even necessary that he become a better man and a better husband. This foreshadows PTG in the course of therapy as this man confronts his failings. The therapist also asks how he can be helpful, to see what the client perceives his needs to be, and where they can join up in a common endeavour. The idea is to become companions in this journey, and the therapist indicates clearly and simply that he is someone the client can talk to: by saying in response to the expressed need to find someone to talk with 'well, we can'. Furthermore, there is the subtle indication by the therapist that he won't be the one trying to solve the problems that were created by the client. When the client states that he has to be a better man and husband, the therapist states that it is up to the client to figure that out, but that the therapist will help.

Beyond initial contact, there is of course much to be accomplished in order to assist trauma survivors. There may be unpleasant stories for the client to tell in which they are victims or in which they commit terrible acts. They may be very emotional in their storytelling. They may have ideas that seem irrational. They may be defensive, self-critical, afraid or otherwise unwilling to tell the truth about things that might put them in a bad light. Then, what emerges needs to be woven into a life narrative that makes sense of all that occurred and connects life before the trauma with life afterward. So, the expert companion working with trauma survivors must, without judgement, tolerate stories that are unusual, difficult to hear or that others might see as crazy. Expert companions see survivors of trauma through a sometimes substantial period of time, more than friend and family may be able to tolerate. That's one thing that makes the expert companion an *expert*.

The expertise of this kind of clinician also involves following the sequence of events outlined in the model of the process of PTG (Calhoun, Cann, & Tedeschi, 2010) to respond to the trauma survivor in ways that help the person move towards PTG. First, it is important to recognize that before traumatic events people had certain coping tendencies, personality traits, experiences and beliefs that perhaps made them vulnerable to trauma but also capable of PTG. Expert companions can ask about those cognitive foundations that have been shaken, or perhaps shattered, by trauma, especially the core beliefs involving identity, meaning, view of the world and the future, or of the life course. Traumas, by our definition, shake up these things – they are 'seismic events' that are psychological earthquakes that can undermine belief systems. The expert companion can talk with the trauma survivor about what they used to believe or always believed. In the case of Clint, introduced above, the clinician approaches the belief system, identity, and other pre-trauma factors this way.

> T: You said that your grandfather taught you about how to live the right way. What did he teach?
> C: Oh, you know, to be honest, and always do God's will.
> T: And God's will is?
> C: To love, always to love. Of course, he doesn't mean it in the way I did it!
> T: Right – to be loving to your wife, and also to Chrissy and Johnny, would have meant to be honest.
> C: Yeah, I wasn't honest at all. Not to Julie or Johnny for sure.
> T: But even to Chrissy?
> C: I guess not – I was leading somewhere with her I couldn't really go.
> T: And you told her you loved her, but now you said you doubt that.

C: That's confusing. I guess I was attracted to her. And getting personal like I was – too personal – I was starting to feel that.

T: Those feelings of love can sure start to develop with the kind of emotional and sexual intimacy you were allowing to occur.

C: Hard to tell the chicken or the egg there.

T: Yeah, I think that may be so. I also think that your grandfather's, or God's idea, about love is something that you haven't gotten to really come to terms with. It's hard to love – there are things that get in the way.

C: Yeah, I obviously have to learn more about that. I sure wish he were still around to talk to about these things. Like I have more lessons to learn – the advanced course or something.

T: It's a terrible loss.

C: He was a great man. I still have a lot to learn. Now I have to figure out another way to learn it I guess.

T: You said you are a sensitive guy, and don't like conflict or hurting anyone. Sounds like someone who might be able to be very loving, but there is something that got in the way of that here.

C: Maybe I have something to build on.

T: I am sure you do.

Clearly, this discussion focuses on Clint's sense of identity, some of his core beliefs, and his patterns of relating – perhaps avoiding conflict and building resentments in spite of his intention to be loving. He begins to recognize some of these things as something to build on while at the same time noting that there must be a flaw somewhere. But the general tenor of the conversation has to do with change or improvement – potential growth. For this person, traditional Christian religious beliefs and teachings are central to the assumptive world. These represent, for this person, an important way of trying to understand what happened and, in addition, perhaps, they offer to him an avenue for the experience of PTG.

Another step in the PTG process is the management of emotional distress, and of the ruminations, usually intrusive, that prevent trauma survivors from making more constructive progress. With Clint, this part of the process was explored as follows.

T: I am sure this has been on your mind a lot.

C: All the time. Whenever I am around Julie, I wonder what she is thinking about me and whether we'll get into an argument.

T: How about when you are not with her?

C: Oh, it is like I can't get away from this. I just kick myself all the time. Why did I do this? Why didn't I stop when I had the chance? How stupid am I? What is Julie going to do? What would happen to the kids if we split up? All kinds of things. My stomach's in a knot. First I'm guilty, mad at myself, then I'm scared.

T: This isn't really doing you much good, but it is hard to shut this off.

C: I know. I try to get some relief.

T: How?

C: I want to sleep but can't. I've been taking Tylenol PM.

T: I think we need to find a way to turn these thoughts into something more constructive. That's what this therapy can be about.

C: So, what do I do?

T: I will suggest to you to do something with these thoughts rather than just think them. You are actually asking yourself some good questions. We need to start getting to the answers.

C: How?

T: You may know more about the answers than you realize. Let's figure out what you already know and I will help you organize all these clues so we can understand it better. We need to do it like a jigsaw puzzle.

C: What do you mean?

T: Ever put together a jigsaw puzzle?

C: Sure.

T: What do you do first?

C: Usually pour all the pieces out.

T: Then what?

C: Turn 'em over and see what they are. Then maybe look at the picture and see how some will belong in certain places – you know – the colour and what not.

T: Then what?

C: I guess start with the edges.

T: Those pieces are easier to pick out.

C: Right.

T: Same here. We got to dump out of you the pieces – what you already know. Your memories of what you did, how you thought. Then see if we can start putting them together. We might work from a general outline of the kind of person you have been, but get into the middle part that is less clear as we go on. OK?

C: OK. So how do we do that?

T: Are you OK with doing a little homework?

C: Sure, I want to get going on this. My marriage is at stake. I guess my life, you could say.

T: How about you go home after this and write down the questions that float through your mind, like how could I do this, or why did I do it, even how stupid am I. Then try to write down the answers, or pieces of answers the best you can. Bring what you do in here – these are the puzzle pieces. We'll start with those, dig up some more, and start putting it together. Much more constructive.

C: I'll give it a shot. It'll be good to do something useful with all this.

T: That's the idea.

Notice how the expert companion stays close to the client's experience but, utilizing expert knowledge about cognitive interventions and ways to help manage intrusive thoughts, he shows Clint a way to move from intrusive rumination to a more deliberate, reflective and constructive approach to his concerns. This excerpt illustrates not only the blend of companionship on the one hand, but also clinical expertise on the other.

Expert companions also recognize that appropriate and constructive self-disclosure may be useful to move towards PTG. In this disclosure, of experienced emotions, thoughts, and personal understandings that are founded on the individual's assumptive world, it may be possible to engage in new ways of thinking about core beliefs – view of self, of the kind of world this is and how to live in it, perhaps discover new life meanings, and the future or life narrative. The expert companion offers a safe environment in which to discuss these things, and perhaps the trauma survivor will gain the courage to disclose, wisely and appropriately, to other people who might be constructive influences. Standing in the way are embarrassment, fear of the reactions of others and mistrust. Sometimes support groups provide a venue for this. Sometimes people have friends or relatives they feel safe with. Increasingly, people turn to online chat rooms, where the anonymity allows for a sense of safety. Not only other ways of thinking about oneself and the world can come from these sources, but also more distal sources such as the media, religious teachings and general cultural stories and myths. For Clint, Christian religious themes were a powerful component of his core beliefs, and of his reconstructing this assumptive world. Consider how these themes were a source of core beliefs, but how his experience also produced some change, with the help of the expert companion.

T: You said you always tried to follow your grandfather's example, but I got a sense he was a hard act to follow.

C: Yeah, he was a great man. I gave the eulogy, and you know it was easier than I thought, in that there was so much good to say about him. I could go on for hours.

T: He lived almost perfect?

C: Yeah, that's how he was. I'm sure God was glad to have him.

T: You said to me at our first meeting that he now knows what you did.

C: That's what I believe – when you are in heaven you can see it all.

T: So, what do you look like to him?

C: Oh, when you are in heaven, everything is OK. You don't have anything but love for people. So he doesn't focus on my sin, he is just loving me.

T: Feels good.

C: Oh yeah.

T: So, what would he say to you – It's OK son, I love you?

C: I guess so.

T: He wouldn't think you need punishment?

C: I don't think so. My mess is my own punishment I suppose.

T: But you punish yourself.

C: I guess I do.

T: Is there any inconsistency there?

C: Seems like maybe.

T: Have you prayed to God for forgiveness?

C: Sure, a lot.

T: Has he forgiven you?

C: I guess so – I've been sincere.

T: You've sincerely asked for forgiveness, so God forgives?

C: That's what I believe.

T: So you believe you are forgiven.

C: Yes.

T: So, now that you are forgiven by God and your grandfather – now what?

C: I guess I should get on with living better, instead of punishing myself, is what you are saying.

T: I'm not saying it, you are just telling me what you believe.

C: That is what I believe.

T: So can you live now like your grandfather – is that your model? Like Jesus? Who?

C: Well, Jesus was perfect so he is *the* model but I will never be perfect. But I can be better.

T: Maybe more like grandfather. He wasn't perfect?

C: You know, actually he wasn't. He had some slip-ups when he was young, I heard. Before I knew him.

T: Oh yeah?

C: At the funeral, it was funny, people told some stories on him. He used to drive too fast and wrecked his dad's car. He was really good look-ing and had a bunch of girlfriends. There were some funny stories. Too bad I didn't know before. Ah, but I'm not sure I could have kidded him about it.

T: So, your grandfather changed over time.

C: Apparently so. I guess I just knew the final version.

T: So, how about you?

C: I guess I am not my final version. I hope not! So, I can accept forgiveness, and try to do better.

T: OK. And we'll have to figure out what doing better will look like, and what kind of man you will be – the better version of you. Not your grandfather as much as you – the 'you' God made you to be.

C: That's right. That's how it should be. The man God wants me to be. You know I was thinking again about something that granddad said. God wants us to follow his will because it makes a better life for us. I didn't do that and what happens? I make a mess and I'm miserable. I'll be much happier living according to what's right.

T: OK, so that's our focus here.

C: Absolutely, and you help keep me be honest so I get used to doing that better myself.

The expert companion needs to be comfortable working within the framework of the client's beliefs, and it is not unusual, at least in some cultural and geographical contexts, for these beliefs to include religious elements, as they do here (Weiss & Berger, 2010). Being a companion means staying close to the client's belief system, and respecting it. Being an expert means understanding how the beliefs work, seeing where people are inconsistent, where they may be violating their own assumptions, or where these beliefs do not support relief from the distress of trauma and may need revision (Calhoun & Tedeschi, 1999; Knapp, Lemoncelli, & VandeCreek, 2010).

In the later stages of the PTG process, the expert companion highlights changes in the life narrative and, when it is present, of the growth that is emerging. At the same time, the clinician is keeping in mind that any of the five domains of PTG may become evident, and that individuals dealing with particular situations may experience unique forms of growth, that may not necessarily be captured by the PTGI. For Clint, this discussion focused on two of the PTG domains, relating to others and spiritual change.

C: One of the things I am really practicing now is how to treat my wife in ways that don't get me into the same kind of trouble, like not feeling like she doesn't appreciate what I do, and having a grudge against her for that. I really try to focus on not being so selfish.

T: So that translates into how you behave with her?

C: Yeah, I don't complain and don't have a bad attitude, but also, I just have to think differently.

T: So, you look at her and your role as a husband and father differently?

C: Yeah, like I tell myself to grow up. I have a wife and three little kids and I can't expect to be hanging out having fun like a single guy. That's just immature. I decided to get married and have kids, that was my choice so now do it, you know? And it's not like I have to force myself. I appreciate all that. I realize I am really blessed. I thank Julie for hanging in there with me. I tell her she deserved better, and I am going to do better.

T: So, why are you going to do better?

C: Ah, that's the important part, isn't it? Remember we talked about motives? What is my motive to do better? Well, there are lots of them. It's God's will, he has my back, knows what is good for me, and mostly, it is the love thing. That's the way to love. And that's God's will, to love. And, when I am starting to feel ornery, that's my selfishness, and it is harder to love then, but I can't stop. If I let the selfishness take over, I am right back to doing something stupid that will backfire on me, hurt others, make me feel ashamed. That's what I think now. It feels pretty solid.

T: Are these the same things you always believed or different?

C: Same stuff, but I didn't really understand it before. Now I get it because I see what can happen when you don't really get it. I just know it in my gut now, or maybe in my spirit, I guess? Anyway, I guess I had to learn the hard way. I am just so grateful to Julie for seeing that there was still something worthy about me. I have turned around completely. I used to resent her, now I appreciate her. It's a lot better for both of us.

T: So, what is the future for you?

C: A lot better life, I think. The life I thought I would have actually, but wasn't equipped to make it happen. Or I guess I had the basic foundation, but didn't really understand what I thought I believed, if that makes any sense. It's like I had the cardboard version of the married Christian guy, now I have the real one. So my affair served a purpose in the end I guess, though I don't like to think about it as anything good. I think it might be dangerous that way.

T: Maybe you can focus your story of the turnaround more on your efforts in the aftermath of this to be honest with yourself and really learn what your faith was all about. And maybe to remember that you never can be complacent and think you know all you need to know.

C: I'm still not my final version.

Conclusion

In the case of Clint, we see that what is traumatic for him is a situation that is a challenge to his assumptive world, even though his circumstances might not be classified as a trauma, using the narrow focus present in the current version of the Diagnostic and Statistical Manual of the American Psychiatric Association. We used this example to show that PTG emerges out of any circumstances that are psychologically seismic. Clinicians who function as expert companions understand the PTG process, and use the model as a guide for what to focus on in the therapy, while maintaining a close connection with the conflicted thinking, disorientation of a life narrative that has become obsolete and the need for reconstructed core beliefs in the trauma survivor. Within this perspective, the clinician is a companion on what can be a long journey. The clinician is also a person who has expertise that should be used, when appropriate, to help the person manage psychological distress and symptoms, and perhaps also to become a different and better person in the process of struggling to survive. As we shall see in the following chapter, being a close companion to people's change processes carries its own risks.

Summary points

- PTG is a new name for an experience recognized since ancient times.
- PTG is the experience of positive change from the struggle with difficult events.
- Traumatic events are those that challenge or invalidate significant parts of the person's assumptive worlds.
- Trauma clinicians must be both companions and experts.
- Companions see clients as equals, and are willing to learn and be transformed by them.
- Experts have knowledge that can benefit the client.
- The assumptive world can be a fruitful point of focus to understand and perhaps facilitate PTG.
- Models of PTG can guide clinicians in their work with survivors of trauma.

Suggested readings

Calhoun. L.G., & Tedeschi, R.G. (2013). *Posttrauamtic growth in clinical practice.* New York: Routledge.

Calhoun, L. G., & Tedeschi, R. G. (Eds.) (2006). *The handbook of posttraumatic growth: Research and practice.* Mahwah, NJ: Lawrence Erlbaum Associates Publishers.

Joseph, S. (2011). *What doesn't kill us: The new psychology of posttraumatic growth.* New York: Basic Books.

References

American Psychological Association Presidential Task Force on Evidence-Based Practice (2006). Evidence-based practice in psychology. *American Psychologist, 61,* 271–285.

Calhoun, L.G., Cann, A., & Tedeschi, R.G. (2010). The posttraumatic growth model: Socio-cultural considerations. In T. Weiss & R. Berger, (Eds.), *Posttraumatic growth and culturally competent practice: Lessons learned from around the globe* (pp. 1–14). Hoboken, NJ: Wiley.

Calhoun, L.G., & Tedeschi, R.G. (1999). *Facilitating posttraumatic growth: A clinician's guide.* Mahwah, NJ: Lawrence Erlbaum Associates.

Calhoun, L.G., & Tedeschi, R.G. (Eds.) (2006). *Handbook of posttraumatic growth: Research and practice.* Mahwah, NJ: Lawrence Erlbaum Associates.

Janoff-Bulman, R. (1992). *Shattered assumptions.* New York: The Free Press.

Knapp, S., Lemoncelli, J., & VandeCreek, L. (2010). Ethical responses when patients' religious beliefs appear to harm their well-being. *Professional Psychology: Research and Practice, 41,* 405–412.

Norcross, J.C. (2004). Tailoring the therapy relationship to the individual patient: Evidence-based practices. *Psychotherapy: Theory/Research/Practice/Training, 38,* 345–356.

Norcross, J. C., & Wampold, B. E. (2011). Evidence-based therapy relationships: Research conclusions and clinical practices. *Psychotherapy, 48,* 98–102.

Rogers, C.R. (1957). The necessary and sufficient conditions of therapeutic personality change. *Journal of Consulting and Clinical Psychology, 21,* 95–103.

Tedeschi, R.G., & Calhoun, L.G. (1988). Perceived benefits in coping with physical handicaps. *Paper Presented at the Annual Meeting of the American Psychological Association,* Atlanta.

Tedeschi, R.G., & Calhoun, L.G. (1995). *Trauma and transformation: Growing in the aftermath of suffering.* Thousand Oaks, CA: Sage.

Tedeschi, R.G., & Calhoun, L.G. (1996). The Posttraumatic Growth Inventory: Measuring the positive legacy of trauma. *Journal of Traumatic Stress, 9,* 455–471.

Weinberger, J. (1995). Common factors aren't so common: The common factors dilemma. *Clinical Psychology: Science and Practice, 2,* 45–69.

Weiss, T., & Berger, R. (2010) (Eds.) *Posttraumatic growth and culturally competent practice.* Hoboken, NJ: John Wiley & Sons.

8

Vicarious Trauma and the Therapeutic Relationship

Maryann Abendroth and Charles Figley

Introduction

The purpose of this chapter is to set out and consider the effects of vicarious trauma on the relationship between client and therapist during psychotherapy following trauma. Secondly, our aim is to stimulate interest – research and intervention – and explore ways for therapists and other helping professionals to better apply self-care. We will outline the reasons to avoid over-personalization in the therapeutic setting, yet recognize the need to balance this with maintaining the ability to read clients well and remain empathic. We articulate the importance of empathic discernment, a key relational concept to both thriving in trauma work and attaining a valuable life skill. Most helping professions in our field have experienced work-related stress and are thus at risk of vicarious trauma.

Working with the suffering is hard

'I'm finding it hard to get this person's situation out of my head' is a common statement professional caregivers make in disciplines ranging from social work, nursing, medicine and emergency services. Despite acknowledging that this is stressful and challenging work, they often disregard their own reactions and needs when caring for the traumatized (Palm, Polusny, & Folette, 2004). Caregivers may become exhausted and suffer from symptoms of burnout and, in the case of therapists, may develop vicarious traumatization which occurs when these professionals experience the effects of trauma themselves (Culver, McKinney, & Paradise, 2011).

Selye (1976) believed that diseases were due to an inability to cope with stress. Additionally, he believed that the magnitude of stress depended on how one reacts to the stressor. The many observable signs of stress include general irritability, impulsive behaviour, inability to concentrate, headaches, muscle pain and psychoses. In some occupations, stress has reached epidemic levels. Lambert, Lambert, and Yamase (2003) revealed that healthcare providers, military officers, technicians, managers, executives, sports coaches and clergy are most prone to workplace stress in the United States. A stressful work environment can lead to various problems including unhealthy behaviours, lowered job motivation, lost work time, lowered decision-making ability and turnover (Lambert et al., 2003). The work environment especially in the helping professions can be a potential source of stress, yet how people manage their situations and their personality traits are important predictors of conditions leading to job stress (4Therapy, 2011). Difficult work situations are more associated with health complaints than other life stressors which include financial or family problems. Workers that are stressed tend to be fatigued and experience other health complaints which lead to absenteeism. It is not surprising that in the United States work stress-related illnesses cost employers 200–300 billion dollars a year (CDC, 1998; Health Advocate, 2009).

The practice of psychotherapy can be emotionally charged, intense and involve empathic engagement in the pain of the client being helped (Helm, 2010). Despite being taught the principles of psychotherapy which include the importance of professional boundaries, therapists may be in situations where it is difficult to maintain professional distance when they are exposed to the powerful content of the traumatic experiences of their clients (Helm, 2010). The effect of this repeated exposure can lead to the process of vicarious traumatization which can involve countertransference and persist for years after working with traumatized persons (Gibbons, Murphy, & Joseph, 2011; McCann & Pearlman, 1990). The impact of trauma therapy can be profound especially when it can impact the therapists' own mental frame of reference (i.e., identity, beliefs, assumptions about causality, sense of trust/safety) over time (McCann & Pearlman, 1990). Mental health counsellors and others in health professions including nurses may experience anger and resentment towards clients as well as a sense of confusion, helplessness and spiritual distress (Pearlman & Saakvitne, 1995; Sinclair & Hamill, 2007). These situations may result in a loss of a sense of meaning and can damage a counsellor's worldview. In these situations, these professionals can become cynical, emotionally numb and even withdrawn (Pearlman & Saakvitne, 1995; Trippany, Kress, & Wilcoxon, 2004). This symptomology is not only reserved for vicarious traumatization since other constructs are often apparent in the helping professions.

Related constructs

Compassion fatigue is a phenomenon associated with the 'cost of caring' for others in emotional pain (Figley, 1995, 2002, p. 2). Compassion fatigue has been considered synonymous with secondary traumatic stress disorder (STSD) and vicarious traumatization. Both the constructs of vicarious trauma and compassion fatigue are phenomena that are often used interchangeably (Huggard & Huggard, 2008).

Figley (1995) defined compassion fatigue as a secondary traumatic stress reaction resulting from helping or desiring to help a person suffering from traumatic events. This concept is parallel to vicarious trauma which is 'a transformation of the helper's inner experience, resulting from empathic engagement with client's trauma material' (Helm, 2010; Saakvitne & Pearlman, 1996, p. 40). Both phenomena can have similar symptomology which occurs when healthcare professionals develop a preoccupation with their patients by re-experiencing their trauma, and may exhibit symptoms of avoidance of reminders, numbing in response to reminders, anxiety and persistent arousal.

A growing interest in understanding the clinical phenomenon of compassion fatigue and its impact on healthcare providers has existed in all disciplines reaching as far afield from psychological helping professions to veterinary medicine (Huggard & Huggard, 2008). Numerous studies have cited the effects of compassion fatigue in other disciplines such as social work, religious ministry, emergency management and nursing (Abendroth & Flannery, 2006; Lombardo & Eyre, 2011; McCann & Pearlman, 1990; Prous, 2006; Roberts, Flannelly, Weaver, & Figley, 2003).

Working with those who suffer can affect professional caregivers throughout the world as they care for patients in hospitals, clinics or at home through the course of many types of illness. Healthcare providers may also care for patients in emergency shelters in the aftermath of hurricanes, tsunamis, earthquakes and acts of terrorism. In all of these settings and across many professional disciplines, the therapeutic relationship between those helping and those being helped is crucial in the experience of providing optimal care. Attention to this relationship is essential and if left, a unchecked secondary traumatic stress reaction such as compassion fatigue can result from these relationships. In some situations, the symptoms of compassion fatigue can be exacerbated among healthcare workers who must leave their own families and friends who are experiencing devastation in order to help others. This situation can be seen in natural disasters such as hurricanes (Frank & Adkinson, 2007). Thus, the potential for compassion fatigue as well as vicarious traumatization can emerge anywhere in the helping professions.

Relational processes and compassion fatigue

The Compassion Stress and Fatigue model developed from social science research contains several variables to predict compassion fatigue and hence can be used to prevent and treat the phenomenon as it occurs (Figley, 1995, 2002). The model is diagrammed using the 11 variables associated with preventing or enhancing the risk of developing compassion fatigue. Initially, the caregiver is exposed to the client and directly experiences the emotional energy of suffering and pain. The caregiver, thus, provides empathic concern which is the motivation to respond professionally to those in need. Following the concern is empathic ability; this is the aptitude of noticing the pain of others. This ability to empathize is the hallmark to helping others, yet it also puts one at risk for compassion fatigue. Following empathic ability is the empathic response which is based on the caregiver's insight into the feelings and thoughts of the client. In order to accomplish this, caregivers often project themselves into the clients' perspective. This may cause caregivers to have strong emotions similar to those that are experienced by clients (Figley, 1995, 2002). The concepts of satisfaction or a sense of achievement and disengagement are used as measures to prevent compassion fatigue in this model. When caregivers are satisfied with their ability to help the client, there is an understanding as to where the caregiver's responsibilities end and the client's responsibilities begin. Disengagement is a healthy way in which caregivers can promote self-care by distancing themselves from the client/family. They do this by letting go of the thoughts, and feelings associated with their interaction with the client in order to focus on their own lives (Figley, 1995, 2002).

Meyers and Cornille (2002) conducted a study to assess the prevalence of secondary traumatic stress symptoms in child protective service workers, and to identify factors that were linked to secondary trauma. A sample size of 205 male (17%) and female (83%) child protection service workers were surveyed to examine relationships of (a) family of origin functioning, (b) personal traumatic history, (c) exposure to child abuse victims' trauma and, (d) gender to secondary traumatic stress symptoms of the professional. The findings revealed that workers who were employed five or more years experienced a higher degree of secondary traumatic stress symptoms than those working less than five years. Veteran workers, defined as those employed more than one year, reported more symptoms of nervous tension and panic attacks than those working less than one year. Findings also revealed that female workers had more symptoms of anger, irritability and exaggerated startle response compared to males in the study. Females also reported more muscle pain, cardiovascular, gastrointestinal and respiratory problems.

Meyers and Cornille (2002) noted that the child protection service workers were genuinely affected by their family of origin history. For example, those who had enmeshed family-of-origin relationships (i.e., families who become intrusively involved with one another) had more nightmares, intrusive thoughts and images than child protection service workers who were raised in a less enmeshed environment. Many of these workers (82%) also reported experiencing a trauma prior to being employed in this field.

Moreover, Figley's (1995) theories of compassion fatigue/secondary trauma emphasized that persons exposed to traumatized children are especially vulnerable to the side effects of secondary traumatic stress. These professionals tended to endure this pain on a daily basis throughout their careers. These types of therapeutic relationships can be stressful and are not exclusive to those professionals in a psychotherapy setting.

Helping professionals such as nurses in all settings can be vulnerable to work-related stress especially since this is also a profession that focuses on the importance of therapeutic communication and trust in the client–nurse relationship. Care providers' declining ability to provide empathy in a therapeutic relationship is considered a key factor in compassion fatigue (Sabo, 2011). The need to address resilience in compassion fatigue research initiatives is important in the area of nursing especially since nurses are also first responders who may have no formal support to combat the effects of compassion fatigue (Boyle, 2011). Moreover, available assessment tools are limited in scope to use with nurses who are in dire need of onsite workplace interventions (i.e., counselling, support groups, de-briefing sessions) that address compassion fatigue (Boyle, 2011).

Lombardo and Eyre (2011) brought an interesting case study approach to their discussion of compassion fatigue. They emphasized how compassion fatigue can impact job satisfaction and healthcare providers' health resulting in decreased productivity and increased turnover. This is an essential consideration since nurses comprise the largest group of healthcare providers in the United States. The findings echoed that imbalanced empathic relationship-based care is a factor in compassion fatigue. Interventions to support nurses that include knowledge of symptomology and a healthy workplace environment could bring compassion fatigue to the forefront before it adversely affects the healthcare provider (Abendroth, 2011).

Compassion fatigue may exist in populations of informal (e.g., family) caregivers as well as among professionals. Day and Anderson (2011) compared Figley's model of compassion fatigue and found that it could be an informative framework for understanding compassion fatigue in the informal caregiver population. Understandably, family caregiver distress and prolonged consequences of poor physical and emotional health among this population have been well documented in the literature (Caron & Bowers, 2003; Pinquart & Sorensen, 2006; Tsukasaki et al., 2006).

Recent evidence is now suggesting that compassion fatigue exists in this informal caregiver population. When nurses, for example, become family caregivers, the complexity of this added variable of attempting to fulfil both the formal and informal caregiving role can become daunting (Ward-Griffin, St-Amant, & Brown, 2011). This type of caregiving also leads to blurred boundaries between professional and personal care which, in this study, ultimately predisposed the nurse/daughter to compassion fatigue. The research also promotes a greater focus on the socio-economic and political contextual factors associated with compassion fatigue. For example, society's expectations of daughters as caregivers compounded with nursing responsibilities never allow these individuals to temporarily break free of the role of caregiver (Abendroth, 2011; Ward-Griffin et al., 2011). With many of the professional disciplines such as psychology and psychotherapy being populated with more women than men, this issue becomes of central importance. Additional research is needed to better understand the impact of compassion fatigue on informal caregivers, and the role of gender in compassion fatigue, in order to provide an empirical basis for developing multidisciplinary interventions for vulnerable family caregivers.

Empathy, discernment and resilience

'I don't know how you can do this!' is a common exclamation hospice nurses hear from families of dying patients. That statement, of course, is not exclusive to nursing. Other professions such as persons working in the criminal justice system especially in child protection services or therapists working directly with abused children or sexual offenders may also hear those comments reflecting the difficult nature of their work. For example, families have difficulty imagining how helpers can work in an environment where they are surrounded by patients experiencing trauma and terminal illness. Healthcare staff working in multiple settings face many daily stressors. They can become too empathic towards their patients leading to blurring of professional boundaries. A healthy sense of empathy and the strong coping mechanisms of compassion satisfaction and healthy detachment play a role in protecting the self and promoting resilience (Abendroth & Flannery, 2006). These professionals develop an acceptance of death as part of a life's journey as they care for their patients following trauma or when entering hospice care and during the dying process. They are often present at the time of death and fulfil the task of consoling grieving loved ones.

One of the joys of nursing in a setting that regularly faces trauma is a sense of fulfilment when a patient's suffering is diminished. Barbato-Gaydos (2004) writes that end of life nursing care is defined as a choice that provides meaning to nurses' lives rather than it being a job or a career. Cicely Saunders, founder of the modern hospice movement, described nursing as the 'cornerstone of hospice care' because of the subtle multifaceted presence of these professional caregivers as they help patients live as normally as possible despite disease limitations (Krisman-Scott & McCordle, 2002). There is nothing more fulfilling for nurses than to realize that they were instrumental in giving their patients a 'voice' to their fears and grief which subsequently gives meaning to their suffering (Krisman-Scott & McCordle, 2001).

Empathy is an important characteristic in working with the traumatized. Riggio and Taylor (2000, p. 353) identified that empathy is an essential aspect of hospice nursing when it takes the form of 'perspective taking' and 'empathic concern'; however, once empathy becomes unhealthy, it leads to 'personal distress', which negatively affects nursing care and leads to stress and burnout. In a recent study of social work, trainees' reflective ability was a factor that played a role in predicting resilience and psychological well-being. When these trainees reflected on their thoughts/experiences, they were able to better address the needs of their clients and communicate effectively with others. Moreover, empathic concerns such as feelings of warmth, compassion, and empathy appear to enhance stress resilience among this population (Kinman & Grant, 2011).

One of the newer constructs in trauma research is empathic discernment which is the effectiveness in accurately selecting and using the best empathic response for both client and self in the therapeutic setting (Radey & Figley, 2007). It is important to look at the broader context of caregiving that emphasizes positive social work. Radey and Figley (2007) introduced a model reflecting compassion satisfaction rooted in positive psychology. They felt that seeking positive fulfilment in social work was essential to the profession especially since this is a protective mechanism from the negative consequences of working with trauma sufferers. Hence, maximizing positivity can also maximize compassion satisfaction.

Similarly, findings from a study of social workers ($N = 62$) revealed that among the factors contributing to their functioning (i.e., states of mind) included working with suffering: degree of exposure to intense emotionality and disturbance, levels of job satisfaction, burnout, secondary stress and the perceived value attached to the work. However, they found that posttraumatic growth and other positive outcomes were possible and should be explored. Specifically, those professionals who felt more valued had higher job satisfaction, lower burnout and greater positive changes despite being at risk for vicarious traumatization (Gibbons et al., 2011). These findings were consistent with other studies of trauma workers (e.g., Weiss & Berger, 2010).

Self-care

Self-care is an essential counter measure to strain and possibly compassion fatigue or vicarious traumatization among formal as well as informal caregivers. Informal caregivers who became intensely involved with their loved ones needing care often neglect their own basic needs and become strained. It was interesting to note in a recent study that many caregivers spoke about the need to care for self or to have a sense of self-preservation but were unable to do it because of the overwhelming responsibilities of caring for the relative with Parkinson's disease (Abendroth, Lutz, & Young, 2012). Some caregivers had difficulty separating themselves emotionally and physically from their loved ones. Their lives were so intertwined that there was no time for their own needs, as illustrated by the following quote from a caregiver.

I've had a lot of years of painting and it's just, I know it helps me as far as my well-being and contentment within myself. It helps me to paint. But if it's going to take getting me stressed out to get out here and paint while I'm worried about him, I'll just set this aside and make sure he's taken care of.

Lack of self-care and self-preservation put caregivers at risk for exhaustion and inability to manage unexpected events such as the need for long-term care placement (Abendroth et al., 2012).

The importance of self-care among formal caregivers is evident in many studies (Harrison & Westwood, 2009; Hunter & Schofield, 2006; Palm et al., 2004). The model for creating compassion satisfaction (Radey & Figley, 2007) also emphasized self-care to increase positivity among therapists specifically by increasing:

1. positive affect (i.e., keeping a positive attitude towards clients)
2. resources in managing all types of stress
3. self-care that comes from happiness and inspiration

These three conceptual ideas lead to increased positivity and compassion satisfaction among practitioners. Harrison and Westwood's research (2006) emphasized the importance of holistic self-care which is crucial in both the professional and personal realm and interestingly, the ability to separate these two realms of life is also a form of caring for the self.

Resilience promotion approaches

Given the enormous secondary traumatic stress experienced by caregivers noted in this chapter, it is not surprising to find a considerable array of strategies for assessing, treating and preventing such stress. Chu (1990) was among the first to talk about the traps of trauma therapists in treating trauma survivors, including the over identification with the victim and countertransference. McCann and Pearlman (1990) introduced the concept of vicarious trauma and offered a framework for not only understanding how it develops but also provided specific guidelines for monitoring the impact on therapists' work and ways for more effectively managing these impacts by focusing on the therapists' internal dialogue about the meaning of their reactions to the trauma material. This and other strategies were discussed in a compendium of treatment methods useful in counteracting compassion fatigue (Figley, 2002).

Munroe et al. (1995) offer a team approach to not only treating the traumatized but by also enabling the team to tolerate and be more resilient as a team and as individuals. Neuman and Gamble (1995) and later Norcross (2000) were early advocates for promoting the professional development of psychotherapists that extends to counteracting the effects of countertransference and vicarious traumatization. Southwick, Litz, Charney and Friedman (2011) more recently emphasized the importance of resilience promotion approaches in working with the traumatized. The final section, Training for Resilience, identified ways of working with clients to enhance self-regulation, self-care, stress management, self-talk and other strategies. Similarly, Reissman, Kowalski-Trakofler and Katz (2011) offer a useful framework for resilience development by making it a part of a worker protection strategy.

At a more practical level, the first step in preventing or ameliorating compassion fatigue is to recognize the signs and symptoms of its emergence. Being aware of these factors can help psychotherapists, nurses and other helpers to both prevent and recover from compassion fatigue by (a) being aware of the costs of empathic responses; (b) more effectively managing the cumulative effects of compassion stress; (c) engaging in self-care and stress-management strategies that increase caring disengagement at work and at home; (d) being more aware on a daily basis the satisfactions of dispensing compassion to patients and fellow staff members; (e) not over extending and overworking; (f) being aware of and processing any unwanted traumatic memories; and (g) being aware and patient of and accepting various life disruptions.

Pfifferling and Gilley (2000) have offered a useful list of 'warning signs' of compassion fatigue. These include abusing drugs, alcohol or food; anger; blaming; chronic lateness; depression; diminished sense of personal accomplishment; exhaustion (physical or emotional); frequent headaches; gastrointestinal complaints; high self-expectations; hopelessness; hypertension; inability to maintain balance of empathy and objectivity; increased irritability; less ability to feel joy; low self-esteem; sleep disturbances; and workaholism. Another more rigorous method is utilizing one or more tools available to measure compassion fatigue (see Bride, Radey, & Figley, 2007 for a review).

There are three tools in particular that are the most widely used in the ongoing monitoring of compassion fatigue. The first is the Secondary Traumatic Stress Scale (STSS) (Bride, Robinson, Yegidis, & Figley, 2004). All of the 17 items of the STSS are designed to tap one of the Diagnostic and Statistical Manual (DSM-IV-TR: American Psychiatric Association, 2000) criteria for PTSD, but are worded in such a way that they assess symptoms due to indirect exposure to traumatic events through clinical work with traumatized populations.

The second is the Compassion Fatigue-Short Scale (Adams et al., 2006), which has evolved from Figley's (1995) original Compassion Fatigue Self Test. The Compassion Fatigue-Short Scale is a 13-item measure that is comprised of an 8-item burnout subscale and a 5-item secondary trauma subscale. Both instruments have documented evidence of reliability and validity (Adams et al., 2006, 2008; Bride et al., 2004; Ting et al., 2005).

The third is the Professional Quality of Life (ProQOL): Compassion Satisfaction and Fatigue Subscales, R-IV (Stamm, 2005). It is a 30-item measure designed to determine estimates of compassion fatigue, compassion satisfaction, and burnout. The most current version is the ProQOL 5, which is currently being translated into several languages (Stamm, 2009). In addition to ongoing monitoring of STS reactions, there are a number of strategies that caregivers can implement in their personal and professional lives to reduce the impact of Compassion Fatigue.

Professional coping strategies include: (1) balancing a clinical caseload with other professional activities; (2) developing realistic expectations for working with traumatized clients; (3) engaging in advocacy activities for traumatized populations; and (4) being aware of unresolved personal trauma issues (Pearlman & Saakvitne, 1995).

Organizations must take responsibility for their part in preventing and ameliorating compassion fatigue and vicarious traumatization (see Chapter 9 of this volume). Alert administrators must be observant of trauma workers who exhibit signs of this phenomenon. These practitioners who often define themselves as 'being their job' may be at particular risk because they may easily begin to blur the professional/personal boundaries with their patients. Administrators must also be open to listening to the voices of trauma services workers when they say things like ' no relief when you have multiple deaths in a day or week, not recognizing the nurse needs time to refill the well' [unsolicited comment from a survey instrument] (Abendroth, 2005). The research literature suggests, over and over, that a supportive organizational culture is essential in order to help healthcare providers validate their feelings through supervision (see Chapter 9 of this volume). As we will see in the next chapter, supervision can be integrated into organizations to help protect workers from the effects of compassion fatigue and vicarious trauma. Indeed, in the field of psychotherapy in the UK supervision remains a mandated requirement for all practitioners. Specifically, Linley and Joseph (2007) in their study ($N = 150$) found a range of occupational and psychological factors associated the positive and negative well-being of practitioners and specifically noted the value of therapists receiving clinical supervision as a facilitator of personal growth (Linley & Joseph, 2007).

Conclusions

The purpose of this chapter was a discussion of the effects of vicarious trauma and compassion fatigue on the relationship between client and therapist during psychotherapy following trauma. We have attempted to demonstrate the impact of the work on psychotherapists and others providing services to the traumatized, such as nurses. The importance of the therapeutic relationship between those helping and those being helped was emphasized as a pivotal factor in optimal care; however, it is crucial to realize that special care or vigilance is needed to maintain a healthy relationship without crossing professional boundaries in any care setting. We attempted to show that the full impact of secondary trauma or vicarious trauma on the professional is a consequence not only of the toxic nature of trauma but also the context in which trauma services are delivered and the psychosocial and emotional status of the professionals themselves.

Our second purpose was to stimulate the readers' interest in the topic not only as researchers but also as providers of care to other trauma workers validating to them that this is difficult work that needs to be shared with other colleagues in order to help manage these responsibilities sufficiently. We attempted to show that with proper attention by both employers and employees, trauma workers can thrive in this work and even have positive growth from experiences in trauma therapy.

We are confident that with proper measure in place to care for trauma workers they can avoid over personalization in the therapeutic setting; attend to their own emotional needs while following good standards of care to provide the best care for the traumatized. We believe that good empathic discernment and balancing one's own needs with those of others are critical in not just surviving as a trauma therapists but thriving and enjoying the experience as well.

Summary points

- Empathy is a key relational component in trauma work.
- There are risks for the helper in being empathic.
- Vicarious traumatization can be the result of compassion fatigue.
- Using skills and strategies can be an effective way to preserve the therapeutic relationship from vicarious trauma and compassion fatigue.

Suggested reading

Figley, C. R. (Ed.) (1995). *Compassion fatigue: Coping with secondary traumatic stress disorder in those who treat the traumatized.* New York: Brunner/Mazel.

Figley, C. R. (2002). Compassion fatigue: Psychotherapists' chronic lack of self care. *JCLP/In Session: Psychotherapy in Practice, 58*(11), 1433–1441.

Munroe, J. F., Shay, J., Fisher, L., Makary, C., Rapperprot, K. U., & Zimering, R. (1995). Preventing compassion fatigue: A team treatment model. In C. R. Figley (Ed.). *Compassion fatigue: Coping with secondary traumatic stress disorder in those who treat the traumatized* (pp. 209–231). New York: Brunner/Mazel.

References

Abendroth, M. (2011). Overview and summary: Compassion fatigue: Caregivers at risk OJIN: *The Online Journal of Issues in Nursing, 16*(1), Overview and Summary. doi: 10.3912/OJIN.Vol16No01OS01.

Abendroth, M. (2005). *Predicting the risk of compassion fatigue: An empirical study of hospice nurses.* Masters Thesis. Florida State University, Tallahassee, FL.

Abendroth, M., & Flannery, J. (2006). Predicting the risk of compassion fatigue: A study of hospice nurses. *Journal of Hospice and Palliative Nursing, 8*(6), 346–356.

Abendroth, M., Lutz, B. J., & Young, M. (2012). Family caregivers' decision process to institutionalize persons with Parkinson's disease: A grounded theory study. *International Journal of Nursing Studies, 49*(4), 445–454.

Adams, R. E., Boscarino, J. A., & Figley, C. R. (2006). Compassion fatigue and psychological distress among social workers: A validation study. *American Journal of Orthopsychiatry, 76*(1), 103–108.

Adams, R. E., Figley, C. R., & Boscarino, J. A. (2008). The compassion fatigue scale: Its use with social workers following urban disaster. *Research on Social Work Practice, 18*(3), 238–250.

American Psychiatric Association [APA], (2000). *Diagnostical and statistical manual of mental disorders: DSM-IV-TR*: 4th edition text revision. Arlington, VA: APA.

Barbato-Gaydos, H. L. (2004). The living end: Life journeys of hospice nurses. *Journal of Hospice and Palliative Nursing, 6*(1), 17–26.

Boyle, D. (2011) Countering compassion fatigue: A requisite nursing agenda. OJIN: *The Online Journal of Issues in Nursing, 16*(1), Manuscript 2. doi: 10.3912/OJIN.Vol16No01Man02.

Bride, B. E., Radey, M., & Figley, C. R. (2007). Measuring compassion fatigue. *Clinical Social Work Journal, 35*, 155–163.

Bride, B. E., Robinson, M. M., Yegidis, B., & Figley, C. R. (2004). Development and validation of the secondary traumatic stress scale. *Research on Social Work Practice, 14*(1), 27–36.

Caron, C. D., & Bowers, B. J. (2003). Deciding whether to continue, share, or relinquish caregiving: Caregiver views. *Qualitative Health Research, 13*(9), 1252–1271.

Chu, J. (1990). Ten traps for therapists in the treatment of trauma survivors. *Dissociation, 1*, 24–32.

CDC (1998). *Stress at work.* DHHS (NIOSH) Publication No. 99–101. Retrieved from http://www.cdc.gov/niosh/docs/99-101/.

Culver, L. M., McKinney, B. L., & Louis V. Paradise, L. V. (2011). Mental health professionals' experiences of vicarious traumatization in post-Hurricane Katrina New Orleans. *Journal of Loss and Trauma, 16*(1), 33–42. doi: 10.1080/15325024.2010.519279.

Day, J. R., & Anderson, R. A. (2011). Compassion fatigue: An application of the concept to informal caregivers of family members with dementia. *Nursing Research and Practice. Volume 2011*, Article ID 408024, 10 pages. doi: 10.1155/2011/408024.

Figley, C. R. (Ed.) (2002). *Treating compassion fatigue: Coping with secondary traumatic stress disorder in those who treat the traumatized.* New York: Brunner/Mazel.

Figley, C. R. (Ed.) (1995). *Compassion fatigue: Coping with secondary traumatic stress disorder in those who treat the traumatized.* New York: Brunner/Mazel.

Figley, C. R. (2002). Compassion fatigue: Psychotherapists' chronic lack of self care. *JCLP/In Session: Psychotherapy in Practice, 58*(11), 1433–1441.

4Therapy (2011). *What is work related stress?* Retrieved from http://www.4therapy. com/life-topics/stress/what-work-related-stress-2245.

Frank, D. I., & Adkinson, L. F. (2007). A developmental perspective on risk for compassion fatigue in middle-aged nurses caring for hurricane victims in Florida. *Holistic Nursing Practice, 21*(2), 55–62.

Gibbons, S., Murphy, D., & Joseph, S. (2011). Countertransference and positive growth in social workers. *Journal of Social Work Practice: Psychotherapeutic Approaches in Health, Welfare and the Community, 25*(1), 17–30. doi: 10.1080/02650530903579246.

Harrison, R. L., & Westwood, M. J. (2009). Preventing vicarious traumatization of mental health therapists: Identifying protective practices. *Psychotherapy Theory, Research, Practice, Training, 46*(2), 203–219. doi: 10.1037/a0016081.

Health Advocate (2009). *Stress in the workplace: Meeting the challenge.* Retrieved from http://www.healthadvocate.com/downloads/webinars/stress-workplace.pdf.

Helm, H. M. (2010). *Managing vicarious trauma and compassion fatigue.* Retrieved from http://www.lianalowenstein.com/artcile_helm.pdf.

Huggard, P. K., & Huggard, E. J. (2008). When the caring gets tough: Compassion fatigue and veterinary care. *VetScript*, 14–16. http://www.compass/Onflllgue.org/pagesfHuggardVetScriptpdf.

Hunter, S. V., & Schofield, M. J. (2006). How counselors cope with traumatized clients: Personal, professional and organizational strategies. *International Journal for the Advancement of Counselling, 28*(2), 121–138. doi: 10.1007/s10447-005-9003-0.

Kinman, G., & Grant, L. (2011). Exploring stress resilience in trainee social workers: The role of emotional and social competencies. *British Journal of Social Work, 41*, 261–275. doi: 10.1093/bjsw/bcq088.

Krisman-Scott, M. A., & McCordle, R. (2002). The tapestry of hospice. *Holistic Nursing Practice, 16*(2), 32–39.

Lambert, V. A., Lambert, C. E., & Yamase, H. (2003). Psychological hardiness, workplace stress and related stress reduction strategies. *Nursing and Health Sciences, 5*, 181–184.

Linley, P. A., & Joseph, S. (2007). Therapy work and therapists' positive and negative well-being. *Journal of Social and clinical Psychology, 26*(3), 385–403.

Lombardo, B., & Eyre, C. (2011) Compassion fatigue: A nurse's primer. *OJIN: The Online Journal of Issues in Nursing, 16*(1), Manuscript 3. doi: 10.3912/OJIN.Vol16No01Man03.

McCann, L., & Pearlman, L. A. (1990). Vicarious traumatization: A framework for understanding the psychological effects of working with victims. *Journal of Traumatic Stress, 3*(1), 131–149.

Meyers, T. W., & Cornille, T. A. (2002). The trauma of working with traumatized children. In C. R. Figley (Ed.), *Treating compassion fatigue* (pp. 39–55). New York: Brunner-Routledge.

Munroe, J. F., Shay, J., Fisher, L., Makary, C., Rapperprot, K. U., & Zimering, R. (1995). Preventing compassion fatigue: A team treatment model. In C. R. Figley (Ed.), *Compassion fatigue: Coping with secondary traumatic stress disorder in those who treat the traumatized*, (pp. 209–231). New York: Brunner/Mazel.

Neumann, D. A., & Gamble, S. J. (1995). Issues in the professional development of psychotherapists: Countertransference and VT in the new trauma therapist. *Psychotherapy, 32*, 341–347.

Norcross, J. C. (2000). Psychotherapist selfcare: Practitioner-tested, research informed strategies. *Professional Psychology, 31*, 710–731.

Palm, K. M., Polusny, M. A., & Follette, V. M. (2004). Vicarious traumatization: Potential hazards and interventions for disaster and trauma workers. *Prehospital Disaster Medicine, 19*(1): 73–78.

Pearlman, L. A., & Saakvitne, K. W. (1995). *Trauma and the therapist: Countertransference and vicarious traumatization in psychotherapy with incest survivors.* New York: WW. Norton.

Pfifferling, J. H., & Gilley, K. (2000). Overcoming compassion fatigue. *Family Practice Management, 7*(4), 39–44.

Pinquart, M., & Sorensen, S. (2006). Helping caregivers of persons with dementia: Which interventions work and how large are their effects? *International Psychogeriatrics, 18*(4), 577–595.

Prous, C. (2006). Burnout, vicarious traumatization and its prevention. *Torture, 16*(1), 1–9.

Radey, M., & Figley, C. R. (2007). The social psychology of compassion. *Clinical Social Work Journal, 35*, 207–214.

Reissman, D. B., Kowalski-Trakofler, K. M., & Katz, C. L. (2011). Public health practice and disaster resilience: A framework integrating resilience as a worker protection strategy. In S. M. Southwick, B. T. Litz, D. Charney, & M. J. Friedman (Eds.), *Resilience and mental health: Challenges across the lifespan* (pp. 340–358). New York: Cambridge University Press. Chapter doi: http://dx.doi.org/10.1017/CBO9780511994791.025.

Riggio, R. E., & Taylor, S. J. (2000). Personality and communication skills as predictors of hospice nurse performance. *Journal of business and Psychology, 15*(2), 351–359.

Roberts, S. B., Flannelly, K. J., Weaver, A. J., & Figley, C. R. (2003). Compassion fatigue among chaplains, clergy, and other respondents after September 11th. *The Journal of Nervous and Mental Disease, 191*(11), 756–758.

Sabo, B. (2011). Reflecting on the Concept of Compassion Fatigue. *OJIN: The Online Journal of Issues in Nursing, 16*(1), Manuscript 1. doi: 10.3912/OJIN.Vol16No01Man01.

Saakvitne, K. W., & Pearlman, L. A. (1996). *Transforming the pain.* New York: W.W. Norton.

Selye, H. (1976). *The stress of life*, revised edition. New York: McGraw-Hill.

Sinclair, H. A., & Hamill, C. (2007). Does vicarious traumatisation affect oncology nurses? A literature review. *European Journal of Oncology Nursing, 11*, 348–356. doi: 10.1016/j.ejon.2007.02.007.

Southwick, S. M., Litz, B. T., Charney, D., & Friedman, M. J. (Eds.). (2011). *Resilience and mental health: Challenges across the lifespan.* New York: Cambridge University Press.

Stamm, B. H. (2005). *The ProQOL Manual. The professional quality of life scale: Compassion satisfaction, burnout, compassion fatigue/secondary trauma scales*, (pp. 1–24). Retrieved from http://compassionfatigue.org/pages/ProQOLManualOct05.pdf.

Stamm, B. H. (2009). *Professional quality of life: Compassion satisfaction and fatigue.* Version 5 (ProQOL). Available at: www.proqol.org.

Ting, L., Jacobson, J. M., Sanders, S., Bride, B., & Harrington, D. (2005). The secondary traumatic stress scale (STSS): Confirmatory factor analyses with a national sample of mental health social workers. *Journal of Human Behavior in the Social Environment: Special Issue on Measurement and Assessment, 11*(3), 177–194.

Trippany, R. L., White-Kress, V. E., & Wilcoxon, S. A. (2004). Preventing vicarious trauma: What counselors should know when working with trauma survivors. *Journal of Counseling and Development, 82,* 31–37.

Tsukasaki, K., Kido, T., Makimoto, K., Naganuma, R., Ohno, M., & Sunaga, K. (2006). The impact of sleep interruptions on vital measurements and chronic fatigue of female caregivers providing home care in Japan. *Nursing and Health Services, 8,* 2–9.

Ward-Griffin, C., St-Amant, O., & Brown, J.B. (2011). Compassion fatigue within double duty caregiving: nurse-daughters caring for elderly parents. OJIN: *The Online Journal of Issues in Nursing 16*(1), Manuscript 4. doi: 10.3912/OJIN.Vol16No01Man04.

Weiss, T., & Berger, R. (2010). *Posttraumatic growth and culturally competent practice: Lessons learned from around the globe.* Hoboken, NJ: John Wiley and Sons.

9

A Reciprocal Supervisory Network: The Sanctuary Model

Sandra L. Bloom, Sarah Yanosy and Landa C. Harrison

Introduction: Adapting to paradox

The treatment of trauma survivors begins with a paradox: relationship is at the heart of healing from traumatic experience while relational damage is at the core of our clients' problems. Similarly, supervision of psychotherapeutic work has always been thought to be an essential component of clinical care. But today, with increasingly diminished economic resources going to mental health and social services, supervision of clinicians is frequently focused on 'productivity schedules' and 'billable hours' and not on the actual relationships unfolding between clients and clinicians.

Adding to this paradoxical situation is the fact that the clients with the most severe and complex problems related to a past history of exposure to childhood adversity, toxic stress and disrupted attachment end up in the foster care system, in residential treatment programmes, hospitals, substance abuse facilities, homeless shelters, juvenile justice facilities and prisons. Historically, caregivers in these settings who spend the most time with the clients are the least well-trained and the least supervised. To make things worse, we live in an age when most forms of intensive relational treatment particularly those that occur in complex multirelational situations such as hospitals and residential treatment programmes are discouraged, depleted or completely unavailable when they are most needed.

For these reasons, we must take a radical approach to creating an effective methodology for sustaining supervision within organizations like these. This method we subscribe to is part of the Sanctuary Model, a clinical and organizational, trauma-focused intervention. Using Sanctuary to re-think supervision includes redefining the field's traditional understanding of 'therapist' of 'supervisor' and of 'supervision' itself. This chapter will outline the scope of the problem facing supervisors and therapists in the current service delivery climate in putting the therapeutic relationship at the heart of trauma therapy, and present a proposal for improving the support that trauma therapists so desperately require to serve their clients.

The gaping hole

Another dimension of the many-sided paradox of trauma healing is the call for 'evidence-based practices' (EBPs). Though admirably scientific in intent, it has led to the simplistic notion that if one employs any of these EBPs, the clients for whom these practices have been created should get better (see Chapter 2 of this volume for a critique of the evidence-based treatment approach to trauma therapy). Likewise, clinicians who are not providing an EBP are slightly suspect, subject to a condescending scepticism about their approach as if they had suggested herbal supplements as a cure for AIDS. Unfortunately, even the most studied of evidence-based procedures frequently fail to achieve the hoped for results in the treatment of 'simple' PTSD, much less the more complicated cases that populate our social service delivery systems. Worse yet, clients who suffer from complex mixtures of Axis I and II disorders are frequently excluded from the very research studies that prove the efficacy of EBPs.

Thus, a fundamental question must be asked and ultimately addressed as we evaluate the effectiveness of today's human service practices: Do the current trends – evidence-based and mandated practice parameters – place appropriate emphasis, value and relevance on understanding our world? Has our field addressed this complexity or with the best of intention, unwittingly created a large gaping hole as a result of 'worldview blindness'. As one philosopher of science has noted,

> our scientific theories have failed to explain what matters most to us: the place of meaning, purpose, and value in the physical world. Our scientific theories haven't exactly failed. Rather, they have carefully excluded these phenomena from consideration, and treated them as irrelevant. This is because the content of the thought, the goal of an action, or the conscious appreciation of an experience all share a troublesome feature that appears to make them unsuited for scientific study. They aren't exactly anything physical, even though they depend on the material processes going on in brains.
>
> (Dean, 2011; p. 22)

The experience of penetrating behind what is our self-protective wall of denial about the fragile nature of human existence is what happens to survivors of traumatic life experience at a deep and existential level. For them, the shield that we each maintain between ourselves and the loneliness and unpredictability of existence is shattered, often suddenly and irrevocably. Healing from this kind of insult requires healing not just the body and not just the mind but the soul as well. Mechanistic approaches to trauma healing may significantly reduce symptoms such as chronic hyperarousal, flashbacks and nightmares. For some people, symptom reduction may be enough to enable them to reconstitute a world that has made sense to them in the past and makes sense to them once again. But for others particularly those who have had multiple experiences of betrayed trust, loss of safety and disrupted attachment, symptom relief alone is likely to be insufficient. They have gone down the rabbit hole, have been changed profoundly by their experience, and there is no going back. They can only go forward. But for a social species going forward into what is experienced as the dark unknown is so filled with terror that it is far more likely that without supportive relationships they will stay in place, treading water, often repeating a traumatic past because it is all that they know how to do and because they must keep picking at an unhealed wound.

Largely as a result of this large gaping hole, complex problems are frequently viewed as simple problems; minds are seen as machines and parts are viewed as wholes. We often do our best to avoid recognizing the social, economic and political contexts within which traumatic experiences inevitably occur. Our social environments seem to undergo such rapid change, and the problems are so complex that the individual is left feeling unable to exert control. Subsequent feelings of helplessness and incompetence across systems drive the need to apply what are often believed to be easily replicable, manualized treatment approaches. In the process, the context of experience can be lost and the issues of meaning and purpose that derive from extended relationships are relegated to unimportance. In this way, it becomes possible to believe that the application of specific manualized treatment is all that needs to be done.

Restoring order

Pioneers in the traumatic stress studies world have consistently recognized this serious gap in standard professional discourse. Helping clients to make meaning out of their traumatic experiences has been central to many practitioners involved in the treatment of survivors of overwhelming life experiences. Shay (1994) has spent his career working with combat veterans. Much of his work has focused on the undermining of our sense of humanity that trauma brings in its wake, as he writes 'war destroys the trustworthy social order of the mind' (p. 32). Herman (1992) describes the 'central dialectic of psychological trauma', and the conflict between the 'will to deny horrible events and the will to proclaim them aloud' (p. 1). As she makes clear, to study psychological trauma is to come face-to-face both with human vulnerability and the natural world and with the capacity for evil in human nature. To study psychological trauma means bearing witness to horrible events.... It is impossible to remain neutral in this conflict. The bystander is forced to take sides.

(ibid; p. 7)

The 'bystander' that Herman refers to here includes the therapist who bears witness to the trauma narrative.

Bearing witness both solidifies trust and connection within the therapeutic relationship and renders the therapist vulnerable to his or her own psychological turmoil. It is essential that supervision acknowledges, respects and addresses these risks without succumbing to the inherent risk of denying or dismissing these realities (Bloom & Reichart, 1998). After traumatic experience, a fundamental part of healing is restoring a sense of social and moral order. Without that restoration, the survivor is likely to continue to feel outside of normal human relationships, unable to adequately integrate their past and present experience. For many survivors, the journey of healing requires what has been called 'trauma transformation' or 'posttraumatic growth' accompanied by the development of a 'survivor mission' (Herman, 1992; Tedeschi & Calhoun, Chapter 7, this volume).

There is no known manualized treatment programme that can bring about such crucial existential change. Childhood adversity can be devastating because children are still trying to make sense of the world they live in. The impact of negative previous experiences can splinter across the life span and present significant challenges to the development of healthy relationship (Dube et al., 2002). Holism is a theory that postulates the universe and especially living nature as interacting wholes. To be effective, a therapist must deal with the wholeness of each individual client. But this requires a level of supervision that is supported through a safe, emotionally intelligent, collaborative and reciprocal network of supervisory relationships. Helping trauma survivors – particularly those who have experienced complex trauma – to heal from their moral, spiritual, characterological and existential posttraumatic injuries requires a relational scaffolding that the survivor and helpers must build together. This scaffolding must provide pathways to a different future, a future that doesn't yet exist but that is only a possibility, a co-created possibility.

The complex problem of supervision

Helping people who have lost a sense of meaning and purpose in their lives is an awesome responsibility. Supervising people whose job it is to help do this is equally challenging, particularly during these arduous economic times when funders are seeking to expend shrinking resources. Let's assume, for a moment, that a traditional, individualized, regular supervisory relationship is still available and accessible. To what will supervisors need to attend? And how will supervisors collaborate with and engage supervisees in a reciprocal relationship that aims to support all parties involved?

Complex traumatic stress disorders

Clients who suffer from what can be most aptly described as 'complex traumatic stress disorders' have significant problems in developing and maintaining therapeutic relationships (Courtois & Ford, 2009). Healing and recovery is dependent on the establishment of a therapeutic relationship and yet the failures in earlier relationships often sabotage the possibilities of creating healthy therapeutic relationships. It is these clients who present the greatest challenges to caregivers and hence to any supervisory relationships.

Chu (1998), a psychiatrist with extensive experience in treating people with complex trauma disorders, described these as the *Ten Traps for Therapists in the Treatment of Trauma Survivors*: difficulties with interpersonal trust, maintaining too much or too little distance in the therapeutic relationship, poor boundaries, insufficient limits, flaws in the therapeutic contract, unclear expectations for clients, reluctance to penetrate the client's wall of denial, difficulties in managing intense countertransference, inability to successfully manage idealized transference and setting unrealistic goals. So challenging are the therapeutic tasks necessary for healing that he has observed, 'given the extreme emotional pain that is often a part of the therapy of patients with abusive pasts, it often seems quite remarkable that patients can tolerate their own treatment' (p. 30). Supervision that appreciates the fragmentation, information overload, and intensity of trauma responses in clients will also comprehend client 'no-shows' as a multifaceted issue that can be explored and use the supervisory relationship to explore them.

Complex countertransference

These treatment traps illustrate the challenges that clients present to the therapeutic relationship that are inherent in the nature of complex trauma exposure and the damage such exposure inflicts on the capacity for healthy relationship. But there are other layers of difficulty. There are those that are inherent in the person of the therapist widely described using the term countertransference. Countertransference problems may arise secondary to therapists' past life issues and their own experiences of trauma that are triggered by the clients' narratives. Therapists are people too, going through their own present life challenges in real time, and they may be more vulnerable at key life stages relevant to the presenting material of their clients, such as when a therapist's daughter has her sixth birthday just as a client is revealing a history of sexual abuse when she was that age. And then there are the emotions that therapists experience upon hearing about, empathizing with, and trying to help trauma survivors referred to variously as 'vicarious traumatization', 'compassion fatigue' or 'secondary traumatic stress' (Figley, 1995; Pearlman & MacIan, 1995; Stamm, 1995). Then there are the countertransference beliefs secondary to the therapists' own familial or cultural beliefs that may interfere consciously or unconsciously with the therapeutic relationship, as when the therapist's cultural group endorses the role of corporal punishment while the client experienced corporal punishment as traumatic. Supervisors need to be attuned enough to explore, without being invasive – to balance the line between offering supervision and therapy.

As if this were not enough, there is also the reality that most of the people working in the social service delivery system in the United States will have been exposed to Adverse Childhood Experiences before they themselves were fully mature (Felitti & Anda, 2010). People who have experienced the impact of toxic stress as children do not just 'leave it at the door' when they enter the workplace. In our own informal surveys of people working in health care, social services, education and mental health service delivery for children and for adults, we have found that most of the staff members we surveyed had suffered some kind of serious childhood adversity. This suggests that many of the providers of services to traumatized people will be themselves vulnerable to the same symptoms as their clients. Supervisors need to look for these symptoms, not only in the clients, but also in the workers they supervise – and not only in the workers, but also in themselves.

A recent US Justice Department survey has confirmed that most children in the United States are exposed to violence in their daily lives, over 60 per cent of them in the previous year alone. Nearly half of the children and adolescents had been assaulted at least once in the year prior to the study (Finkelhor et al., 2009). Recognizing this reality, the National Academy of Science has asserted that a growing proportion of the US workforce in the future will have diminished cognitive and social skills secondary to being raised in disadvantaged environments (Knudsen et al., 2006). National reports declare that at present and in the foreseeable future, the social services are experiencing a workforce crisis (Hoge et al., 2007). This crisis is evident in high turnover rates in many social service organizations – sometimes as high as 50 per cent. If we want to keep good workers and attract more, then we must create organizations within which their deficits are minimized and their strengths maximized. We do not believe that our present human service delivery environments can measure up to those expectations. Supervising these workers then means balancing the need to demand what may be perceived by workers as unachievable results in billable hours or client outcomes with maintaining quality services. This also must be accomplished within a context of constant turnover, requiring supervisors to oversee cases through the eyes of worker after worker after worker.

Trauma-organized systems

Finally, there are the challenges that occur when our organizations and systems of care are themselves traumatized, something my colleagues and I have referred to as 'trauma-organized systems', building on the original work of Bentovim, who applied the term 'trauma-organized system' to families (Bentovim, 1992; Bloom & Farragher, 2010). Organizations are, like individuals, living systems (Senge et al., 2004). Being alive, they are vulnerable to stress, particularly chronic and repetitive stress. Chronic stress stealthily robs an organization of basic interpersonal safety and trust and thereby robs an organization of health. Similarly organizations, like individuals, can be traumatized and the result of traumatic experience can be as devastating for organizations as it is for individuals. Supervising in such an environment poses further complications.

For decades, the social service delivery system in the United States has been under stress. Clients with increasing numbers of diagnoses and multiple treatment experiences have vastly increased the complex demands put on all helping professionals. There has been an alarming increase in rates of injuries to clients and staff with subsequent demoralization of staff accompanied by an increase in hostility towards clients. An increase in aggressive behaviours has resulted in staff counter-aggressive responses and the subsequent development of punitive environments that can be difficult to supervise when the dangers are real and apparent. When professional staff and non-professionally trained staff gather together in an attempt to formulate an approach to complex problems, they are not on the same page, while every behaviour is attributed to conscious intent and unconscious motivation is denied. They may share no common theoretical framework that informs problem-solving. Without a shared way of understanding the problem what then passes as treatment is often little more than labelling, the prescription of medication and behaviour management. The inherent trap for supervisors in this scenario is being cast in one of the roles in the re-enactment, most likely that of persecutor to the staff person's victim role (Bloom & Farragher, 2010).

In a supervisory context, the impact of chronic stress and adversity on organizations has been thus far minimized and denied except in the most dramatic of circumstances. As a result, supervisors, managers and organizational leaders remain largely unaware of the multiple ways in which organizational adaptation to chronic stress creates a state of dysfunction that can significantly impede, if not prohibit the beating of the organization's heart: safe, consistent and ethical client service delivery. In many systems, there is loss of memory of former competencies. Direct care staff are often working at cross purposes with clinical staff, if they are grounded in any theory at all, and supervision for these staff members is minimal and usually directed at specific problems or egregious infractions of rules and policies. It is not uncommon to find a mishmash of training approaches all diluted without any attempt at integrating these different approaches. Under these circumstances, leaders become variously perplexed, overwhelmed, ineffective, authoritarian, avoidant, hostile and burned-out. Then when troubled clients fail to respond to what passes as 'treatment', they are labelled again given more diagnoses and termed 'resistant to treatment'. The damaging consequences of such dysfunction for clients, workers, supervisors and even communities ultimately impair their ability to heal and move forward.

In many settings, supervision does not focus on any of these critical issues but on productivity demands and whether or not the therapist has met those demands. Training programmes are still not adequately preparing therapists to deal with the complexity that they will inevitably encounter in any kind of social service or mental health setting so that when the supervisor and supervisee encounter each other, they do not necessarily have a common framework of understanding or meaning to inform their interactions. When this is the case, the supervisees are more likely to keep hidden any conflicts they are having with their clients that relate to their own countertransference and just tell the supervisor what they think the supervisor wants to hear.

Economic challenges and high turnover rates have meant that at the same time supervisors are unlikely to have had much training or experience in supervision themselves and it is highly unlikely that they have had any management training. As a result many people placed in supervisory roles know little themselves about countertransference relationships and find themselves far more comfortable in focusing on productivity, bill collection, and scheduling, rather than the more demanding issues that really need to be addressed. Supervisors with clinical training may find themselves uncomfortable with these conversations, but follow the same route as they succumb to organizational pressure for financial rather than clinical performance and the business or sustainability models that human service systems adopt to survive.

Parallel processes

A useful way of defining this set of complex interactions between troubled clients, overwhelmed staff members, and chronically stressed organizations is the concept of 'parallel process'. The definition used here derives from work done in industrial settings:

> when two or more systems – whether these consist of individuals, groups, or organizations – have significant relationships with one another, they tend to develop similar affects, cognitions, and behaviors, which are defined as parallel processes.... Parallel processes can be set in motion in many ways, and once initiated leave no one immune from their influence.
>
> (Smith, Simmons, & Thames, 1989; p. 13)

The effect of chronic and repetitive stress on social service and caregiving organizations is that these workplaces tend to have problems that parallel or mirror the problems of their clients. Chronically stressed organizations are crisis-driven, unsafe and hyperaroused, having lost the capacity to manage emotions institutionally. As a result of poorly managed emotions, interpersonal trust is absent. This results in a failure to learn from experience, a form of 'organizational learning disability' that is accompanied by 'organizational amnesia' as knowledge formerly gained is systematically lost. Under such circumstances, the most emotionally charged information in any organization becomes 'undiscussable' resulting in a form of 'organizational alexithymia'. As this dysfunction unfolds, organizational leaders are likely to become more authoritarian and punitive, while workers respond with more aggressive and passive-aggressive behaviour, and an attitude of learned helplessness, while the entire environment becomes progressively more violent, punitive and unjust. Despite this apparent deterioration, the likelihood is that unless this process is stopped, chronically stressed organizations will simply continue to repeat the past, engaging in reenactment and as a result, steadily deteriorate in function. In this way, an entire organization and even the larger system, within which it is embedded, become organized around a past history of chronic stress, adversity and trauma, unable to adapt to changing circumstances and therefore chronically failing (Bloom & Farragher, 2010).

As a result, our systems frequently recapitulate the very experiences of abuse of power that have proven to be so toxic for the people we are supposed to help. 'Sanctuary trauma' is the term that has been used to define the experience of expecting a protective environment and finding only more trauma (Silver, 1986). This perplexing combination of forces – complex exposure to trauma of the clients, complex problems among the staff, combined with organizational dysfunction – creates a toxic and interactive set of problems.

In the face of the overwhelming nature of these problems, a model that relies on individual supervision set within fixed, hierarchical supervisory structures cannot hope to succeed. Given these multiple difficulties and the economically treacherous times we live in, what is to be done? Should we go on pretending that supervision, just by scheduling it, is effective? Should we give up on the idea of supervision entirely? Should all treatment only be explicit and manualized so that supervision can be more easily structured and certified? Under the circumstances we must adapt to, how do we get many people from diverse backgrounds, with a wide variety of experiences, on the same page speaking the same language sharing a consistent, coherent and practical theoretical framework?

If we are to make our clients' problems better and not worse, then we need a supervisory network where everyone in the system is supporting and empowering client healing in a consistent, trauma-informed way. The reciprocal network model of supervision that we are suggesting requires increased innovation, leadership and knowledge to promote a socially responsible, interactive supervisory network that is supported, nurtured and continuously evaluated by the organizational culture.

Redefining supervision

Bloom and her colleagues operated an acute-care psychiatric unit and an out-patient setting for 20 years between 1980 and 2001. Beginning in 1985, we recognized that most of the clients we were seeing as adults had experienced extensive exposure to childhood adversity (Bloom, 1997, 2013). This recognition radically changed our approach to treatment, to each other, and to our understanding of the world around us. We were undergoing this change process at a time when the ability to implement the innovations we were discovering was becoming increasingly difficult. Beginning in 1991, we called our programme 'The Sanctuary' and specialized in treating people with complex traumatic stress disorders usually secondary to childhood abuse. Most of our clients had multiple diagnoses, had previously had negative therapeutic experiences, and were admitted to the hospital because they were a danger to themselves and/or others. One of the 'discoveries' we made was in recognizing how frequently we were caught up in the reenactment behaviour of our clients – how often we were helping them to repeat destructive relational patterns simply because we did not recognize these patterns, when our most critical job was to change those patterns. It became obvious to all of us that to keep them safe and to keep ourselves safe, while still creating opportunities for change, we needed to watch out for each other. We needed to be 'supervising' each other all the time, not just via some structured and limited supervisory system. We needed to be able to constructively criticize each other, regardless of where each one of us existed in the typical medical hierarchy. It had to be safe for our clients to critique us, even while we were setting limits on them.

Out of this interactive, prolonged and communal group experience, we began to develop what is now called 'The Sanctuary Model', a theory-based, trauma-informed, evidence-supported, whole culture approach with a clear and structured methodology for systematically introducing organizational change (Bloom & Farragher, 2013). At this writing, we have trained over 200 mental health and social service organizations in our model, which has given us extensive experience in wrestling with the thorny issue of supervisory systems (www.thesanctuaryinstitute.org).

360-degree supervision

In the industrial world, there is now extensive experience with what has become called '360-Degree Feedback' (Luthans & Peterson, 2003; Rogers, Rogers, & Metlay, 2002). Many Fortune 100 programmes find such processes time-consuming, people-intensive and rife with conflict and expensive but worth the investment because of the many benefits particularly when it comes to staff development, coaching, positive influence and leadership development. Companies that derive the highest benefit from it use individual development as a primary goal with the emergence of a 'development culture' as the payoff for the company as a whole. The major benefits include: providing people with information on how they are perceived by others; providing information on improvement by addressing weaknesses; and offering feedback from a variety of sources and points of view (Luthans & Peterson, 2003). Programmes that take a 360-degree approach have also been recommended as a protection against what has been termed 'abusive supervision' because they help to create a culture of civility that is incompatible with abusive behaviour (Tepper, 2007). Major problems associated with the method include: providing an overwhelming amount of information that is hard to process; differences between self-ratings and others' ratings; need for someone to resolve the conflicting information (Luthans & Peterson, 2003).

Another problem of these approaches, particularly in a variety of high-impact, intensive mental health and social service programmes, is that formal systems of supervision are usually point-in-time evaluations. These serve many useful purposes but can only begin to address the need for rapid-response, immediate innovation and concerted teamwork that is basic to working in these settings to bring about significant change. Thanks to the efforts of several hundred programmes and thousands of people, we can state that a method exists that enables entire organizations to develop interactive networks of supervision and accountability. We believe a network model of supervision is the most economically feasible and appropriate to the times we live in. Networks are self-organizing they scale up to networks of networks, they take advantage of the power of peer influence, they can last indefinitely, even when individual members sever their connections, they fill in gaps, they are intelligent and they have memory (Christakis & Fowler, 2009). To accomplish this, it is necessary to work at the level of organizational culture, while still respecting individual development and experience. Organizational culture represents a pattern of shared basic assumptions that group has learned as it solved its problems and that has worked well enough to be considered valid and taught to new members. It represents how we do things around here, the accumulated wisdom of the group and in most cases organizational culture is largely unconscious (Schein, 1999).

Reciprocal supervision

In light of the overwhelming challenges that confound traditional supervision and the growing evidence that there are more effective methods, we propose a departure from the conventional construction of supervision that offers a richer and more holistic interpretation of the support needed to enhance the therapeutic relationship that grounds trauma treatment. This construction offers an expanded understanding of the term 'therapist', to include an entire team of service providers. In the Sanctuary Model, it is understood that clinicians often have much less direct contact with clients than other types of support staff (i.e., milieu workers, foster parents, paraprofessionals, youth counsellors, peer counsellors, etc.) do. This reality requires that we consider the need for every member of this team to have a therapeutic impact on clients. In short, the team is the treatment.

If the team is the therapist, then we must also consider an expanded understanding of 'supervisor'. Weighted by the challenges presented earlier in this chapter, individual supervisors cannot be expected to provide for all the needs of a multidisciplinary team. For this reason, the Sanctuary Model expands the role of supervisor to encompass the whole community to supplement the support of individual supervision.

Finally, the concept of 'supervision' through the Sanctuary lens is not simply a dyadic relationship, but a complex dynamic web of reciprocal relationships within a community and an organic interplay among multiple parties. In the context of the reciprocal supervisory network, supervision from the community includes client critique in shaping feedback and acknowledges client contributions to shaping the therapeutic environment. It involves equal focus on individual performance and relational dynamics, recognizing that treatment is a collaborative and participatory process in service of the therapeutic relationship between the client and the treatment team, community and organization as a whole.

Another component of reciprocal supervision is the constant acknowledgment of traumatic reenactment and active rescripting of these events (Bloom & Farragher, 2013). That means that every member of the team is aware of how easy it is for any of us to be drawn into playing a role in the other person's life that recreates a previous problematic relational dynamic and that it is our mutual responsibility to work within this knowledge base to bring about significant change. There is also a shared ownership of clinical practice, client care and excellence. In addition, reciprocal supervisory networks include building trust among staff through praise and celebrations of their successes. To operationalize this definition of supervision, Sanctuary relies on its relational value system, known as the Seven Commitments.

Operationalizing reciprocal supervision

The Sanctuary Model rests on four main 'pillars': trauma theory, the seven Sanctuary Commitments, S.E.L.F. and the Sanctuary Toolkit. Together, these four domains create a consistent, scientifically based framework from which everyone in an entire organization can derive meaning, purpose and practice so that everyone can be 'on the same page' and can see when someone is not on that 'page'. To do so, however, requires universal training of everyone including the board of directors, administrators and managers, clinicians, direct-care staff, indirect-care staff (everyone else in an organization), clients and families.

Trauma theory

Trauma Theory is the foundation for creating a trauma-informed environment. Simply put, trauma, adversity and chronic stress are universal to the human experience and affect individuals and organizations in predictable ways. Understanding the ways in which trauma impacts functioning and health and the use of the Sanctuary Model to mitigate these effects are at the core of the Sanctuary Model. A Sanctuary Agency understands trauma theory and uses the lens of Sanctuary to make connections about behaviours and events, to problem solve and ultimately to create a high-functioning, compassionate, healthy community.

The Sanctuary Commitments: Creating a system of meaning

The value system of the Sanctuary Model is embodied in the seven Sanctuary Commitments: to Nonviolence, to Emotional Intelligence, to Social Learning, to Open Communication, to Social Responsibility, to Democracy and to Growth and Change. They serve as the ground upon which all meaningful decisions, strategies, supervisory interventions and conflict management occur.

The Sanctuary Commitments work together and interactively. They help us think systemically, placing relationships and meaning-making at the heart of healing and also at the core of all interactions. They engage everyone in the community or organization and they are supportive and positive, focusing more on what *to do* and less on what *not to do*. These values guide every interaction at every level in every situation throughout an organization. These are the terms with which our community agrees to operate in order to thrive. Adoption of the Sanctuary Commitments creates processes that are a vehicle for 360-degree supervision. Team members use these guiding principles as anchors for evaluation, reflection, deliberation, hypothesis formation, experimentation, conflict management and as the touchstones for measuring their construction of a trauma-informed community.

The commitment to nonviolence

The commitment to nonviolence represents the commitment to creating a safety culture. To create a safety culture, there must be physical safety, psychological safety (safe with oneself), social safety (safe with other people) and moral safety (safe to know what the right thing is and to do it). Dr Martin Luther King described the commitment to nonviolence not as a lofty value but as a practical solution for humanity's greatest problem. As he wrote, 'We have learned through the grim realities of life and history that hate and violence solves nothing. Violence begets violence; hate begets hate; and toughness begets toughness. It is all a descending spiral, and the end is destruction – for everybody' (King, 1958; p. 87).

The commitment to nonviolence represents a shift towards the group social body, analogous to the immune system in the physical body as the means to protect its members. The social immune system is the social body's ability to recognize and respond to threats to its well-being. When such a threat enters the social body, complex social activities are set into motion to defend and protect the social body against the emergence of violence. It must include everyone to be effective. Just as good trauma treatment focuses on building a therapeutic alliance, the commitment to nonviolence means building that same alliance of trust among the team through a strength-based approach and an agreement not to hurt each other with words or actions.

The commitment to emotional intelligence

Emotional intelligence has been defined as the ability to perceive accurately, appraise and express emotions; to access and/or generate feelings when they facilitate thought; the ability to understand emotions and emotional knowledge; and the ability to regulate emotions so as to promote emotional and intellectual growth (Mayer & Salovey, 1997). As this definition implies, there are many elements of emotional intelligence. Clients and staff must identify and have words for feelings and understand their feelings. They must be able to integrate thoughts and feelings and accurately read the emotions in others. They must accurately interpret emotions and other people and manage strong emotions in themselves. They must be able to regulate their own behaviour develop empathy for others and establish and sustain healthy relationships.

An emotionally intelligent culture is inherently contagious. Clients and staff alike assimilate to their environment. A therapeutic and supervisory relationship that takes into account how I am feeling, how you are feeling and what the impact of my behaviour is on you is a relationship that enables all members to thrive.

Emotional intelligence in our world is especially vital because caregivers must perform what has been termed emotional labour (Hochschild, 1983). This means work performed by any service employee was required, as part of his or her job, to display specific sets of emotions with the aim of inducing particular feelings and responses among those for whom the services are being provided. Emotional labour is what clinicians do. People who cannot adequately perform emotional labour should not choose any form of caregiving as a profession. Rude, emotionally unintelligent behaviours are often replicated by those people who have been targets of such behaviour. As a result, individuals sabotage themselves and others. Collaboration at both the treatment level and the supervisory level produces positive emotions that help an individual negotiate future challenging dynamics.

Emotional intelligence also requires the ability to manage conflict successfully. There are different kinds of conflict. These include task-related conflict and interpersonal forms of conflict. Interpersonal conflict creates tension between members, impedes group performance, decreases the possibility of synthesis and results in oversimplified solutions. Task-related conflict on the other hand means that people disagree on specific tasks and how to accomplish those tasks. Task-related conflict stimulates discussion, stimulates creativity and synthesis and makes it more likely that the system will be able to deal with complex problems.

The commitment to social learning

The commitment to social learning requires that an organization become a learning organization that adapts to changing conditions, values staff and extends the learning environment to everyone. A social learning environment is what Maxwell Jones, one of the founders of the original therapeutic community movement, called a 'living-learning environment', one that promotes good decisions and good decision makers who search for alternatives, consider short- and long-term consequences of decisions, are sensitive to group process, learn from past experience, rely on multiple sources of information, are able to weigh the pros and cons of the situation, are still able to listen to gut feelings and are aware of their own blind spots.

Good decisions often require what is been called 'double loop learning' in which we review our basic assumptions, beliefs and values to understand what is behind what we do and the results that we get rather than just having a simple feedback loop where we try to improve upon what already exists (Argyris, 1977). A social learning environment is not only about adopting evidence-based practice, but it is also about using practice-based evidence to constantly informed innovations in approach and in relationship, in order to get better results.

The commitment to open communication

In the Sanctuary Model, the commitment to open communication is about building organizational transparency and creating a culture of candour (O'Toole & Bennis, 2009). A transparent organization is a place for information sharing. When individuals get stuck in repetitive, tedious environments, they lose desire, momentum and inspiration. There is no reason to take risks and challenge yourself if you cannot see the future and how it will be replicated. A place where it is okay to reflect, brainstorm, experiment and evaluate your experience of the work and the emotions that come with the work is vital. Such a climate facilitates and promotes understanding by decreasing uncertainty.

We recognize that communication among and between human beings is difficult and that there are many physical, psychological, social and philosophical barriers that can interfere with good communication. In order to communicate adequately, we have to mean what we say and say what we mean while not being mean when we say it. It is important to gather information from a variety of sources, be able to manage our emotions, while being able to let our guard down and be vulnerable to the influence of others. It means admitting mistakes, apologizing when necessary, learning how to deliver bad news well and routinely showing care and concern for others.

The commitment to democracy

There are several reasons why we need more not less democracy in our care-giving environments. Staff at every level as well as clients are energized by the ability to provide information and make decisions that affect their life and work. We constantly confront adaptive problems – problems that we have never seen before, that are different day to day, that require adaptive change. Maintaining a high level of adaptability is tiring for lone individuals. It is a drain on the brain. We are more likely to maintain adaptive change if we do not have to do that alone. In the Sanctuary Model, we use the definition of democracy described by Dr John Gastil 'democracy represents the ideal of a cohesive community of people living and working together and finding fair, nonviolent ways to reconcile conflicts' (Gastil, 1993, p. 5). Empowering clients and staff through collaborative and reciprocal therapeutic relationships with individuals gives them a greater sense of control, an increased say in how things get done and more opportunities to learn, grow and change. The same is true for the relationship between the therapist and supervisor. The chal-lenge in human services is to avoid decreasing empowering interactions when mistakes happen and productivity levels wane.

Democracy evolved in order to minimize the abusive use of power so it is a vital component of helping people to heal who have been exposed repeatedly to the abusive use of power, often at the hands of people upon whom they were supposed to be able to depend. In many ways, democratic participation is an antidote to the effects of trauma because it requires: patience; the ability to manage emotions; using words as a substitute for action; building trust; and exercising social skills including learning how to negotiate and compromise. Democratic participation is a demonstration of fair play and restorative justice in action. Democratic workplaces tend to be those where there is more com-munication, or interaction, more coordination, greater information richness, greater commitment, more analysis of results, more productive conflict, and more innovation and creativity.

Reciprocal supervision is an inherently democratic process because it insists that each of us, at times, may have to supervise the other, regardless of where we are placed in the organizational hierarchy. This is the most radi-cal part of what we see happening in the adoption of the Sanctuary Model, that people who have little formal power can civilly and nonviolently con-front problems they see unfolding, even with people who have power over them. In interaction with the commitment to democracy, the commitment to emotional intelligence, to growth and change, to open communication and to nonviolence makes such change possible. The commitments to social learning and to social responsibility make such change necessary.

The commitment to social responsibility

In the Sanctuary Model, the commitment to social responsibility is about balancing the needs of the individual with the common good of the entire community. This implies that even as an individual therapist, you can't ignore your role in the community or in the ways in which other therapeutic relationships play out in the community. This commitment holds every individual accountable to look for opportunities to make more meaningful impacts and to take risks. It also implies that it is important to create and maintain an organizational justice climate that enhances trust, predicts performance, and predicts good citizenship within the community. In the context of the supervisory relationship, supervisors are a critical part of maintaining this balance within the context of the overall environment.

The commitment to growth and change

In any supervisory relationship, all parties must keep in the forefront of their actions that the goal of therapy is growth and change, not just stabilization and acceptance of the status quo. We must always be asking ourselves and each other – 'Are we getting change or are we helping the other person to repeat what he or she has always done?' In cases of trauma and particularly chronic exposure to traumatizing circumstances, there is a very high likelihood that clients will repeat their past, an exaggeration of what comes naturally to human beings. It is vitally important that everyone in any therapeutic environment understand the dynamics of re-enactment. Without that understanding, we are always in danger of simply helping our clients stay arrested in time, reliving destructive relational dynamics. Likewise, in the supervisory relationship, it is important to routinely consider the commitment to growth and change, expecting that learning must be occurring for all of us, all of the time.

S.E.L.F.: The Sanctuary Directional Compass

The road to recovery from trauma and adversity can be a long one for both individuals and organizations. When you are lost, it's useful to have a compass and that's what S.E.L.F. is – a compass on the road to healing. S.E.L.F. is an acronym that represents the four interactive key aspects of recovery from bad experiences. S.E.L.F. provides a nonlinear, cognitive behavioural therapeutic approach for facilitating movement – regardless of whether we are talking about individual clients, families, staff problems, or whole organizational dilemmas.

The four key domains of healing: *Safety* (attaining safety in self, relationships and environment); *Emotional management* (identifying levels of various emotions and modulating emotion in response to memories, persons, events); *Loss* (feeling grief and dealing with personal losses, recognizing that all change involves loss and understanding that signs of grief are embedded in re-enactment of the past); and *Future* (trying out new roles, envisioning a different future). Using S.E.L.F., the clients, their families, and all levels of staff members are able to embrace a shared, non-technical and non-pejorative language that allows them to see the larger recovery process in perspective. The accessible language demystifies what sometimes is seen as confusing and even insulting clinical or psychological terminology that can confound clients and staff, while still focusing on the aspects of pathological adjustment that pose the greatest problems for any treatment environment.

S.E.L.F. is a vitally important tool for Reciprocal Supervision because it is such a useful problem-solving tool. It can simultaneously be employed in a parallel process manner to deal with problems that arise within the treatment setting between staff and clients, among members of staff, between staff and administration, and between supervisor and supervisee. Applied to such issues as staff splitting, poor morale, rule infraction, administrative withdrawal and helplessness, and misguided leadership, S.E.L.F. can also assist a stressed organization to conceptualize its own present dilemma and move into a better future through a course of complex decision making and conflict resolution.

The Sanctuary Toolkit

The Sanctuary Toolkit comprises the concrete activities that individuals and organizations use to inoculate themselves against the effects of trauma and chronic stress. Think of them as the medicine or vitamins used to ensure the health and functioning of a community. They are vital for the implementation and sustained success of Sanctuary and they are inherently supervisory in nature.

Every organization that adopts the Sanctuary Model has a *Sanctuary Core Team* comprised of usually several dozen people that meets regularly to execute implementation tasks, monitor use of Sanctuary and sustain its use in the organization. Additionally, all staff members must complete the ten modules of *Sanctuary Training* in addition to participating in ongoing training that includes orientation training and booster training, if appropriate.

Community Meetings, held regularly, become the routine way that we check in with each other. Everyone in the community is expected to manage distress without harming others and one of the tools for this is a *Safety Plan*. *Red Flag Reviews* are used to respond to critical incidents and are practised with fidelity. Every staff member participates in a *Sanctuary Team Meeting* which is held regularly, is used to build a strong community, and reinforces the tenets of Sanctuary. *Sanctuary Psychoeducation* about trauma and recovery as well as the Sanctuary Model is used with clients and/or families. *Sanctuary Treatment Conferences* or *Sanctuary Service Planning Conferences* incorporate the principles of Sanctuary and a trauma-informed perspective. Every staff member participates in formal, consistent *Sanctuary Supervision or Coaching*. All community members have a *Self-Care Plan* that they share with each other and are expected to adhere to for the benefit of themselves and the welfare of the community.

Conclusion

In this chapter, we have endeavoured to begin the definition of the way we view supervision in a trauma-informed therapeutic community using the Sanctuary Model, where relationship is at the heart of all that we do. We have used the term 'reciprocal supervision' with the intention of undermining the implicitly hierarchical nature of the term 'supervision' while at the same time not diminishing the importance of how much we have to learn from each other.

Summary points

- Supervision is an essential requirement for maintaining safe, ethical and creative trauma therapy relationships.
- A relational model of supervision is the most relevant for trauma therapy.
- Relational models of supervision can provide relationships based on mutuality and offer horizontal as opposed to vertical forms of person–person contact.
- The Sanctuary Model considers the whole organization with supervision.

Suggested reading

Bloom, S. L. (2013). *Creating sanctuary: Toward the evolution of sane societies*, 2nd Edition. New York: Routledge.

Bloom, S. L., & Farragher, B. (2010). *Destroying sanctuary: The crisis in human service delivery systems*. New York: Oxford University Press.

Bloom, S. L., & Farragher, B. (2013). *Restoring sanctuary: A new operating system for trauma-informed systems of care*. New York: Oxford University Press.

Courtois, C. A., & Ford, J. D. (Eds.) (2009). *Treating complex traumatic stress disorders: An evidence-based guide*. Guilford: New York.

Ford, J. D., & Courtois, C. A. (Eds.) (2013). *Treating complex traumatic stress disorders in children and adolescents: An evidence-based guide*. New York: Guilford.

References

Argyris, C. (1977). Double loop learning in organizations. *Harvard Business Review*, 55(5): p. 115–125.

Bentovim, A. (1992). *Trauma-organized systems: Physical and sexual abuse in families*. London: Karnac Books.

Bloom, S. (1997). *Creating sanctuary: Toward the evolution of sane societies*. New York: Routledge.

Bloom, S. L., & Farragher, B. (2010). *Destroying sanctuary: The crisis in human service delivery systems*. New York: Oxford University Press.

Bloom, S. L., & Farragher, B. (2013). *Restoring sanctuary: A new operating system for organizations*. New York: Oxford University Press.

Bloom, S., & Reichert, M. (1998). *Bearing witness: Violence and collective responsibility*. Binghamton. NY: Haworth Press.

Christakis, N. A., & Fowler, J. H. (2009) *Connected: The surprising power of our social networks and how they shape our lives*. New York: Little Brown.

Chu, J. A. (1998). Ten traps for therapists in the treatment of trauma survivors. *Dissociation, 1*(4): p. 24–32.

Courtois, C. A., & Ford, J. D. (Eds.) (2009). *Treating complex traumatic stress disorders: An evidence-based guide*. Guilford: New York.

Dean, T. W. (2011). *Incomplete nature: How mind emerged from matter*. New York: W. W. Norton.

Dube, S. R., et al. (2002). Exposure to abuse, neglect, and household dysfunction among adults who witnessed intimate partner violence as children: Implications for health and social services. *Violence and Victims, 17*(1): p. 3–17.

Felitti, V. J., & Anda, R. F. (2010). The relationship of adverse childhood experiences to adult medical disease, psychiatric disorders, and sexual behavior: implications for healthcare. In R. Lanius and E. Vermetten (Eds.) *The impact of early life trauma on health and disease: The hidden epidemic*. Cambridge University Press: New York. p. 77–87.

Figley, C. R. (1995). Compassion fatigue as secondary traumatic stress disorder: An overview. In C. R. Figley (Ed.) *Compassion fatigue: Coping with secondary traumatic stress disorder in those who treat the traumatized*. New York: Brunner/Mazel. p. 1–20.

Finkelhor, D., et al. (2009) Children's exposure to violence: A comprehensive national survey. *Juvenile Justice Bulletin*, 2009. October, Accessed 1 March 10 at http://www.ncjrs.gov/pdffiles1/ojjdp/227744.pdf.

Gastil, J. (1993). *Democracy in small groups: Participation, decision making and communication*. Philadelphia, PA: New Society Publishers.

Herman, J. L. (1992). *Trauma and recovery*. New York: Basic Books.

Hochschild, A. R. (1983). *The managed heart: Commercialization of human feeling*. Berkeley, CA: University of California Press.

Hoge, M. A., et al. (2007). *An Action Plan on Behavioral Health Workforce Development: A Framework for Discussion*. Cincinnati, Ohio, The Annapolis Coalition on the Behavioral Health Workforce.

King, M. L. (1958). *The current crisis in race relations*. New South, March: p. 86–89, http://mlk-kpp01.stanford.edu/kingweb/publications/inventory/inv_03.htm.

Knudsen, E. I., et al. (2006). Economic, neurobiological, and behavioral perspectives on building America's future workforce. *Proceedings of the National Academy of Science, 103*(27): p. 10155–10162.

Luthans, F., & Peterson, S. J. (2003). 360-Degree feedback with systematic coaching: Empirical analysis suggests a winning combination. *Human Resource Management, 42*(3): p. 243.

Mayer, J. D., & Salovey, P. (1997). What is emotional intelligence?, In P. Salovey & D. J. Sluyter (Eds.) *Emotional development and emotional intelligence: Educational implications.* New York: Basic Books, p. 3–31. *Pain* (Eds.) New York: Cambridge University Press. p. 286–294.

Murphy, D., & Joseph, S. (Eds.) (in press). *Trauma, recovery and the therapeutic relationship: Context, process and practice.* London: Palgrave MacMillan.

O'Toole, J., & Bennis, W. (2009). What's needed next: A culture of Candor. *Harvard Business Review, 87*(6): p. 54–61.

Pain, C., et al. (2010). Psychodynamic psychotherapy: Adaptations for the treatment of patients with chronic complex post-traumatic stress disorder. In R. A. Lanius, E. Vermetten, and C. Pain (Eds.), *The impact of early life trauma on health and disease: The hidden epidemic.* Cambridge, UK: Cambridge University Press.

Pearlman, L., & MacIan, P. (1995). Vicarious traumatization: An empirical study of the effects of trauma work on trauma therapists. *Professional Psychology: Research and Practice, 26,* 558–565, http://mlk-kpp01.stanford.edu/kingweb/publications/inventory/inv_03.htm.

Rogers, E., Rogers, C. W., & Metlay, W. (2002). Improving the payoff from 360-degree feedback. *HR. Human Resource Planning, 25*(3): p. 44.

Schein, E. H. (1999). *The corporate culture: A survival guide. Sense and nonsense about culture change.* San Francisco: Jossey Bass.

Senge, P., Scharmer, C.O., Jaworski, J., & Flowers, B.S. (2004). *Presence: Human purpose and the field of the future.* Cambridge, MA: The Society for Organizational Learning.

Shay, J. (1994). *Achilles in Vietnam.* New York: Atheneum.

Silver, S. (1986). An inpatient program for post-traumatic stress disorder: Context as treatment. In C. Figley (Ed.) *Trauma and its wake, volume II: Post-traumatic stress disorder: Theory, research and treatment.* New York: Brunner/Mazel.

Smith, K. K., Simmons, V. M., & Thames, T. B. (1989). 'Fix the Women': An intervention into an organizational conflict based on parallel process thinking. *The Journal of Applied Behavioral Science, 25*(1): p. 11–29.

Stamm, B. H. (1995). *Secondary traumatic stress: Self care issues for clinicians, researchers and educators.* Baltimore, MD: Sidran Foundation.

Tepper, B. J. (2007). Abusive supervision, In S.G. Rogelberg (Ed.) *Encyclopedia of industrial and organizational psychology.* Thousand Oaks, CA: Sage Publications, p. 1–3.

10

Reflections and Directions for Future Research and Practice

David Murphy and Stephen Joseph

The tasks that we set ourselves in developing this book were to investigate, illuminate and formulate the varied ways in which the therapeutic relationship contributes to and plays a vital role in psychotherapy with trauma survivors. Of course, as we came to the project we had our own views and understanding of how the therapeutic relationship acts as the primary vehicle for change within nondirective person-centred therapy. This is the approach we know most about and which both of us practise within the trauma centre where we work. From our position, we are aware of the demands, especially in the United Kingdom and the United States, in recent years to move towards empirically supported treatments and how this has driven the training agenda for psychological therapies.

Specifically, we are concerned that this has led to an emphasis on specific techniques for the treatment of trauma over and above the development of the therapeutic relationship. Many approaches to training therapists, particularly cognitive–behavioural approaches, focus on the techniques that therapists may apply in their work but fail to pay full attention to the role of the therapeutic relationship. But as Meichenbaum (Chapter 2) shows, there is already considerable alternative evidence for the therapeutic relationship to be at the heart of trauma therapy.

We were also aware of the increasing recognition given to the role of the therapeutic relationship within cognitive and behavioural therapies. This was especially the case with the advent of third- and fourth-generation cognitive and behavioural therapies such as dialectic behaviour therapy, acceptance and commitment therapy and compassion-focused therapy. To us, this is a logical progression for these therapies as they start to catch up with relationship-based therapies. It is a fact that all therapies are cognitive and behavioural insofar as that they all, to some extent or another, deal with and address a person's problems at the cognitive and behavioural level. This has been shown in this book through Chapters 2, 4 and 6. Each shows that how people think and behave is related to their traumatic stress and the therapy they receive. Likewise, it is a fact that all therapies require the therapeutic relationship. We have explored this across a range of therapeutic approaches in this book and found important areas of convergence and divergence. Through this book, we hope to have shown the *way* in which the therapeutic relationship features in all of the major schools of psychological therapy. There is agreement that the therapeutic relationship is important. Each approach to psychotherapy has however its own understanding of the nature of the relationship and how it contributes to healing. It seems that it is not a question of whether or not the therapeutic relationship plays an important role, but more about where the emphasis lies and how much focus the therapist might give to relational components. Not only this, but it seems also that the important underlying philosophical differences that underpin therapists' views on the role of the therapeutic relationship have been highlighted throughout the various chapters. We have concluded that these subtle differences in emphasis on the role of the therapeutic relationship are related to therapists' views on the nature and meaning of being a person and what it means to have been traumatized. Whatever position is adopted as a therapist, it follows that the relationship created between client and therapist becomes a natural expression of that philosophical positioning.

Within the differences of philosophical positioning, there is also great commonality. What we have also noted is that proponents of all the major schools of psychotherapy that are being represented in some way in this book seem to equally value the relationship even though this may appear to be for different reasons. Our aim has been to recognize, acknowledge and prize each of these perspectives as having worth in their own right.

The chapters in this book have shown how the relational perspective offers an alternative way of thinking about trauma and how to provide help effectively from within many therapeutic approaches. We have highlighted some important issues that indicate the therapeutic relationship has the potential to transcend dividing lines between various models of psychotherapy. Often, these lines are drawn and interpreted as placing territorial markers of defensive battle grounds. The therapeutic relationship provides a unifying construct for understanding successful approaches to psychotherapy for trauma survivors. Collaboration not competition will take us further towards our shared goals of helping clients recover and grow towards their potential and enabling a range of psychotherapies to be available for clients to select from and match their individual needs as closely as possible. In supporting the range of trauma clients with what they need, the relational approaches can step in and offer something different and effective. This has certainly been the case in our own trauma centre where we have worked with clients whose previous attempts at therapy through the 'recommended treatment' have been less than satisfactory.

A further point of reflection is around the purpose of psychological therapy. It seems to us there has been a generation of psychotherapists and psychologists that have become fixated on doing therapy to their clients rather than being a companion alongside their client. Such an emphasis on doing and delivering the technological aspects of psychotherapy with trauma survivors seems at odds with the understanding, both ours and the other contributors to this book, of psychotherapy. But times are changing as evidenced by the chapters. Practitioner scholars such as Tedeschi and Calhoun (Chapter 7) have been important pioneers in offering us a new vision where therapists are expert companions. Others have challenged the very notion of the illness ideology. As Bloom, Yanosy and Harrison (Chapter 9) show, to understand recovery from trauma as being about symptom reduction is to misunderstand the existential rabbit hole down which trauma takes us. We hope that readers will now be encouraged by these and the other writings in this volume to seek deeper and richer understandings of the very nature of trauma therapy.

*   *   *   *   *

Each of the chapters has shown how the therapeutic relationship is a critical element of trauma therapy. In our own work, we have been interested in exploring the meta-theoretical stance of the therapist (see Chapter 4) and how depending on their view of the nature of suffering following trauma, some approaches operationalize the relationship in a utilitarian manner to enable the administration of techniques; whereas others view the relationship as the active agent of healing in itself. As such the most important target for future research into clinical practice needs to be to gain a better understanding of the balance *between* relationship and technique rather than relationship *or* technique. Specifically, three issues stand out as in need of research and clinical development.

First, is the role of the therapeutic relationship to provide a context within which therapeutic techniques can be delivered? Or is the therapeutic relationship itself the vehicle for change? As already noted, all of our authors offer perspectives on the importance of the relationship, but differ on how they may answer this question. Some chapters (Chapters 3 and 5) propose the relationship provides a platform for the use of new techniques whereas others (Chapters 4 and 7) propose the relationship as a vehicle for recovering following a trauma in its own right. Importantly, none of these are suggesting that there is no place for technique within the therapy.

Existing evidence as reviewed by Donald Meichenbaum in Chapter 2 shows the need to take more seriously the idea of the common factors approach and that it is likely that the role of the therapeutic relationship within trauma therapy has been seriously underestimated. As such, further theory and research is required. The answers will have significant clinical implications. For example, if it is shown that the therapeutic relationship itself is responsible for the highest proportion of change in trauma survivors, over and above the use of techniques alone, then the emphases in training will need to be oriented more towards relational ways of working. This first question is however complicated when we consider what is meant by change, whether it be posttraumatic stress-symptom reduction, posttraumatic growth, or however else we may want to conceptualize human functioning.

Second, the therapist's relational stance needs further research. As noted above, there are already some authors who see the relationship as a vehicle for recovering following a trauma in its own right. But there are differences in how this is interpreted. Joseph and Murphy (Chapter 4) discuss the difference between instrumental and principled non-directivity. Whereas instrumental non-directivity refers to using a non-directive approach to prompt the client towards a goal held by the therapist, principled non-directivity is an ethical stance in relation to the client in which the therapist has no goal in mind for the client in the belief that such an attitude is respectful of the client's right to self-determination. These two distinct approaches both recognize the central role of the relationship but lead to different stances to practice.

Third, there are constraints that affect the therapist's actions. As already noted in Chapter 1, the illness ideology of the medical model has been dominant for many years within mental health services. While the medical model is consistent with previous historical frameworks for helping in the field of trauma, the illness ideology itself is not beyond criticism. For example, the medical model focuses on diagnostic categories as opposed to seeing the person as a whole system reacting to adverse events. This can be seen as unhelpful. Diagnosis often removes agency from clients, keeping them in the role of victim and diverting the therapist's attention away from growthful aspects of the client's functioning. Technique-driven therapeutic approaches fit within the medical model paradigm and are more consistent with the current context of mental health services than relational ways of working. For relational approaches to be more fully integrated into mental health services, changes need to be made to the social and professional context of trauma work. Relational therapies as opposed to technique-driven therapies also require greater attention to the person of the therapist as discussed by Abendroth and Figley (Chapter 8), and by Bloom, Yanosy and Harrison (Chapter 9) in their chapters on vicarious trauma and supervision processes, respectively. The demands of training and supervision for relational practice are different to those required for technique-driven approaches and need to be based on a deep awareness of relationship dynamics.

In summary, as relational ways of working become more firmly established within the field of psychological trauma, attention will need to be paid to the above issues – exactly what the role of the therapeutic relationship is in relation to the use of technique, the stance of the therapist and finally how an understanding of relational ways of working may provide a challenge to the illness ideology that currently dominates the field of psychological trauma. Again, we hope this volume will encourage researchers and practitioners to think outside the illness ideology and to begin to explore the relational perspective to psychological trauma.

Trauma practice for tomorrow

Therapists will have seen, first hand, the changes that people make and their recovery and growth. However, how much of this change is attributed to the therapeutic relationship or to the techniques employed?

Below we make some proposals for developing the field of trauma studies through context, process and practice. To do this, we have identified the three fields of training, research and practice as areas for future development.

1. Training

To date a significant amount of training in the field of trauma studies is focused on the development of skills and techniques. Where training has failed to deliver is in the area of relational practice and the development of self-awareness in trauma practitioners themselves. Throughout this book, we have seen evidence presented to support the importance of the therapeutic relationship across modalities and the ways that the relationship features within different approaches to trauma therapy. We have been provided with an insight to the lasting effects on the trauma worker from trauma therapy and also of the need for relational supervision. However, to our knowledge, few training programmes in the field of trauma studies actually focus on the development of the person of the trauma practitioner.

Our proposal is that training courses for trauma practitioners need to incorporate a strong element and focus on practitioner's self-awareness. This can of course be achieved through a number of options. First, by operationalizing and instituting a system of group work focused on self-awareness development. This model is perhaps closely aligned with counsellor/psychotherapy training in the humanistic and psychodynamic traditions. An alternative to this, and one we have used ourselves, is for the learning group to operate as a self-directing and self-organizing system employing specific relational components. It has been our experience that in such a relational atmosphere students move towards the satisfaction of needs, support for one another and are able to identify learning needs and organize their learning to meet these needs. The learning that seems to take place in this kind of environment is often transformational and brings about personal as well as intellectual development. Students learn about their relational capacities at the same time learning about trauma in their field of practice. Due to the community learning atmosphere, students also learn about the areas that are of most interest to each other too.

Assessments are based on portfolios meaning that students select assessment tasks that most suit their needs; both needs for a topic of focus and the most appropriate task for the topic. The learners are able to self-direct, and this is proved to be a very effective learning process.

2. Research

We think that research in the field of trauma practice needs to consider the therapeutic relationship in a number of ways. As we have stated earlier, there are some obvious starting points for empirical studies to begin to consider. First, we think there is a need to look at the nature of the association between the therapeutic relationship and therapeutic techniques applied within trauma-focused therapy. How these two aspects of therapy can support one another is of vital importance for developing our knowledge in work with trauma survivors. Not least because how one finds themselves using techniques in trauma therapy will be intimately linked to the philosophical view on the nature of being human, of distress, and of trauma itself, but also because the therapy relationship and techniques used within therapy are always related to one another in ways dependant on these philosophical positions. This has implications for the reasoning employed by the therapist leading to the decision that a technique is presented to the client. For example, if a technique-driven approach to therapy is preferred, then the relationship is secondary; whereas, in a relationship-driven therapy, the technique is presented to further enhance the quality of the relationship. Understanding through research, the possible way that these two perspectives impact upon psychotherapy outcomes is very important for the development of future therapeutic approaches to trauma work.

We also see the need to develop research in the field of trauma studies and the therapeutic relationship that incorporates both qualitative and quantitative methods. For an extensive period of time, the research that has dominated the field of general psychotherapy, and to some extent trauma psychotherapy, has been concerned with demonstrating superiority. However, it is now being increasingly recognized that psychotherapies are largely equivalent in their effectiveness and that the therapeutic relationship as a transtheoretical construct plays a significant role in outcomes across all approaches. Hence, what also needs to be present in the field of trauma and therapeutic relationship research is high quality and focused qualitative research studies that develop our understanding beyond where it currently lies. That the therapeutic relationship contributes to outcomes is a well-accepted fact of trauma therapy. We need to learn how the experience of being in a compassionate therapeutic relationship enhances psychological growth.

It is also highly likely that this research becomes driven by the development in technology that is available today. While we are positive about the benefits of human-to-human contact and more questioning of the notion of techno-practice being the answer to healing deep emotional wounds, we do believe that the technology can be used wisely to further our understanding of how human to human contact releases client self-healing potential. It is clients that make therapy work. We think that therapists in the trauma field need to be researching what it is they can do to most effectively enable clients' potential to be actualized.

3. Practice

As has been highlighted through the chapters in this book, the therapeutic relationship spans the entire range of therapeutic approaches. Within the field of trauma therapy, the role of the therapeutic relationship becomes increasingly important, whether this is to facilitate the development of the positive therapeutic alliance required for a good outcome, to facilitate the regulation of difficult affective experiences, to provide the opportunity for growth or for the reparative experiences that can only occur within a close therapeutic relationship. We suggest that each of the chapters in this book make a strong case for all psychotherapists working with trauma survivors to become relationally aware practitioners. Whether practising using one of the 'trademarked' acronym-based therapies that encourage specific techno-practice or those therapies in which the relationship is seen as a means to an end, we think that even here by being more relationally aware the quality of therapy experience will be enhanced for the client.

Working in a relationally aware way involves commitment to your work that goes beyond the simple technological application of therapeutic techniques. Literally 'anyone' can do that. We have heard so many, trainees, students, even experienced practitioners saying things such as 'all I did was *just* listen empathically'. We look on in amazement as these practitioners underestimate the power of their empathic listening for the other person. Whenever a student or supervisee, for example, says that 'all I do is *just* be there with my client in their despair, their pain and their trauma', we invite them to reflect that back without the 'just' in their sentence. Nearly always this prompts a reflection on how important it is to 'be' with their client, to not push or not judge them or not try to make them another way. We think the pressure to 'do more' might be born out of a feeling of being under pressure to always be 'doing to' the client as many of the more directive approaches promote. Stepping back from this pressure to do more can be a very helpful process for trauma therapists. Spending time to reflect on the relationship between the therapist and client is essential work for the trauma therapist. Awareness is the key to developing effective therapeutic relationships with clients and practitioners have a responsibility to keep themselves self-aware and in good shape for practice.

We hope that in this book you will have found something to support you in your therapeutic work with trauma survivors. The therapeutic relationship is the core component of psychotherapy, and we think that in this book we have shown that to be the case in trauma therapy. The therapeutic relationship plays a significant role in whatever the approach to trauma therapy that is being practised; and it is our view that the therapeutic relationship must always be placed at the heart of trauma therapy.

Index